The Bodies of Others

Thinking through Theatre seeks to advance theatre and performance studies by exploring the questions performance itself is uniquely capable of asking, and by interrogating the ways in which it asks them. The series seeks to problematize the distinction between "making" and "thinking" by stressing their interrelation and by identifying in theatre and performance practices aesthetic and political forms of thought and action.

The *Thinking through Theatre* series aims to examine theatre and performance practices as material forms of thought, and to articulate the knowledge embedded within them. The series examines the ways in which theatre is continually rethinking the possibilities of movement, space, action, image, voice, etc., exploring the logics of creative invention and critical investigation that enable performance to operate as a mode of thought *sui generis*.

Series Editors

Maaike Bleeker (Utrecht University, Netherlands), Adrian Kear (Wimbledon College of Arts, University of the Arts London, UK), Joe Kelleher (University of Roehampton, London, UK) and Heike Roms (University of Exeter, UK)

Thinking Through Theatre and Performance
edited by Maaike Bleeker, Adrian Kear, Joe Kelleher and Heike Roms

Nomadic Theatre: Mobilizing Theory and Practice on the European Stage
by Liesbeth Groot Nibbelink
9781350051034

Forthcoming titles

In Solitude: The Philosophy of Digital Performance Encounters
by Eirini Nedelkopoulou
9781350051034

Performance Criticism as Political Event: Nonconforming Practices and Covert Poetics
by Diana Damian Martin
9781350178595

Theatres of Powerlessness: Acts of Knowledge and the Performance of the Many
edited by Edit Kaldor and Joe Kelleher
9781350233584

The Bodies of Others

Essays on Ethics and Representation

José A. Sánchez

Translated from the Spanish by David Sánchez Cano

Series Editors: Adrian Kear, Heike Roms, Joe Kelleher and Maaike Bleeker

methuen | drama
LONDON • NEW YORK • OXFORD • NEW DELHI • SYDNEY

METHUEN DRAMA
Bloomsbury Publishing Plc
50 Bedford Square, London, WC1B 3DP, UK
1385 Broadway, New York, NY 10018, USA
29 Earlsfort Terrace, Dublin 2, Ireland

BLOOMSBURY, METHUEN DRAMA and the Methuen Drama logo are trademarks of Bloomsbury Publishing Plc

First published in Mexico 2016 as *Ética y representación (Ethics and Representation)* by Paso de Gato and Universidad Iberoamericana, and in Spain 2017 as *Ensayos sobre ética y representación* by La Uña Rota and Universidad de Castilla-La Mancha

First published in Great Britain 2022
This paperback edition published 2023

Copyright © José A. Sánchez, 2022

Translation, organization and editorial matter
Copyright © David Sánchez Cano, 2022

The author and translator have asserted their right under the Copyright, Designs and Patents Act, 1988, to be identified as the author and translator of this work.

Cover image: You Are My Destiny, Angélica Liddell
(Photography © Brigitte Enguérand)

All rights reserved. No part of this publication may be reproduced or transmitted in any form or by any means, electronic or mechanical, including photocopying, recording, or any information storage or retrieval system, without prior permission in writing from the publishers.

Bloomsbury Publishing Plc does not have any control over, or responsibility for, any third-party websites referred to or in this book. All internet addresses given in this book were correct at the time of going to press. The author and publisher regret any inconvenience caused if addresses have changed or sites have ceased to exist, but can accept no responsibility for any such changes.

A catalogue record for this book is available from the British Library.

A catalog record for this book is available from the Library of Congress.

ISBN: HB: 978-1-3502-5062-8
PB: 978-1-3502-5066-6
ePDF: 978-1-3502-5064-2
eBook: 978-1-3502-5063-5

Series: Thinking Through Theatre

Typeset by RefineCatch Limited, Bungay, Suffolk

To find out more about our authors and books visit www.bloomsbury.com and sign up for our newsletters.

Contents

Preface to the English edition (2022)   vi
Acknowledgements   xxxiii

1	Representing ourselves	1
2	Ethics and morality	5
3	Ethics and artistic practice	9
4	The problem of sincerity	15
5	What does 'represent' mean?	23
6	Representation and alterity	31
7	Frauds	41
8	Body and representation	47
9	Ethics of the body	53
10	'Putting the body on the line'	59
11	Hell	65
12	Document and monument	71
13	Representation and sacrifice	75
14	Fiction and pain	85
15	Fabrications	93
16	Dis/appearances	99
17	Presences	105
18	Memory and care	113
19	Memory and violence	121
20	Memory and humour	127
21	Histories and memories	133
22	End of the party	143
23	The fascination of evil	151
24	The ethics of the witness	157
25	The apparatus of memory	163
26	The history of this book	169
27	Without / End	181

References   189
Index   195

Preface to the English edition (2022)

I write this preface in a state of semi-confinement, like millions of people whose economic situation has allowed them to protect themselves in order to slow down the pandemic. We contemplate death from a distance and are anxious about the effects of this disease on bodies and on the social paralysis of the economy. We bemoan the cancellation of our projects, in some cases lifelong ones, while we see cultural and teaching activity reduced to a minimum. Many of our loved ones we hear or see only on the other side of headphones or a screen. In such a context, the ethical relationship is only projected, mediated or in modes of representation.

Distance hinders empathy, it makes it difficult for us to put ourselves in the place of others, because each one of us is confined to their home, a comfortable and stable one for some, for many others an oppressive place or one harbouring the threat of expulsion. Separation, in addition to hurting us, angers us, because we know that even if temporary, sometimes even trivial, it is symptomatic of graver and more urgent rifts, rendered in discriminations on account of class, race, gender, colonial relationships or even generational relationships.

We isolate ourselves to conserve our biological health, despite being aware of the hazards of distance for our social wellbeing. Perhaps for this reason, the desire to take care of others has grown, as has the responsibility towards the vulnerable and the gestures of telematic care. Negative reactions have multiplied as well, calls for individualist liberty that only recognize the rights of the strong, of the healthy, and that reject measures that contribute to the relative safeguarding of the common good. The gestures of care are answered by others of hate, incited by fascist ideologies recently on the upswing in Europe and the Americas.

This tension has reconfigured the perception of the public sphere. During the lockdown two collective demonstrations occurred every evening in the streets of Madrid and other Spanish cities: applause from balconies, sometimes accompanied by songs and other expressions of support, for medical personnel, and later also for other essential workers, at eight o'clock. At nine o'clock noisy protests with pots and pans against the leftist government coalition, a protest that exalted a centrist, exclusive nationalism and grew in intensity and time, adding unease to the lockdown experience. They are the expression of two fundamental ethea that result in two extreme modes of politics: a politics that celebrates separation, identity (religious or national) and the rights of the (supposedly) stronger; another that assumes responsibility for equality, works for the common good, prioritizes care and affirms tolerance. Both nightly demonstrations fizzled out when public spaces were reopened: streets and squares, restaurants and entertainment places, universities, museums, cinemas, theatres.

Going to the cinema or to a class at the university, adhering to the strict measures on capacity and security, were quickly re-signified as political gestures. Not only in response to the attempts to occupy public spaces with expressions of hate, but also to put into practice that desire for care that had been growing in the isolation. Reduced to domestic space, our homes were transformed into classrooms, studios, workshops, stages. At the same time we rediscovered our need of the public sphere, we verified how right Hannah Arendt was when she lamented the blurring of the 'dividing line' between the private realm (the sphere of the family) and that of the public realm (the sphere of politics) (Arendt 1958: 28).

It is true that the revolution in everyday life in the 1960s and the ensuing feminist movements have proposed a politicization of the private realm that radically changed the framework of understanding originally delineated by Arendt. Nevertheless, her observations point in another direction: at the occupation of the public sphere by part of the private sphere that she described as 'pacified', in accordance with the bourgeois concept of the 'domestic', of the home as a protected (and isolated) place of affectivity and repose. The occupation of the public sphere (that acts through dissent) by part of the social sphere (that acts through consensus) has served to stifle debates, camouflage injustice and divert attention from violence. In a way, the pandemic has produced an inverse movement, exposing the domestic space and bodies themselves as spaces of tension and of conflict, generalizing the theses of those who for decades have worked for a political re-signifying of the domestic sphere and of the body.

Ethics and politics constantly intersect here, to the extent that in some cases it may be futile trying to establish a distinction. Félix Guattari (1977) proposed the category of 'micropolitics' to map the territory that Michel Foucault (1975) investigated under the category of 'microphysics of power' and 'bio-power'. In a more recent elaboration, the Brazilian philosopher Suely Rolnik (2019) has updated the conceptual framework put forward by Guattari. Her aim is to comprehend the evolution of the forms of domination brought about by neoliberalism and neo-conservatism in their various and at times unexpected alliances, as well as the modes of resistance against what she terms the 'unconscious colonial-capitalistic'. Rolnik proposes distinguishing two modes of subjectivity: a subjectivity conceived as subject, relating to an external world by means of representations and operating in it within established limits; a subjectivity conceived as receptive to a flow of affects, situated in a fluid world, that can only operate as a node in a complex network or for a common good.

There exists a subjective experience of the world, of what affects us, an experience that exceeds the limits of individuality and that immerses us in a flux of connections with other beings and the signs that those beings generate, that is, with material and symbolic reality. This is, evidently, an experience of the body. However, this body that we are, each one of these persons that we are as bodies, is likewise a subject, that is, a subjected being, dominated by the learning of culture, or by the different cultures that make up the one in which each of us is inscribed and lives. This subject is not something bad, it is the other dimension of our subjectivity. This subject that each one of us is represents the world to itself, talks, communicates with others. When doing so it interrupts the flow of emotions, sets limits, frames, abstracts, translates, speculates.

Subjected subjectivity has been the traditional subject of macropolitics, the subject that inhabits the public sphere and affirms itself by means of property and identity. Affective subjectivity occupies the territory of micropolitics. The intersection – or collision – of macropolitics and micropolitics is where the space of ethics opens up. The more active are the forces that operate in the sphere of micropolitics for affirming and preserving life, the multiplicity and complexity of life, or when macropolitical action is traversed or guided by the defence of those values that emerge in the micropolitical sphere, the more the importance of ethics grows. In fact, the concept of 'micropolitics' developed by Rolnik owes much to the *Ethics* of Baruch Spinoza (1677) as well as to the reading that Gilles Deleuze (1970) made of Spinoza's theory of affects. There are affirmative affects that produce joy in us, that stimulate desire and that encourage us to live, but that can also be easily co-opted or manipulated. There are also reactive affects that produce sadness in us, that can provoke reactions of anger or rage, but that also can make us swiftly feel solidarity with the oppressed and help us approach death. Micropolitical work consists of maintaining the desire to preserve life, insisting on the intensity of life; it likewise channels the responses of anger, rage or mourning into demands and actions of justice, not letting them drag us into sadness, paralysing melancholy or blind hate.

Rolnik proposes a very precise distinction, based on various factors, between what she terms the 'macropolitical and micropolitical insurrections' (2019: 111): the focus (visible and audible in the former, and in the sphere of the subject; invisible and inaudible in the latter and in the tension between the subject and outside-the-subject); potential agents (only humans versus humans as well as non-humans); motivation (denouncing, versus the impulse of 'announcing' worlds to come); intention (empowerment of the subject versus strengthening of life); modes of operation (negative versus affirmative); modes of cooperation (institutional and organized versus affective). One of these factors of differentiation is the 'measure(s) of evaluation of situations' (121), in the case of macropolitics the 'moral judgement proper to the subject', in the case of micropolitics 'the criterion of the drive and its ethics'.

> [The moral compass] ... points to the value systems of the modes of existence in force: those with which each subjectivity identifies itself in its experience as subject and which it appropriates to situate itself in the social field. . . .
> [The ethical compass] ... points to what life asks for as a condition to persevere each time it is weakened by its suffocation in the prevailing modes of existence and their values, which lose their meaning when this occurs.
> 121–2

This difference between 'moral judgement' and 'ethical compass' constitutes one of the recurring axes of discourse in *The Bodies of Others*, although when I wrote it I was not aware of the precision with which Rolnik had formulated it in relation to the two dimensions of the political. The difference makes even more sense if we take into account that representation-based modes of relation with reality are specific to macropolitics. In the micropolitical dimension, in contrast, representation hinders understanding the affects and the experience of a world in which subjectivity is immersed, without being able to establish a distinction between inside-the-world and outside-the-world. This tension is precisely what I was interested in exploring: how ethics operates in a realm of experience in which representations are necessary, in particular when those representations confront us with a radical alterity, denounce injustice or violations of fundamental rights and testify to experiences of pain. Civil organizations, institutional politics and the justice system respond with legal and moral criteria to such representations. Art, however, responds with ethical criteria, with interventions that usually have more impact in the micropolitical sphere, but that can also be activated in the macropolitical sphere, or in a space of interaction between both, in which, as Paul Preciado points out in the introduction to Rolnik's text, 'the traditional opposition between theory and practice, poetics and politics, representation and action ... is dissolved' (15).

The 'scene of artistic creation' thus reveals itself as a space to think through the moral and political crisis that we are experiencing, but also as a laboratory to put into practice forms that have emerged from desire, as well as to conceive an apparatus for describing worlds to come. The poetic, the construction of the real, which escapes the logic that articulates reality, constitutes a possible manner of expressing the micropolitical disagreement; this disagreement is not reactive, but affirmative, since at the same time that it rebels against the intolerable, it insists on the creative potency of solidarity in the preservation of life. The micropolitics of artistic creation is not incompatible with macropolitical action nor with the construction of representations or big models. Yet it is contrary to the perpetuation of representations and models that are antiquated and oppressive, models which essentially negate the very possibility of micropolitics.

It is no coincidence that in recent years artists have been signalled once more as 'enemies' of society. Between 2016 and 2018 Spain saw a series of arrests and calls for excessive prison sentences against musicians and theatre artists, allegedly for defending terrorism, insults to the crown or so-called crimes against religious feelings. In Brazil the attacks on artists and cultural agents were launched by the president himself, Jair Bolsonaro, in various demonstrations during 2019, at the same time that his government put into practice a politics of disguised censorship, under the motto of a 'machine of cultural war' (Pegna Herçog 2020). 'We are not going to persecute anyone,' Bolsonaro maintained, 'but Brazil has changed. We will not see certain types of artwork around here any more made with public money. This is not censorship, this is preserving Christian values.' The 'types of artwork' to which he referred in particular were those that depicted or affirmed the diversity of gender and sexual orientation, thus confronting Christian morality. Regrettably, the political declarations have not led to economic and institutional discrimination, but to verbal and physical attacks against artists and cultural agents, in particular on LGTBI groups, that have been suffering ongoing harassment for years.

The success of recurrent 'micropolitical insurrections' has contributed to macro-transformations in the form of policies of equality and of care, the conservation of the environment, recognition of the rights of minorities, the rights of one's own body (abortion, euthanasia), animal rights and even the rights of non-living beings, as well as the implementation of multiple transnational commitments. Yet these policies and agreements repeatedly collide against a ceiling established by the neoliberal paradigm, one which we have globally inhabited since the 1970s. Neoliberalism, which rejects regulation, finds in neo-conservatism, based on dogmas of the nation, religion and heteropatriarchy and clinging to old norms of morality, an unlikely ally for the defence of privileges and hierarchies of power. Catastrophic situations ignite not only desires for transformation, but fears of the unknown as well. Those who feel disoriented in the blossoming of life's creative multiplicity, confronted with the necessity of taking ethical decisions according to values that are being redefined, may be tempted to take refuge in familiar spaces of morality, even if these are the legacy of realities that no longer exist.

Since the first publication of this book one of the key macropolitical events has been the rise to power of populist nationalist leaders in the United States and Brazil. One must also add the increasingly authoritarian tendency of the leaders of European countries such as Hungary and Poland, or the 'soft' coup d'état against the democratic government in Bolivia. Ten years ago, when I began to work on this book, the question of ethics arose from ascertaining how the financial crisis not only served to eliminate social rights, but to override respect for basic human rights. The 'evil' then was neoliberal speculation, the dogma of debt containment and the usurping of democratic governments by economic powers not always identifiable. Ten years later, the evil, the real threat to living together and to general welfare, is no longer (or only) neoliberalism, but rather a nationalist populism of totalitarian tendencies, which in Europe and in the Americas enjoys support from radicalized strains of Christianism, whether Catholic or Protestant, and which threatens not only social equality, but the very fabric of democracies. The celebration of inequality and machismo, homophobia and transphobia, the criminalization of the immigrant, as well as racial and cultural hate, have returned to our everyday lives with a virulence that we naively believed had been overcome.

The pandemic has amplified the intensity and visibility of these reactive manifestations. They are responses to a situation that threatens our acquired way of life, a situation often inspiring military metaphors. We talk of war because, in societies descended from enlightened liberalism, only in a situation of war can the suspension of individual rights be justified and the survival of the group over that of individual persons be prioritized. Yet we are not facing a war, but a catastrophe. Svetlana Alexievich warned against this same confusion that spread in Belarus and Ukraine after the terrible accident of Chernobyl: 'There were no words for new feelings and one could not find the appropriate feelings for the new words; people did not know how to express themselves yet, but slowly, they entered the atmosphere of a new way of thinking' (Alexievich 1997: 46). Since there were no words for what was new, people used what was familiar: 'People confuse the concepts of war and catastrophe ... This circumstance prevents us from understanding that we face a new history. The history of catastrophes has begun' (48).

These catastrophes are caused by inhuman agency, with invisible modes of aggression and diffuse chains of responsibility. Wars have visible enemies and more or less justifiable causes; in catastrophes those enemies and those causes can be made visible by means of fictions and simplifications.

What has also become clear in the tendency to understand Chernobyl or the current pandemic as a war is our necessity to employ metaphor and representation in order to relate to reality. It is hard for us to find our way through the realm of the invisible, to communicate what affects us, without resorting to representation. It is likewise difficult for us to produce new representations. This explains the reactive responses that seek refuge in a threatened nationalism, in classism, racial supremacism or machismo, political responses with a moral base, however much this morality contributes to the perpetuation of inequality and injustice.

Yet artists are accustomed to working in such a territory of uncertainty, where new necessities of expression or visibility call for new forms. In such a moment of creation, focusing attention on what exists now is of no use, whether in the moral, political or aesthetic realm. Only ethics can guide the taking of decisions in that process between desire and formalization, between the creative impulse and representation, so that form does not obliterate desire nor representation the creative potency of life. The ethical decision is activated when we take responsibility not only for our desire or for our pain, but also for experiences that affect us collectively or affect others – whom we recognize as equals – more intensely.

States of emergency, the result of armed conflicts, catastrophes or persistent injustice, increase the urgency of expressing disagreement, anger and the demand for a new morality that sometimes involves radical transformations in the administration of the common good. These manifestations yield new ways of naming, new forms of expression, that can be the result of the subjective liberation opened up by participation in rebellion, or it can also be the fruit of artists' involvement in it. The intersection of activism and creativity has demonstrated in the last few decades many paths for articulating the macropolitical and micropolitical insurrection, but also for elaborating the tension between action and representation according to criteria that challenge consensual morality in terms of urgent ethical demands. These types of manifestation and creativity have emerged in the shift from the local to the global during the spontaneous and organized protests against the Vietnam war in the 1960s, the demonstrations for making AIDS visible and against the stigmatization of the groups most affected by the disease in the 1980s, the anti-globalization movements energized by the Zapatista uprising in Chiapas in the 1990s and later flaring up in Seattle, Bangkok and Genoa. Lately the actions of the Black Lives Matter movement during the last decade, which shook us out of our stupor in the midst of the pandemic, have proved that institutionalized racist violence does not let up in exceptional circumstances, but, on the contrary, its discourses and its acts of hate grow, fanned by impunity.

Preface to the English Edition (2022)

One of the outstanding formalizations of the protest that recently had the most impact on a global scale was the choreography *Un violador en tu camino* (A Rapist on Your Path), conceived by the feminist collective Las Tesis and performed for the first time on 20 November 2019 in front of the Second Police Station (Carabineros) in Valparaíso. In parallel with (and in indirect solidarity with) the denunciation of police violence that fuels Black Lives Matter, the Chilean group denounces macho violence. For their title they appropriated a slogan used by the Chilean police during the 1990s, 'A friend on your path', including in their text a literal quote from the force's anthem, which exposes the perverse condescension towards young women and the hypocrisy of a police force that sustains a system profoundly marked by its military and heteropatriarchal heritage.

Analysing the extraordinary impact of Black Lives Matter at a recent conference, Judith Butler (2020) pointed to the importance of two factors. The first has to do with the simplicity with which a specific denunciation, complex thinking and a demand for justice are summed up in three words. The denunciation is a response to the opposite thesis, that 'black lives do not matter', and therefore to the persistence of a racism that justified the practice of slavery, which still persists, but also to any kind of racism and xenophobia intensified by migratory movements. The complex thought underscores the materiality of the body that sustains subjectivity and civil rights, the sacredness of life and the commitment to an ethics of non-violence. The demand for justice is compatible with the mourning for loss, a mourning that, as she already made clear years earlier, is not private, not melancholic, but rather 'generates a sense of political community' (Butler 2004: 21). The second factor has to do with the dual dimension of Black Lives Matter, which is both a slogan and a movement. The movement does not precede the action; it is the action itself that produces the emotion on which the mobilization feeds. Something similar happens with 'Ni una menos' (Not one [woman] less), the Argentinean feminist slogan-movement (2015), or the 'On est plus chaud que le climat' (We are hotter than the climate) chanted at the 'March of the Century' in Paris in 2019).

In the case of *Un violador en tu camino*, it is the lyrics of the song that sum up some of the main principles of the feminist movement, with a simplicity that allows easy appropriation in very different social and political contexts. Yet its mobilizing efficacy lies not so much in the title or slogan, but in the choreography itself. If the form of the words is not subsidiary to the emotional power, in this case neither is the form of the choreography. However, it is a form that only exists in the body of those who in each case participate in the action, a form that only makes sense in terms of political action. What the form allows is repetition, the experience repeated each time as an act of politicization of the body and of political intervention in the public sphere. Through the speaking of the words, the integration of the rhythm and the commitment to performing very accessible movements, the participants engage in an action that is both political and poetic, that allows for their affirmative manifestation as both political bodies and poetic bodies.

The fact that the song and the choreography are repeated does not mean that they are 'interpreted' or 'represented'. This is because each repetition involves each one of the participants in the action in a unique way, arising from an emotion and showing itself as an affect and as a discourse. This unique dimension of each repetition, in whose realization each participant is both herself and a member of a local and global group of affect and discourse, distinguishes action from representation, even if there is a form that is performed. It is the ethical and political commitment, displayed in the words and movements that traverse the bodies, that produces the repetition as action. At the same time, each singular participant does not represent others; she is simply there, exposing the vulnerability of her body and affirming a material subjectivity, a living power. Yet, in these groups without the will to represent, millions of women can see themselves represented, while in the extensive repetition of the action a situation of violence and a denunciation of impunity is re-presented over and over again that requires urgent moral and political transformations. It is probably this repetition that does not become representation, or this representation that is only sustained by its renunciation of representing, which this book seeks to explore through an inquiry into its relationship with ethics.

The ethics that operates in these actions and repetitions is not the ethics of a subjected subject, but the ethics of those who feel confronted by a situation in which pain and anger are recurrent, because the violation, in the literal sense or in the sense of an aggression against a person's rights or integrity, is also recurrent. The ethics at work here does not proceed from a judgement, based on authority or distance, but from letting oneself be affected (Butler 2004: 130). We can be affected by an image, a story or a document – presence is not necessary to experience an affect; an affect, however, occurs in the body. It is through the images and discourses that traverse our bodies that affects are transformed into ethical decisions or ethical positions. The uniqueness of each body makes representation impossible in absolute terms, but the awareness of being a body, one exposed and vulnerable like other bodies, generates in each one of us the awareness of sharing the same condition with those others whom I see, hear and remember, and whom I ethically resist representing.

The pandemic has confronted us starkly with a new experience of vulnerability. No matter how many precautions we take, we depend on the responsibility of others if we are not to be infected; if we fall ill, we depend on the care of others to heal or endure the illness and its effects. This is so fundamental, and yet so incompatible with the dominant ethos of our individualistic and productivist societies, that it allows us to persist in conceiving of ourselves as autonomous and distant subjects. The Chernobyl catastrophe was the first warning about the fragility of our bodies in the face of uncontrolled biological or material processes provoked by our colonizing violence of nature; it heralded the widespread awareness of the unpredictable consequences of climate change. The ensuing precariousness of the middle classes after the financial crisis of 2008, like the rise in poverty as a result of the confinement and of reduced productivity in 2020, are experiences of bodies that are impacted by economic and financial accidents or unilateral and sometimes irrational decisions that escape the control of politics.

The desecration of violated bodies is answered by politicized bodies, poetic bodies, bodies active in gestures and discourse. Political action starts from the recognition of vulnerability and the need for interdependence, but does not exclude forms of protest and of direct action. Poetic creation discovers the inalienable condition of life in vulnerability, aspires to celebratory modes, but does not exclude tragic ones. In such times of pandemic this activation of assaulted bodies has a very specific reference in our collective memory, especially in the memory of the artistic community – the activism against the invisibilization and stigmatization of HIV during the first years of its expansion.

The hegemonic media in the 1980s represented AIDS sufferers as morally condemnable, with a special focus on white homosexual men. Repeated depictions seemed to convey the message that the visible consequences on the bodies resulted from these people's moral betrayal of their own nature. Physical suffering cruelly afflicted those bodies, which were presented as radically other bodies: not only homosexuals, but homosexuals with risky practices, destitute heroin addicts, careless prostitutes. Those affected were depicted as socially dispensable, either owing to their morality, their socially marginal situation, or to a combination of both. As a result, medical authorities failed to react diligently and were criminally negligent.

It was against these modes of representation and against health policies complicit in this stigmatization that the first activist collectives, including ACT UP (AIDS Coalition To Unleash Power), rebelled. 'Stop looking at us, start listening to us' was one of the slogans of this rebellion; representations that put moral judgement before fundamental rights were contested, as were those that induced compassionate contemplation rather than active solidarity. At a very early date (1989), Douglas Crimp warned – anticipating Judith Butler's reflections – that mourning for loved ones is not incompatible with an active demand for justice, as well as that communities of mourning can also be political communities. The condition of this politicization rests on an ethical basis: that the recognition of alterity does not exclude us from responsibility. 'The construction of the us/them dyad is the greatest obstacle to overcome, ... we must accept that AIDS is our problem' (Crimp 1994: 127). Accepting AIDS as 'our problem' does not legitimize us to represent those affected, but rather obliges us to listen to their self-representations, to preserve the memory of their singularities, the memory of their pain, the memory of their struggle and to practise active solidarity.

Giving precedence to listening over the distancing or spectatorial gaze allows us to retrieve the ethical thinking of Emmanuel Lévinas, without ignoring how problematic his transcendent base is. *Totality and Infinity* (1961) presents a synthesis of his efforts to provide an answer to the brutal negation of alterity occurring in the Shoah and in World War II. 'Totality' referred to the objectification of human relationships, the suspension of the face-to-face, the reification of bodies and, consequently, the unleashing of violence against them. Opposing this rule of totality, Lévinas proposed recuperating the idea of the 'infinite', which can only be accessed through the recognition of the transcendence manifest in the 'face of the Other' (Lévinas 1961: 24, 51). The face is the site of the epiphany of the Other; in the face-to-face encounter I become aware of the limit of selfhood and discover the impossibility of continuing to contemplate that face as an object, as an image. The transcendence of the Other's face resists representation and demands its revelation via language: 'The face opens the primordial discourse whose first word is first obligation, which no "interiority" permits avoiding'; the face-to-face founds language and its first words are 'you shall not commit murder' (201 and 207).

Acknowledging the 'critical consternation' caused by the metaphor of the face, Judith Butler nevertheless returned to Lévinas to consider a Jewish ethics of non-violence in the face of Zionist radicalization and discrimination against Arabs in the post 9/11 global context. Butler starts from Lévinas' observation that an ethical relationship cannot be based on representation, but rather on listening, for the face is primarily discourse. Yet such a formulation, according to Butler, cannot be understood in absolute terms. 'There is something unrepresentable that we nevertheless seek to represent, and that paradox must be retained in the representation we give. In this sense, the human is not identified with what is represented but neither is it identified with the unrepresentable; it is, rather, that which limits the success of any representational practice' (Butler 2004: 144). The ethical relation does not require the annulment of representation, as it can lead to invisibilization, nor is it enough to find adequate representations, as they can cancel differences and singularities; what is at stake is to accept 'the challenge to representation that reality delivers' (146).

ACT UP accepted this challenge by resorting to an image, the inverted pink triangle created by the Silence = Death Project, which directly referred to the badge identifying homosexuals detained in Nazi concentration camps, and by producing self-representations, such as those that can be seen and heard in *Voices from the Front* (1991). The body itself, including the image of the body or the images that mark or signal it, is the first means of representation. This is something we encounter again in the actions of Black Lives Matter or in the re-presentations of *A Rapist on Your Path*. All these movements have in common the affirmation of an embodied subjectivity, of an ethics that operates in bodies, that does not require transcendent thought to justify an idea of good embedded in material life and its different manifestations. They all recognize the materiality of the body as a place of experience, thought and action: the body in its materiality suffers, the body in its materiality is affected, the body in its materiality acts. These movements also have a double objective: a project of transforming morality through normative changes and active policies, and a project of reparation through legal actions and processes of recovering and sustaining memory.

The ethics at work in these movements is an ethics of non-violence that does not renounce justice, but actively demands it. It articulates the two models of morality described by Carol Gilligan (1982) in her psychological studies focused on gender difference: a morality based on rights and justice (determinant in the formation of male psychology) and a morality based on responsibility and care (determinant in the formation of female psychology). Both conceptions of morality are necessary for society, but the predominance of the former throughout history led to regarding the ethics of care as a defect, as a hindrance to understanding the meaning and foundation of justice.

> To understand how the tension between responsibilities and rights sustains the dialectic of human development is to see the integrity of two disparate modes of experience that are in the end connected. While an ethic of justice proceeds from the premise of equality – that everyone should be treated the same – an ethic of care rests on the premise of nonviolence – that no one should be hurt. In the representation of maturity, both perspectives converge in the realisation that just as inequality adversely affects both parties in an unequal relationship, so too violence is destructive for everyone involved.
>
> Gilligan 1982: 174

It is necessary to transform morality, since many crimes and aggressions are committed because of disagreement over the limits of good and evil, as a result of discrimination or contempt for certain bodies due to their status as women, homosexuals, blacks, migrants, transsexuals, prostitutes or subalterns. The transformation of morality, moreover, requires legislative changes, but also behavioural models and the construction of new representations. Reparation is necessary here, not only as a process of healing or subjective consolation, but because of the need to sustain the new models and representations within a collective memory of evil and pain, but also of mobilization and justice.

There are multiple ways of achieving these objectives, but in all of them two basic dispositions probably coincide that intertwine and overlap: one that emanates from pain or grief and manifests itself as rage, anger, demand and persistent claim; one that arises from a desire for change, and manifests itself as solidarity, celebration and affirmation of life. These two dispositions were very evident during the performance of the choreography invented by Las Tesis: putting the body on the line in a public space in a gesture of collective empowerment produces a positive affect, which encourages enthusiasm for a life without violence and that is lived together. Nonetheless, the celebratory dimension cannot make us forget that this desire combats a deficiency: impunity, social apologies for certain selective aggressions, the persistence of evil entrenched – to the point of going unnoticed – in institutionalized morality, in family inertias, in hegemonic representations. The celebratory dimension also rebels against the suffering that this deficiency produces. It is necessary to insist on the duality, on the simultaneity of rage and celebration, of mourning and militancy, of justice and transformation, of memory and desire. This duality is inherent in a representation understood as a means and not as an end, a mode of representation that is not incompatible with action, but which incorporates the repetition of what has been, of what is left behind. Nor could action in itself be conceived as an end, since the end is change, the moulding of modes of coexistence in which there would be minimal recourse to justice, because evil would be marginal, or in which there would be no need to propose a morality and it would be possible to rely on an ethics based on life.

* * *

Marielle Franco, a councillor in Rio de Janeiro, was executed on 14 March 2018 after being repeatedly threatened for her political action in defence of human rights, her activism against violence in the favelas and her legislative proposals to help vulnerable children, black women and LGBTI groups. The proud affirmation of her black and lesbian identity must have intensified the hatred of the militias and those motivated by the discourse of the then presidential candidate, Jair Bolsonaro. Her death was a very painful blow, as was the death the following day of Mame Mbaye, a young Senegalese man who, after twelve years in Spain, had not been able to legalize his residency status and continued to survive as a street vendor. Pursued by the police through the streets of central Madrid, he collapsed after suffering a cardiorespiratory arrest that ended his life.

We wish Marielle were still alive. That Mame were alive. And so many other persons, murdered for having put their bodies on the line in the defence of justice, the preservation of life and of the common good. But they are dead. Their determined action put them in the crosshairs of the accomplices of evil. Their ethical firmness encouraged them to carry on, not to cease in the face of threats. The memory of their lives demands perseverance in action. The memory of their pain demands justice.

Action for justice can in itself constitute a reason for signalling. Azucena Villaflor (1924–77), one of the founders of the Madres de Plaza de Mayo movement, was kidnapped, tortured and murdered for demanding the return – alive – of those disappeared by the Argentinean military dictatorship. Marisela Escobedo was murdered on 16 December 2010 while demonstrating against the impunity in regard to the femicides in Chihuahua, after two years of demanding justice for the murder of her daughter Rubí Marisol Frayre Escobedo.

On 10 May 2018, Bruno Avendaño disappeared a few kilometres from his home in the Isthmus of Tehuantepec (Oaxaca, Mexico). His brother Lukas then launched, together with his mother, a legal and political search for him, which repeatedly came up against the inefficiency, apathy and even contempt of numerous public servants. Lukas Avendaño is a renowned performance artist and anthropologist, whose solos have represented and elaborated, with a strong poetic and sensual charge, the traditional Zapotec *muxhe* identity. This third gender denotes people whose assigned sex at birth is male, but who assume roles culturally delegated to women. Anthropological research intersects in Avendaño's performances with queer theory and with the legacy of poets such as Allen Ginsberg and Pedro Lemebel. After the disappearance of his brother, Lukas devised an artistic action to reinforce his political activism: *Buscando a Bruno* (Looking for Bruno) was based on a recreation of Frida Kahlo's painting *Las dos Fridas* (The Two Fridas, 1939), for which he himself put forth the body, holding a photo of his brother, and in each case invited another person to incarnate the second person. The action, which was reminiscent of the one carried out by Las Yeguas del Apocalipsis (1989), was only one of the many activist initiatives carried out by Lukas in search of his brother and in solidarity with the tens of thousands of relatives of disappeared people in Mexico.

Bruno's body was found in a clandestine grave on 12 November 2020 (Avendaño 2020).

* * *

Murder is the greatest failure of ethics. And in the above cases, it is also a failure of the state and of the judicial system. However, the law is the only power left to those whom Avendaño, quoting Eduardo Galeano, calls the 'nobodies'; the desire for justice is what encourages them to go on living. When the time comes, or when that time is conquered, it will be necessary to return to the past, for the living to represent the absent, and for the representation to be sufficiently vivid and accurate for a fair judgement.

Judicial decisions are very different from ethical decisions. The former are based on law and must ignore singularities, the latter may be based on moral referents, but must necessarily heed the context and are inseparable from the concern for the singular. Justice aspires to objectivity, ethics cannot disengage itself from subjectivity. Ethics operates in the realm of action, in a continuous present; justice looks to the past, its realm is that of representation.

'*Spilled blood does not reverse itself*' wrote Hélène Cixous (1994a: 3321) in the introduction to *La Ville Parjure: ou Le Réveil des Erynies* (The Perjured City: or The Awakening of the Erinyes), a work in which the character of the Mother calls for justice for her dead sons, denouncing the responsibility of the authorities in distributing blood contaminated with HIV.

> Justice is what makes injustice right. On what heaps of injustice does Justice rise! Justice is not made to be just. It is made to stop. Justice, between men, is necessary. To cut short the pain, which is endless. To cut off everything that goes beyond, to repress the sobs. The victims are scandalous, they never stop complaining. Justice is there to regulate the cries and cut off the complaints. Justice is the good management of Injustice. Justice is our necessary tragedy.
>
> Cixous 1994b: 7

The conception of justice not as restitution but as interruption goes back to the very moment of its mythical foundation in Aeschylus' *The Eumenides* (whom Cixous in her play revives as the guardian of the cemetery): justice interrupts the chain of vengeance instigated by the Erinyes and places the responsibility of judgement on a jury of just citizens. 'It is for you to speak' is the formula Athena uses to inaugurate 'the first trial for bloodshed' in Greek mythical history (Aeschylus 1926, lines 582 and 683). The legitimacy of justice is based on the principle that all those who have something to say should be heard, and the ethics of those who judge is based on active listening.

This is another way of formulating the need to go as far as possible in understanding others, the context of their actions and the determinants that affected their decision-making. Orestes' testimony is heard by the *démos*, that is, the public, on whom rests the decision about the death and life of the accused in the new democratic polis. The audience in a court of justice is, ideally, the citizenry, represented by the 'just'. In the theatre, the audience is that same citizenry, no longer represented, but confronted with representation.

However, the capacity for action of these citizens is very limited and their decisions (even when they are right) rarely satisfy our desire for what is just. Aeschylus' chorus itself warned that this new justice established by Athena could bring about what they considered unjust: the acquittal of Orestes. Two different concepts of justice clash here: in Ágnes Heller's terms, an 'ethico-political concept of justice', based on 'the idea that the good should be happy because they are worthy of happiness and that the wicked should be unhappy because they are unworthy of happiness' (Heller 1987: 48), and a 'socio-political concept of justice', which is achieved in retributive justice (which punishes crimes) or distributive justice (which resolves conflicts over property or economic interests). We want socio-political justice to make happy those who have been honest or ethically just. However, being honest does not guarantee happiness, let alone ward off suffering; on the contrary, ethical consistency can increase the risk of being discriminated against, persecuted or killed.

Justice shares with theatre the impotence of representation, the impossibility of reversing what has happened or of intervening directly in reality. Justice as an ethico-political practice is the act. Justice as socio-political practice is representation. The court is the place where past actions are observed in accordance with morality and the law. The theatre can be the place where past actions are exhibited in order to stimulate ethical reflection. The parallelism between the two spaces has given rise to numerous comparisons, games of representation and the reversal of functions. Beyond the dramatic works (in theatre and film) that use the trial as a basic or central situation, the representation of fictitious trials is a common exercise in the training of lawyers and judges and has also been used in the artistic field.

In *Please Continue (Hamlet)* (2011), Roger Bernat and Yan Duyvendak proposed a mock trial in which Hamlet was accused of murder for the death of Polonius. By interrupting the action in Gertrude's bedroom, tragedy becomes drama, and Hamlet a kind of new Orestes. In each venue the situation was adapted to the local context and only Ophelia, Gertrude and Hamlet were played by actors; the other people on stage were magistrates, lawyers or professional experts. The text consisted of a dossier with police and forensic information, as well as a collection of testimonies, which each participant had to use to interpret at their own discretion. It was up to a randomly selected group of spectators to decide on the guilt or innocence, although inevitably each and every one of the spectators felt challenged to make a decision, not as easy as it might seem. Surprisingly, and contrary to the evidence, Hamlet was acquitted by the jury in fifty per cent of the more than 100 performances held around the world. This reveals – and this is something only understood after the end of the performance – that the issue at stake was not Hamlet's guilt or innocence, but the social and moral determinants that condition the spectators' judgement, as well as the importance of rhetoric and games of representation in ethical and political decision-making. This questioning, which touches the very core of democracy, momentarily returned to the place of theatre, through judicial representation, its original function as a public space or forum for political debate.

The potential of theatre to intervene in the public sphere through the representation of judicial processes without direct validity was used in other instances – relinquishing the fictional dimension – to initiate processes of opinion or reparation on different scales. These are no longer fictional, but symbolic trials, such as the 1967 Russell Tribunal, which judged US war crimes in the Vietnam War, and its successive convocations until 2014, or the hearings associated with the various Truth Commissions, under different names, in territories whose populations were affected by serious violations of fundamental rights caused by armed conflict or state violence. If the execution of socio-political justice is always a recognition of the failure of ethics (due to resistance to agreement or to the persistence of evil), symbolic trials highlight the failures of justice (due to its passivity, incompetence, partiality or inoperativeness).

Several artists have used the representation of the oral hearing to launch debates with an impact on the public sphere. Adberrahmane Sissako did this with his film *Bamako* (2004), in which a group of residents of a working-class neighbourhood, acting as representatives of African civil society, put international financial institutions – the World Bank and the IMF – on trial. Similarly, the Swiss director Milo Rau, in one of his most ambitious projects, *The Congo Tribunal* (2015), organized two public hearings, held as theatrical stagings, but where all the witnesses and documents were real, in Bukavu and Berlin. Two years earlier he had organised *The Moscow Trials* (2013), as a way of contesting three previous trials in which different curators and artists (including members of Pussy Riot) had been prosecuted, and in some cases convicted, for crimes against morality and religious feelings (Bernstein 2014). Once again, judges, prosecutors and practising lawyers, as well as experts in art history and theology, representatives of different political parties and nationalist associations, and some of the defendants, participated in this case. The fact that the trial took place in the room of a museum (the same room where some of the works that had justified the charges had been exhibited), and that the sentences had no validity, did not detract from the power of this initiative to have an impact on the public sphere. Paradoxically, the fictional framework, which delimits the space of autonomy of representation, allowed for sincere debate between ideologically very distant persons, who outside this space normally related to each other with hatred. It is the awareness of the fictional framework that allows the participants to openly present their ideas, to argue calmly, to question each other in microdebates, and even to exercise criticism and self-criticism, free of the constraints of the strict regulations of procedural law. Furthermore, the list of witnesses can be extended to other social agents not directly involved in the criminal case, but who participate in the social debate. Fiction thus allows the constitution of an autonomous space for collective debate and criticism in search of the truth, or at least of a minimum agreement.

The Moscow Trials also echoes the spectacularity of the historical trials of Trotskyist leaders (1936–39). The show trials have a political objective and the function of the hearings is not to determine the truth in order to deliver a just verdict (for the verdict is predictable and in fact decided prior to the trial), but to consolidate power through exemplary punishments and to publicize an ideology or an edifying doctrine. Jacques Vergès studied this type of trial to affirm his commitment to rupture strategies in his defence of those accused of political crimes (Vergès 1968). In contrast to a strategy of connivance, in which the established order is respected and the aim is to obtain the mildest sentence, the rupture strategy opts for challenging the legitimacy of the court. Clarifying the facts takes second place and the goal is to transfer the debate, through polemic and spectacle, to the realm of opinion and the public sphere. This was the strategy that Vergès himself adopted in his defence of Djamila Bouhired and the FLN defendants (1957), which resulted in the reprieve of her death sentence and, ultimately, her pardon and release.

'My law', wrote Vergès, 'is to be against laws, because they seek to stop history; my morality is to be against morals, because they seek to paralyse life' (15). If mock trials and symbolic trials employ the theatricality of the hearing to generate debates in the public sphere, the rupture strategy shifts the spectacularity to the very interior of the judicial process with the same objective. In both cases, the outcome is a challenge to the judicial system and to the morality associated with it, which can be rendered in exposing the obsoleteness of some laws, or the absence of legislation that effectively prevents systemic violence.

In no case can judicial courts (real, fictitious or symbolic) intervene in the past to prevent evil. They are all trapped within the limits of representation, in its double sense of repetition and theatricalization. They can never bring back life or lost time, or erase suffering or trauma. This is not to say that they cannot effect transformations in the lives of those involved in the process (in the form of restitution or partial healing), with potential social and political consequences. Although condemned to return to the past without the possibility of changing what has already happened, representation (be it judicial or artistic) is not impotent in relation to reality, not even when representation is based on fictions. For trials or stage performances are in themselves also situations of reality, in which ethics is activated. An ethics that does not replace the one that operated or should operate in the realm of action, but which is necessary for the representation to be just, that is to say, honest.

The court as much as the theatre is meaningless if regarded as an institution turned towards the past, in which representation is exhausted within itself and only results in punishment or applause. The meaning of both institutions derives from their contribution to an effective transformation or to the emergence of transformative thinking. Ensuring the possibility of either of these outcomes constitutes one of the fundamental indicators of that 'ethical compass' that has to operate in the interior of representation itself, to prevent representation from fraudulently substituting action or acting against the creative forces of life.

Conceived in this manner, this 'ethics of representation' makes up the axis that drove and guided the writing of the essays that constitute this book. In the same way that justice does not return life nor erase injury, theatre cannot replace justice nor life itself, nor become a substitute for the space of mobilization, political action or even of the claim for justice. Nonetheless, theatre can activate the potency of representation to generate spaces of communication, expression, play and debate that highlight the losses, encourage desire, celebrate difference or promote the articulation of a thinking at the service of emancipatory action. The ethical response becomes urgent when representation implies appropriating memories that are not one's own, faraway struggles and sufferings, experiences of other bodies.

This book assembles real and represented memories and experiences with the aim of producing thoughts and encouraging desires. It is a practice of mediation, like so many others in the fields of art, education and culture. It does not pretend to postulate a theory, nor a systematization, and from the outset renounces any claim to being exhaustive. On the contrary, it is an exercise in writing that arises from listening to or accompanying creative processes that respond to experiences of violence. As author, I assume the

Preface to the English Edition (2022)

risk of writing from a distance and proposing thoughts that are formalised in representation. Whether or not the ethical decisions taken in relation to the momentary appropriation of voices and experiences have been correct or not will be for each reader to judge. I am aware that such judgements will be diverse, and that each reading will detect shortcomings and excesses, as well as potential itineraries of accompaniment and discourse. This is why I have preferred to avoid at all times the closure of representation rendered in the form of a 'final text', choosing instead a writing that preserves the traces of learning and thinking in their respective processes, as well as of the movement that nourishes them, including the movement of the body itself. I have thus relinquished correcting or completing what has already been written and have decided instead to write this extensive preface, which gives an account of new urgencies and of artistic and discursive encounters that have necessarily shifted my own position.

This permanent movement of writing and discourse is made explicit in the chapter 'The History of This Book', which I have decided to keep at the end of the book, but which can also be read at the beginning. It sets out the motivations, the successive contexts in which it was conceived and the circumstances of its writing. As can be seen from those pages, the successive phases of research and writing coincided with various invitations to conferences and stays in Latin American universities, which partly explains the choice of referents and interlocutors. It explains it only partly because the desire to think 'from the South' (Sousa Santos, 2010) arose as a dissatisfaction that affected my teaching and research work. This dissatisfaction arose from realising that the way in which I had written the history of the performing arts in my texts and books of the 1990s was determined by ideas of modernity and contemporaneity that cannot be conceived of as global; rather, they are imposed as a consequence of structural, economic, linguistic, racial and academic imbalances.

In its Spanish edition, the book begins, without prior introduction, with the chapter 'Representing Ourselves'. It is an attempt to establish a relationship of conversation in absence, to reduce the distance between the act of writing and the act of reading the text, to reveal the materiality that sustains these essays as a fabric in which experiences, intuitions, readings, thoughts and affections have been woven. The chapter also introduces the first section of the book (Chapters 2 to 7), in which I propose an approach to the two core concepts, 'ethics' and 'representation', in constant dialogue with artistic practice.

The distinction between 'ethics' and 'morality', which is one of the argumentative axes of the book, is based on Alain Badiou's (1993) reading of Hegel, but coincides with the difference established by Rolnik between the 'ethical compass' and the 'moral compass', one of the differential criteria of micropolitics and macropolitics. One could establish a correlation between ethics and artistic practice (operating mainly at the micropolitical level) and one between morality and culture (at the macropolitical level). It might seem coherent to extend this correlation to the pairs ethics and action, on the one hand, and morality and representation, on the other. However, the term 'representation' entails a complexity of meaning that affects the concepts it refers to and the experiences it categorizes.

In Chapters 4 to 6, I offer a rereading of Jean Renoir's *La carosse d'or* with a twofold intention: to highlight the pleasure and power of representation, while at the same time unravelling its meanings, following the analytical clues offered by Jacques Derrida (1989), in contrast to the studies on social theatricality by Erving Goffman (1959) and Richard Sennett (1976). Situating Merimée and Renoir's fable in its possible location (Lima) and transferring it to the present permits a dialogue with contemporary referents, such as the films of Claudia Llosa (2006 and 2009) or the performances by Yuyachkani (2000 and 2001). The study of representation leads to the question of radical alterity, as posed by Gayatri Chakravorty Spivak (2013):

> Radical alterity – the wholly other – must be thought and must be thought through imaging. To be born human is to be born angled toward an other and others. To account for this the human being presupposes the quite-other. This is the bottom line of being-human as being-in-the-ethical-relation. By definition, we cannot – no self can – reach the quite-other. Thus the ethical situation can only be figured in the ethical experience of the impossible.
>
> Spivak 2013: 98

The need to think the quite-other through representation marks the impossibility of ethics, yet the mandate of representation already implies an ethical decision: 'the image of the other as self produced by imagination supplementing knowledge or its absence is a figure that marks the impossibility of fully realising the ethical' (104). Spivak elaborates this aporia through the concept of the 'double bind', the obligation to heed two contradictory mandates, which is not a logical or abstract contradiction, but a moral experience.

Judith Butler was confronted with this experience of the 'double bind' when considering, in her re-reading of Lévinas, the 'unrepresentability' of the Other in the face:

> For representation to convey the human, then, representation must not only fail, but it must *show* its failure. There is something unrepresentable

that we nevertheless seek to represent, and that paradox must be retained in the representation we give.

In this sense, the human is not identified with what is represented but neither is it identified with the unrepresentable; it is, rather, that which limits the success of any representational practice.

Butler 2004: 144

This 'double bind' can explain why Baroque irony or the 'fake' have been a way of addressing the challenge of the representation of radical alterity in such fake documentaries such as *Agarrando pueblo* (The Vampires of Poverty, 1978) by Carlos Mayolo and Luis Ospina, or *Adieu Monde* (Goodbye World, 1997) by Sandra Kogut.

The second section comprises Chapters 8 to 14 and focuses on the 'ethics of the body', interweaving two linked themes: the staging of one's own body as an ethical justification for representing alterity on stage, and the 'putting the body on the line' of activist practices. The first theme is raised specifically in relation to the work of playwrights who put their own bodies at risk as a condition for manifesting the challenge of representation in its impossibility: Angélica Liddell, who appropriates conceptual body art practices of a sacrificial nature, or Eduardo Pavlovsky, who in response to the Argentine dictatorship elaborated what he termed an 'ethics of the act', which takes up the Bakhtinian conception of the 'ethical act'. The second theme is raised in dialogue with activist artistic and social practices, with particular emphasis on the actions of the Chilean group Las Yeguas del Apocalipsis. In both stage performances and in actions in public spaces, it becomes clear that the will to intervene in the real is the result of an ethical decision, which does not exclude the use of representation or fiction.

In Chapters 11 to 14 I deal specifically with the function of fiction and its legitimacy in the representation or elaboration of experiences of extreme suffering and violence, based on a reading of the novel *2666* (2004) by Roberto Bolaño and the play *La casa de la fuerza* (The House of Strength, 2009) by Angélica Liddell, both of which refer to the femicides that have taken place in Ciudad Juárez since the early 1990s. In both cases, the idea of 'putting the body on the line' responds to the limits of representation proposed by Susan Sontag in *Regarding the Pain of Others* (2003) and is translated into the concepts of 'anti-monument', in the case of Bolaño, and of 'sacrifice' (with a direct trace of Antonin Artaud's thoughts on pain) in the case of Liddell.

In *Dolerse. Textos desde un país herido* (Grieving: Dispatches from a Wounded Country, 2015), Cristina Rivera Garza reflected on the possibility of poetic writing in the face of the 'horrorism' of the femicides and the systemic violence unleashed in Mexico since 2006. After paralysis and falling silent in the face of violence, it is necessary to 'grieve yourself'; to say 'you pain me' becomes an 'aesthetic urgency' (Rivera Garza 2015: 14).

> Pain not only destroys but also produces reality: thus its social languages are above all political languages: languages in which bodies decipher their relations of power with other bodies. It is frequently through religion and social reproduction that the language of pain becomes a generator of signifiers and of legitimacy.
>
> 44
>
> And then is when you, which is another way of saying I, see us.
>
> 56

Bolaño's poetic response to horror was one of mourning and resistance, using humour as an instrument of resistance and healing. Liddell's response, which also went through mourning and rage, leads to an ethics of care, as announced by Gilligan and later elaborated by other authors, such as Adriana Cavarero (2013). Her proposal of a 'postural ethics' (121) provides a very interesting tool of analysis that could certainly be applied in the analysis of the scenes of sisterhood present in *La casa de la fuerza*. The explicit 'inclinations' of the actresses manifest that necessary putting-oneself-outside-oneself, which is the correlate of 'putting the body on the line' as a condition of representation. Their bodies make visible an ethical act, which is embodied, materialized and revealed as physical: 'the center of gravity of the person moves, first of all, to the loved person, and when love disappears, that movement "outside of the self" remains, even though that position is difficult to maintain', because 'to be a man means to be steady, to weigh on something' (6–7).

The third section, the longest, deals with practices of representation referring to absence, disappearance and memory, and is divided into three sub-sections.

Chapters 15 to 17 extend the study of fiction as an instrument of representation, in this case the representation of the invisible, the disappeared or the inaccessible. The concept of 'fabrication', taken from an exhibition by Rabih Mroué (2012), allows us to approach his work in collaboration with Lina Majdalanie, in parallel to the construction of the fictional archives of Walid Raad and the Atlas Group. A re-reading of *The Invention of Morel* by Bioy Casares offers a clue for thinking about the use of audio-visual devices as a means of making absence discernible through ghost presences. The phantasmatic does not refer to the transcendent, but to the violence that prevents the reunion of bodies in life or in presence. Hence the reference to the documentary by Mohamed al-Atassi on the Syrian dissident Riad el Turk, which both illuminates and problematizes the practices of Mroué and Majdalanie.

I have recently returned to this theme in an article entitled 'Presence and Disappearance' (Sánchez 2019), in which I proposed a correlation between the absence of actors on stage and the commitment to tackle an impossible task: that of making the disappeared present. Stage absence can take the form of telematic presence, of withdrawal into the background, without direct participation in the action, or even in the form of literal disappearance. In each case, the violence to which it refers is different, but most importantly such absence, in the works analysed, does not imply relinquishing representation or abdicating responsibility. In order to understand this, the distinction proposed by Hannah Arendt (1958) between an active appearing and a passive appearance was decisive. By defining the act of appearing as a condition of political action (208), one might think that for Arendt there is no room for action based on disappearance, which is even common sense: how can one intervene in the public sphere by renouncing visibility? However, the gesture of appearing is not the same as the condition of appearance; for the same reason, one can conceive of a gesture of active disappearance, different from that of passive disappearance. It is this gesture that can be identified as a political act of resistance, but also as an artistic action, which exercises violence on the very nature of the actor, and which in this violence manifests (or represents in its impossibility) the absences and forced disappearances.

The pandemic has placed all of us in the situation of mediated communication, of communication at a distance, similar to those described in the chapter 'Presences' in relation to the theatre of Rabih Mroué and Lina Majdalanie, the cinema of Mohamed al-Atassi or the installation (and its activation) by Beatrice Catanzaro. We have all, on a global scale, experienced isolation, the rupture of our physical network of affections and the extreme dispossession of public space; at the same time, we have the possibility of real involvement with other distant people. We have also assumed a theatre without presences, mediated by virtuality. However, there is a political reason that cannot be ignored. Just as the decision to appear in absence is, in the case of the artists mentioned, a response to political violence and a will to intervene in a transformative way, the virtualization of communication should be understood as a possibility of action. It should not descend to an accommodation in immobility (in the practice of a new format, regarded merely as a format), ignoring the underlying violence and disregarding the contexts and material situations that differentiate the places we each inhabit.

Chapters 18 to 20 deal with different responses to the memory of violence, taking up some of the concepts already mentioned in the previous section: the ethics of care, the ethical limits of representation and humour as a technique of resistance and as a means of dispelling the horrible and making it accessible to representation. The ethics of care, present in the practices of Liddell, Mroué and Majdalanie, appears in a different light in the cinema of Apichatpong Weerasethakul, particularly in the representation of the main character in *Uncle Boonmee* (2010), whose body harbours the memory of violence as an agent of evil and as a victim of trauma. The concept of 'ethics of care' here refers to the epistemological proposal of Boaventura de Sousa Santos and his commitment to an 'axiology of care' (2010: 26) as the basis of a new postcolonial humanism. A problem arises, however, which was already present in Gilligan's formulation: how to establish a balance between justice and care, what are the limits of empathy? In addition, does the desire to understand evil or the causes of violence justify giving a voice to its agents and placing the means of presentation in their hands? These questions were answered in opposing manners by Rithy Pahn, creator of *S-21, la machine de mort du Khmère rouge* (2003) and Joshua Oppenheimer, Cristine Cynn and 'Anonymous', directors of *The Act of Killing* (2012). Humour is shown here as a third way of offering a response, as shown in Basilio Martín Patino's film *Queridísimos verdugos* (1973). This portrait of the last three executioners of General Franco's regime appears as a revealing antecedent to the enquiry into the banality of evil, in which the highlighting of the grotesque present in reality itself acts as a distancing factor, one that shields us from an empathy that could make judgement dispensable.

The third subsection, finally, deals with the representation of the past at the crossroads between memory and history, between subjective memory and collective memory. In Chapter 21 I deal with the specific context of state violence in Latin America, with special attention on the evolution of the treatment of historical memory in Argentine cinema in the post-dictatorship period.

Chapters 22 to 25 propose a detailed analysis of *Tríptico de la violencia en Colombia* (2010–14) by the group Mapa Teatro. A new concept emerges here, that of the 'ethics of the witness', as coined by Heidi and Rolf Abderhalden to refer to their own practice. The witness is an embodiment of the 'double bind': they are present, involved through their presence, but avoid direct intervention; they facilitate re-presentation, opening the place of enunciation to 'guests', without falling into the temptation to represent by usurping the voice or corporeality of others; they assume responsibility without claiming prominence, multiplying mediations that relativize authorship. The analysis of the *Tríptico* allows us to return to many of the questions raised in the three sections of this book, in a certain way serving as an exercise in synthesis. But it also highlights two aspects that have not been sufficiently underscored: the potentiality of Baroque aesthetics and its play of representations, and the link between ethics and micropolitics in the sphere of stage representation.

In a subsequent essay I had the opportunity of contrasting the artistic work of Mapa Teatro with the theorization of Baroque modernity proposed by Bolívar Echeverría. The 'Baroque ethos' was, according to this author, the way in which capitalist modernity was configured in the Latin American sphere, in opposition to the hegemonic mode of a realist ethos, characteristic of Protestant capitalist modernity, and in contrast to other possible types of ethea, such as the classical or the romantic (Echeverría 1998: 38–9). The Baroque affirms representation, but a representation conceived as an 'absolute staging'. Representation is not understood as a substitution for the world, but as the production of a world. Bolívar refers to this phenomenon as a 'transgressive radicalization of representation' (Echeverría 2011: 278). Radicalizing representation implies giving precedence to the ritual, ceremonial, festive, cyclical and ludic dimension over the labour, routine, productive, linear or legal one. Hence, the 'bracketing' of reality characteristic of the Baroque ethos can be read not only as a religious, escapist or transcendent option, but also as a political positioning and as an aesthetics of resistance.

The opting for a baroque aesthetic is central and evident in Mapa's project, but it is also visible in Angélica Liddell's performances and, in a different way, in those of Rabih Mroué and Lina Majdalanie. In all of them, the primacy of micropolitical action can also be detected in the linking of personal and collective memory, in the realization of an ethics of care in the processes of research and staging, or in the attention put on the affect as driving the processes. 'What emerges first in the works of Mapa Teatro to its directors . . . is purely and simply an affect. An affect pulsing in their bodies, which, at that very moment, causes a tension in them' (Rolnik 2018: 24).

The last chapter, 'Without / End', is part epilogue, part an attempt to come to a provisional conclusion. It was written a few weeks after finishing the book, the consequence of being affected by attending a performance by Angélica Liddell, *You are my Destiny (Lo stupro de Lucrezia)* (2014). The work literally situates itself beyond morality in its defence of a love arising from a rape (in stark contradiction with the discourse previously formulated in Liddell's *La casa de la fuerza*). The paradox that probably moved me, however, was discovering that the immersion in pain and violence constituted a means of expressing a singular mode of love and desire for life.

The question of ethics inevitably leads to the question of evil. Evil permeates our daily lives in varying degrees of intensity. We put up with it when it is incidental, even if recurrent. It scares us when it becomes normalized, when it surfaces in subjective models hostile to difference, in moralities deaf to alterity and in policies based on exclusion and hate. All of these result in the transformation of Others into mere bodies, into de-subjectivized bodies, expelled from ethical relations, but also from the *polis*. Evil has contextual causes, yet it can be pointless to attempt to discover its ultimate cause. Since it does not realize the ethico-political principle of justice, as formulated by Ágnes Heller, it is a question that only leads to the abysm or to melancholy. The only thing worth fighting for is for justice – in its socio-political development – to come as close as possible to the ethical principle. Ethical action will continue to be necessary as long as the insuperable chasm remains between these two concepts of justice. Sometimes theatricality, fiction, art and thought can modestly contribute to this task.

Madrid, December 2020

Acknowledgements

The translation of this book has been carried out with the aid of the financing of research activities for groups within the framework of the UCLM's (Universidad de Castilla-La Mancha) 'Plan Propio' (FEDER Funds) and with the support of the project 'La nueva pérdida del centro', financed by the Spanish Ministry of Science, Innovation and Universities (PID2019-105045GB-I00).

1

Representing ourselves

As I write these words, I try to imagine the situation in which they are read. While you read these words, you can try to imagine the situation in which they are written. In this double exercise of representation, temporality becomes paradoxical. For in my representation the imagination of reading is prior to the writing of the words that you are now reading. And in yours, the present of reading occurs – even if just for a few seconds – before the imagining of the act of writing. In a certain sense, for me the words are the memory of an image. For you, they constitute an invitation to imagine a plausible fiction.

I can imagine the situation in which you read, in your home, sitting on a couch or a chair, holding a book that you have just been lent. I can also situate the scene in a cafeteria, in front of a cup of tea or a glass of beer, beginning with the reading of the book you have just bought while you wait for someone, or simply enjoying a moment of solitude in the company of others. Yet perhaps you are not reading a book, but on a screen, or even some photocopies, which suggests you are a student and someone has recommended reading this book, or even insisted on it. You can also be lying on the grass, while around you people discuss today's news, or plans for tonight, the weekend, a joint project, a romantic rendezvous or disagreements. Or you might be lying on a stage, maybe sitting against the wall of a studio, at the beginning, at the end or during the break, of a class, workshop, seminar or rehearsal.

'Representation' in this case is synonymous with 'imagination', the imagination of a situation or a scene. Since we are imagining, let us imagine something at this moment unreal, yet not impossible: that I am writing at the same time that you are reading. This would be a bizarre situation. Because if I existed not here, but yet now, connected, on the other side of the page or the screen, then it would be very strange if you did not respond to me, if you did not interrupt my discourse to agree, differentiate, debate or negate. On the other hand, if we both shared the same time, if the time of writing was the same as that of reading, perhaps with a slight delay between production and reception, then why use the written word and not the spoken one? Why resort to the mediation of the visual code when an aural one would allow more immediate communication? Above all, since it would free our eyes to look at each other. This would provide us with more information on the intentions of each one of us: on my honesty as author and yours as reader. Evidently, the criteria of honesty differ immensely from those of truth.

If in such a situation of co-temporality we would insist on using the written word and if we, moreover, accepted that one of us (in this case, me) writes while the other reads, then we would be condemned to a representation that is apparently useless. It would be a present in which the presence of bodies would be superfluous, since all the attention would be focused on the emergence of words, on the materiality (or virtuality) of the written language.

It is true that we can find in everyday life and in the cultural sphere examples of situations similar to the one described above. In everyday life they generally arise from an intent to establish a distance or ensure protection between persons who do not know each other or are in a delicate situation. In the cultural sphere, they instead arise from the opposite: bringing the writer closer to the readers, forcing a certain spontaneity in the writing. In the first years at my secondary school I had a teacher whose working method consisted of writing the text of his lecture on the blackboard. He did not speak, he simply wrote, with his back to us, and we had to copy everything that he in turn copied from his notes. Only after finishing writing would he turn to us and ask what we did not understand. Perhaps it was shyness that drove him to use such an exhausting method. The fear of presenting himself made him submit to a representation that made it unforgettable; without a doubt his action of writing persists in my memory much more clearly than his words and maybe his teaching unexpectedly passed through the body that he wanted so much to hide. At the other extreme, we could situate the writers who attend improvisation sessions, who write 'live' on the stage or in front of a camera, at the request of the audience or following certain rules. In this case, the writer presents themselves as a writer, but that which defines them becomes secondary and the spectacularity of the act acquires greater relevancy. A representation once again, not decided by the writer but imposed by the apparatus, it anticipates the presentation: what is written is less important than how one writes.

This is not the intention of this introduction, much less that of plunging us into an abyss of reflection in which you will undoubtedly not accompany me. Yet reflecting on writing does not necessarily have to lead to an abyss, in the same way that reflection in general does not necessarily lead to self-absorption. Are we condemned to representation? Why not forget all of the foregoing and return to the immediacy of discourse? The problem of representations is that once created, they do not disappear that easily. Moreover, I seriously doubt that such an 'immediate' discourse even exists.

The imagination that you read about while I write, or that I write about while you read, is a fiction that makes us conscious of representation. I agree to assume the role of writer, offering myself to your imagination to be represented as the author; you accept the function of reader, offering yourself to my imagination to be represented as the reader. The good thing about this representation is that when the reading is over (and the reading can be interrupted, paused or ended at any moment), then you will stop embodying the role of the reader, in the same way that I will cease embodying that of the author when I stop writing. We will only recover those functions, moreover, if at some moment we encounter each other physically. Perhaps then other functions have superimposed or will superimpose themselves on those of the writer and of the reader. The acceptance of this provisionality keeps us from falling into Baroque games, those that very effectively allowed fictional representations to be superimposed on physical or social realities, with the aim of negating the reality until it imploded. Today we know that physical and social realities are likewise representations and we know what interests they serve.

Certainly, we could do without all of the above. Then I should write in the simplest manner possible what I want to communicate. Not ask you to imagine, but only to think. Why not definitively abandon the mode of representation and adopt the much more pleasant one of presentation? In presentation we would be in the present and in presence. Both imply the availability of those who make themselves present; in the present of those who prepare for dialogue, moreover, lies generosity (the present as a gift) and enthusiasm in giving time, as well as each one of us opening themselves to experience.

In recent decades, many artists have attempted to abandon representation to simply present their works or just present themselves. They believed that representation condemned them to insincerity, as well as that temporal, physical and symbolic mediations distanced them from the possibility of sincere communication and of an authentic experience in artistic practice. Representation, moreover, always implies a certain hierarchy: usually there is someone who represents and someone who observes the representation. This exclusivity is coherent with an economic logic based on accumulation, very different to the logic of the gift inherent in the presentational model. In contrast to these models, the goal was a certain immediacy and a certain horizontality in relationships, based on the modesty of the interlocutors: one presents what one has or expresses what one feels, does not pretend to be something else, nor that their representation is worth more than that of others.

Yet, is representation really tied to non-experience, to distance and to arrogance? Would it not be possible to conceive of modes of representation equally based on interchange? When we speak of 'presence', are we not actually saying commitment, involvement and not literally 'presence'? What is more, 'representation' is, as has already become clear, a chameleonic word: which of the chameleon's skins is problematic? Is the chameleon itself the problem or rather is it the light artificially projected on the captive chameleon that provokes intolerance?

What is certain is that these pages could not have been written without a certain confidence in the effectiveness of representation, without the confidence in that your reading will make reflections present and activate new representations, of which I will not be the author. Although, in a strict sense, I am the author of very few of the pages that follow in this book, in which I interpret, quote, comment on and appropriate what has been realized or written by others, who in turn developed, copied or intensified images, ideas and sensations that were seen, read or learned.

I cannot deny that a ludic impulse underlies these pages. One of the reasons that motivates the writing of these texts and the interest in many of these artistic and non-artistic realizations that serve as stimulus for reflection is the recognition of representation as play. It has traditionally been thought that play is what is left after the transcendental nucleus has been extracted from ritual. But the inverse hypothesis is increasingly becoming more productive: that first religions and subsequently art were the outcome of injecting transcendence into play. The critique of transcendence cannot lead to the elimination of play simply because it served as the support for ritual.

All human activity not driven by the necessity of survival, nourishment, defence or protection has a ludic foundation. Culture is play, art is play. We could also add: culture is a necessary game, art is a possible game and sometimes a gratifying one. A few years ago we would have said that the game of culture is necessary to affirm the human condition. Now we know that we share this condition with many animals. Consequently, we should acknowledge that play in culture is necessary to affirm the consciousness that allows us to conceive the human condition. Where there is no play, there is only brutality. Brutality is not a condition of animals, but of animals and humans deprived of the ludic impulse. Brutality is not the result, as determinists believed, of scarcity, ignorance and endogamy; brutality can sublimate itself in barbarism, in the survival instinct, evolve into a will to dominate, colonize, exploit and dispossess. Play is the antidote to brutality; representation based on provisionality, on modesty and on the acceptance of consensual realities, is one of the modes of practising play, without relinquishing experience.

2

Ethics and morality

Ethics operates in the sphere of practice, not in that of representation. One acts in accordance with an ethics. Does representation accept ethics? Only to the extent that representation is conceived as a practice, not as the closure of a practice. That is to say, only to the extent that representation is a moment of thought, of production or of action – not the place where thinking, production and action are detained.

The relationship between 'ethics' and 'representation' can be considered in various spheres of experience, with special relevance in those where representation implies people, where people represent other people. This habitually occurs in the sphere of theatre and film practices (in both cases taken in a broad sense, ranging from performative practices to television series). It also undeniably occurs, and has become an urgent problem, in the sphere of political action (trade unions, parties, citizens etc.).

I understand ethics as the operation activated when an individual has to make decisions that affect others in a specific social context, as well as the set of values and reflections that condition or justify the making of those decisions. Ethics cannot be reduced to a set of norms dictated by an institution, whether religious, academic or political. Such a reduction, in fact, means its annulment, as it would renounce the debate that arises in the immediacy of practice, as well as relinquish judgement of whether such behaviour is good or evil and of the decisions made in that practice. 'Ethics' defined as a normative set would be entirely compatible with 'representation' defined as the closure of action. The function of representation then would consist precisely in the fixing of those norms. In this hypothetical case ethics would see itself supplanted by moral science or moral doctrine. Yet this contradicts experience. For ethical conflict does not occur in reflection, but in action. Ethical behaviour, moreover, is more a habit that occurs in the flux of experience, one that cannot be based merely on contemplation or criticism of the acts of others.

If ethics occurs in practice, then one can only speak of ethics in relation to others, in a behaving for others, or at least conditioned by others. Good and evil cannot be regarded as absolute universalities that an individual or a group approaches through thinking or isolated action, but rather as relative terms, solely definable by the consequences that our decisions have on the life, happiness, joy or well-being of those whose lives we can affect.

According to Jean Jacques Rousseau, the human condition is acquired when one is capable of distinguishing between good and evil. Such a distinction, however, only occurs when a human being lives in society, since in isolation the human being's sole worry would be survival. The distinction between good and evil is not theoretical, but practical. It is not a question of recognizing what is good and what is evil, but of deciding to do one thing or another thing, taking into account the good or evil that result from such actions. For this reason, the moral distinction is inseparable from action. And action is only moral when the individual decides in freedom, not compelled by or submitting to any force or doctrine. 'To renounce liberty is to renounce being a man' according to Rousseau's maxim (Todorov 2009: 126).

Rousseau's ethical reflection is coherent with a humanist stance. As Tzvetan Todorov observes, it differs from a traditional ethics that situated the individual in relation to nature and is instead closer to Christian ethics, which situated the individual in relation to others. Christian morality justified behaviour towards others in the connection of all human beings with a transcendental being: love of your neighbour is also love of God. The challenge for Enlightenment thinking lay precisely in justifying a humanism shorn of transcendence.

In a democratic society respectful of individuals' autonomy, ethics can neither be based on transcendental principles nor be imposed as a set of norms. Ethics manifests and conditions the consideration that each person has for others as subjects of rights and feelings. In contrast to transcendental ethics, fixed and represented in a positive morality, the concept of ethics proposed here is more one of an immanent ethics, which does not serve as the basis of morality, but is manifested instead as morality in the time of an individual life and in the time of social life.

Alain Badiou attempted to lay the foundation of an immanent ethics based on his concept of the 'event'. He reminds us that it was Hegel who established the precise difference between 'morality' and 'ethics', placing the former in the realm of 'reflexive action' and the latter in the realm of 'immediate action' (Badiou 1993: 2). Proceeding from this, he elaborates a critique of the ethical models dominant at the end of the twentieth century, beginning with the resurgence of a humanist ethics that strives to ignore poststructuralist criticism and the 'death of man' proclaimed by Foucault and Lacan. According to this ethical model, the victim, the object of ethical thinking or doing, is contemplated as a body, hardly distinguishable in its organic animality from the victimizer, both of them equal in their being for death. Badiou therefore proposes that the consequence of the ethical decision must be the manifestation of the 'Immortal'. Secondly, he criticizes the ethics of transcendent alterity, inherited from Lévinas' thought, which in itself cannot escape a religious foundation. What is more, it is corrupted in an ethics of sameness that achieves its most reductive formula in 'become like me and I will respect your difference' (25). Thirdly, Badiou unmasks the ethics of human rights as a substitute for politics understood as disagreement and as a manifestation of the nihilism concealed behind the announcement of the end of ideologies.

In radical opposition to this new nihilism, Badiou proposes an 'ethics of truths', which would be grounded not on the subject, recognized as non-existent, but in the relationship with the event, in the 'fidelity' to the event and in the 'perseverance' of the rupture created by the event. Each person would enter into an ethical relationship not as a human subject, but as a singularity affected by the event, who takes decisions based on the 'fidelity' to the event and to 'persevere' in it (71).

Giorgio Agamben formulated the immanent condition of all ethics from another point of view. The ethical discourse exists in return for recognizing that the human being lacks essence and does not have to realize any historical, spiritual or biological essence, that is, that human existence is the possibility and the potentiality of being one way or another (Agamben 1990: 39). The ethical experience occurs in a space of freedom, of free relationships and, what is more, of egalitarian relations: a relationship in which I recognize the other as equal to me in terms of a subject of rights, action and desire, but also of feelings and passions.

Ethics is inseparable from freedom, it manifests itself in the moral decisions that are taken in specific situations. It is consolidated in time, in the succession and in the coherence of such decisions. Yet it always manifests itself in the present, it becomes effective in the present of the making of decisions. Is there an ethics beyond presence in the present? Ethics is not a 'reserve' that generates future benefits, it cannot be understood in terms of production, but in terms of practice. Neither is it a knowledge that serves to judge and analyse the decisions of others, but rather something that becomes effective in doing, in action.

I will use the term 'ethics' below to refer to a practice dependent on the taking of practical decisions, or on the sum of practical decisions, and the reflection on this practice by a person or a group of persons. I will use the term 'morality' to refer to the normative or descriptive dimension, in other words, the study of behaviours proceeding from the judgement of good or evil, or to their determination according to such a criterion. This will avoid the confusion so exploited by religions and churches, who have attempted and continue to attempt to impose their doctrines on the political regulation of moral affairs. When religions speak of ethics in reality they are referring to a moral restriction, to a moral law. Yet in the absence of freedom one cannot speak of ethics.

To impose moral law, churches need power and it is the striving for power that drives them to politics. In political struggle morality forgets ethics in order to make room for the interests of power, without whose alliance the alleged moral law cannot be imposed. Morality is the *natural* access route of religions and their surrogates towards political power and their *legitimate* weapon in political debate. Religious leaders appear before the powerful, cloaked in authority, to demand laws conforming with their moral dogmas. If necessary they dispense with the necessary political debate for the passing of such laws, submitting any superficial incoherence to an ultimate coherence that only they, as representatives of divine will, can sanction.

In contemporary societies these tasks have been displaced to the agents of the construction of subjectivity: transcendence is no longer materialized in heaven or in hell, but in the community of good people who are rewarded with the fulfilment of small desires that never provide real satisfaction.

Obviously, these moral transactions never have to do with ethics. Ethics can never be politically determined. Neither can it be determined by a religion. Religion imposes absolute truths, from which dogmas of behaviour are derived. Political power imposes limits on behaviours. Religious law annuls ethics to the extent that the imposition of the dogmas threatens the liberty of the individual. Political power annuls ethics when the legal limits are so restrictive that they eliminate the margin of individual decision. And ethics is contrary to limits.

That ethics, religion and politics are incompatible does not imply that religious actors or those in power are free of ethical decisions, unless they themselves believe entirely in the role they represent and in the reason (or in the essence) of their representation. The possibility of an ethics of representation implies, first of all, the recognition of the artifice that all representation involves, that is, the acceptance that representations are not contrastable with criteria of truth and that the sense of representations lies in their utility. They can be useful as a means of knowledge, as the manifestation of invisible realities, as games or entertainments, as means of generating aesthetic pleasure, or as tools for the creation of community.

3

Ethics and artistic practice

Radically democratic societies will be societies in which no privilege of truth shall be conceded to representations. Representations will be conceived as transitory modes of being or as temporary means of communication. Their legitimacy shall not depend on any type of criteria of truth or transcendence, but on political agreements following debates or conflicts. The transitoriness of representations prevents the existence of religions based on transcendent entities, since these arise from their hypostasis. Discussion of morality ceases to be a translation of dogmatic principles and is transformed into a discussion on limits.

The criteria for the establishment of limits are derived in many cases from ways of understanding the coexistence established in ancient religions or old humanisms. The progressive liberation of those principles for the elaboration of free agreements, grounded in debate and the resolution of conflicts, will give rise to a moral democracy. Morality is necessary for coexistence, as long as morality does not become a legal system that completely annuls the freedom of individual decision and, consequently, the living out of singularities. Without shared moral limits, conflicts of behaviour would end up making effective relations and communication impossible and, as a result, prevent the development of politics as well: moral conflicts would devour politicians. On the other hand, the necessity of establishing precise moral codes in certain spheres of responsibility seems obvious, as in research with human beings or the management of common goods (the current sphere of professional politics).

Moral codes are necessary in those spheres in which the actors/representers work in relation with persons (or the interests of persons) who do not act in representation, but who are themselves. The patient will continue to be the same body when the surgeon takes off their mask and gown and returns home to eat dinner or watch a film. Citizens affected by political decisions will remain affected by those decisions when the politician abandons the parliament or ministry office to dedicate themselves to their profession or business.

What ethical committees that regulate experiments with stem cells, or establish protocols for assisted dying, essentially do is free others from ethical decisions, imposing a code that annuls the ethical conflict. Once the code or protocol is established, the individual persons are theoretically excused from any decision, from the effort of assuming and maintaining an ethical position. The code is, consequently, a tool that protects society from individual immoral decisions, but which also frees a person from ethical responsibility.

There must be moral codes because differences of responsibility and influence exist and because diverse degrees of representation exist. Consequently, they owe their existence to the unequal distribution of the sensible; they belong to the political debate. Nevertheless, when codes or protocols are elaborated by experts they not only deprive the involved person or group in question of the capacity for an ethical decision in a specific situation, but also rob the questions they regulate of political debate. Politics cannot be privatized by committees of experts in the name of ethics.

With religion excluded from the public sphere, morality becomes a political question, or rather, a matter of political order. Ethics is definitively freed of dogmatic restrictions and assumes a place in the sphere of specific practice. Although ethics can also operate in extreme situations in the sphere of political representation, it normally operates in the sphere of everyday life and in the sphere of micropolitics. Ethics operates in the decisions of action and performance not determined by moral and legal limits, or where the moral and legal limits conflict with specific situations that require urgent action.

In those cases where the actors/representers are unequivocally situated in a sphere of representation, without the possibility of actually affecting people they do not represent or who are external to this sphere, then there is no place for the imposing of moral codes. This permits the representation of immoral behaviours, even criminal ones, their justification and defence, on the condition that the limits that separate representation from reality or from actual life are not questioned. These limits, however, are becoming increasingly blurred (if they ever were clear): firstly, by the undifferentiation of the public and private spheres in contemporary urban societies; secondly, by the amalgamation of reality and fiction in all spheres of our experience (from autobiography to politics). The confluence of private and public life has provoked an indistinctness between ethics and morality, micropolitics and politics. The same effect results from the incursion of the real in spheres traditionally reserved for fiction, as well as by the incursion of fiction in spheres traditionally reserved for effective action.

All of the foregoing may sound very abstract. In fact, it proceeds from a theoretical supposition that has never been realized until now: the existence of radically democratic societies, neither determined by religions or moralities imposed by economic interests, nor governed by power groups capable of 'buying' political representatives and social agents. One could then succumb to the temptation of regarding ethical responsibility as secondary to political responsibility, every effort being channelled into the effective transformation of our societies. Yet, in the absence of transcendent principles (and of great ideologies), the only base for political action is ethics.

Artists have taken diverse positions in regards to ethical responsibility. For some, artistic practice is incompatible with ethical responsibility, since it would constrain the freedom of the individual in their experimentation with sensitive issues. For others, the artist, precisely because the artist publicly manifests singularity, has to defend an ethical position confronting conventional morality, but also amorality.

The first position is pragmatic – it proceeds from the idea that in current conditions any ethical reflection will always be conditioned by religion or political ideology. Art requires freedom; ethics presupposes freedom. Both art and ethics are resistant to any codes and limits that individuals, as subjects of a practice, have not imposed on themselves voluntarily, as the result of intuition, reflection or habit. Limits that are externally imposed belong to neither art nor ethics, but to religion, replaced in post-Enlightenment societies first by culture and then by morality. The imposition of these limits is made effective by means of power. These limits will only be legitimate when they are the result of debates and political agreements, made effective by means of a radically democratic power. But even then it will be difficult to evade the determination of inherited moralities.

The second option accepts, however, one of these legacies, that of critical humanism or of activist commitment. 'What unites the arts is ethical principles', states the dramatist Angélica Liddell; 'aesthetic renewal is an ethical question' (Liddell 2008: 147). In another passage she adds, 'I believe that ethics is simply the desire to say something about what is good ... true ethics is ungraspable, but as soon as we can name it, ethics, then we can turn it into desire' (Liddell 2014: 61). The ethics of the artist is manifested in their constant struggle against the representations that make up culture. But the means the artist uses for this (and this is especially pronounced in the case of Liddell) is none other than the staging of new representations.

How to overcome the apparent contradiction between ethics and representation? In the first place, by highlighting the decoupling of representation and truth, conceiving of representation as a resource for action and play. In second place, the conflict between representation and ethics arises when we regard artistic activity as production and not as practice. When we think of artistic activity as practice – that is to say, when we accept the social and processual dimensions of artistic creation – then the question of ethics necessarily returns, even if in a paradoxical manner. In third place, the term 'representation' conveys (and at the same time can conceal and confuse) very distinct concepts. It will be necessary to discover when each one of these 'representations' is useful and when it results in closure, which representations are necessary and which representations it would be better to avoid. Finally, in the sphere of live practices (whether they be artistic or not), the mediation of representation is altered by the immediacy of the body and by the real relations between bodies in a space of action or performance, shared with other observing or participating bodies.

The commitment of bodies, the 'putting of the body on the line', has a practical dimension with ethical and political implications. To talk about an ethics of representation is, to a large extent, to talk about an ethics of the practices of bodies. Yet, is not the body precisely that which resists representation? Is the body not the irrepresentable real? It is indeed, in relation to the experience of each one of us. It is also to the extent that the representation of the body serves for the reification of the other, in other words, for the other's alienation as a human being; in Badiou's terms, to deprive the human being of its condition of 'immortal'. Nonetheless, representation is not alien to the body. Or at least that is how neurologists and anthropologists have explained it. Neurologists call 'representation' the way in which the brain relates to the stimuli transmitted by nerves from different parts of the organism (Damasio 1994: 185). Anthropologists observe that, even before being represented in a medium distinct from itself, the body is also an image, inseparable from its image (Belting 2001: 112). Representation is consequently inherent in living bodies. One could object that neurologists employ representation in a metaphoric sense and that anthropologists recur to this concept after it has been elaborated in other disciplines. Other concepts could be used to refer to the processes described by each of them. But the fact is that in our current conception, any study of the human being inevitably appears intersected by representation.

The problem lies not in representation, but in forgetting its metaphoric or substitute dimension, in short, its fictional dimension. This forgetting leads to the concession of a status of reality to representation itself and to the experience of separation and absence. This occurs when the representation of the organism in the brain is separated from the organism itself, as though the brain did not form an inextricable part of the organism, or when the image of the body is stripped off, to be fixed in another body or in an inert medium, and the image itself is attributed an immateriality that it lacks.

Literature, dramatic theatre and fictional film are exercises of absence. Representation in those mediums is always of something absent. If they are exercises of absence, how can one conceive of the ethics inside them? Because ethics does not exist without encounter and the encounter cannot occur in absence. It can take place at a distance, in distant co-temporality, but not in absence, nor in asynchrony. For this reason Artaud espoused a theatre of radical presence; for this reason he condemned literature and affirmed the present and the presence, the intense sharing of a time and a space. Nevertheless, the absence implicit in representation does not mean that the event in which the representation occurs is necessarily marked by absence. It will be so only if that which is represented (or the persons that are represented) is conceded an ontological superiority in regards to what takes place in the present moment. This happens, in an extreme manner, in religious liturgies and, by extension, in civil liturgies. But this does not have to occur in other social or artistic events. In this case, the involvement of those who participate in a representation, their being corporally present, can render secondary any absence implicit in representation. Represented absence would then be a mere tool, not the objective of the representational act.

4

The problem of sincerity

Let us begin with an old story. It is about *La carrosse d'or* (The Golden Carriage), a film from 1952 by Jean Renoir. Like his other films, it is based on a literary work, *La carrosse de Saint-Sacrament* by Prosper Merimée. Freely adapting the novel, Renoir presents an amusing set of Chinese boxes, which function, according to Erich Rohmer, like a 'jeweller's case' that 'holds the precious jewels "commedia dell'arte", Vivaldi and Magnani' (Bazin 1971: 231).

Vivaldi returns us sensorially to the Baroque and to the game of representation. 'Commedia dell'arte' is a mode of popular theatre recovered in the eighteenth century by the major Italian and French playwrights, as well as by some theatre reformers at the beginning of the twentieth century. The latter rejected the notion that actors should be limited to representing previously written texts, wanting instead physical and sensitive playing to be as important as dramatic representation.

In *La carrosse d'or* we see a troupe of Italian actors who arrive in the capital of a Latin American country during the era of a colonial viceroyalty. These actors, in particular Colombine, played by Anna Magnani, will expose the theatricality of the viceroyalty's political system staged at court. If there were any pretence of historical rigour, it would have been necessary to build a much more splendid and complex set to represent that city which, by all indications, should coincide with Lima, the capital of one of the four viceroyalties that governed the Spanish colonies in Latin America. The action, however, does not take place in history, but inside a theatre. In fact, the film begins with a curtain that is raised to reveal another curtain, which is likewise raised to show a stage representing the interior of a palace. The camera travels inside this interior to transform, 'through the art of film', the theatre into film and the film into a fable. By means of a simple movement the theatrical staging becomes real (or rather, filmic) and the recording of the stage on film a real production of illusions.

A great commotion has arisen inside the palace, stirred up by the announcement of the arrival of the carriage, ordered by the viceroy from Europe, to ride through the streets of the colony and display his power. But the same boat also conveys a company of Italian actors, intent on making their fortune in the Americas. They are deeply disappointed when they arrive at the theatre that has supposedly contracted them, only to discover that in reality it is a farmyard, inhabited by chickens, pigs and llamas and filled with all kinds of debris.

Overcoming this first impression, and after negotiating with the impresario, the actors get to work and 'in a film fade' transform the farmyard into a theatre, announcing the first performance of 'commedia dell'arte'. Don Antonio comes out on the stage before an audience of dumfounded *cholos* (mestizos) to introduce the extravagant characters. In spite of the strangeness of the spectacle, everything appears to go well until Ramón, the famous bullfighter, makes his entrance into the room and immediately incites the enthusiasm of the spectators, who forget the Italians' performance to cheer their idol. Colombine has to resort to her most potent weapons to recapture the audience's attention. In a duel of charisma with the torero she manages to win a smile and applause from him. From this moment on she becomes the new focus of admiration for the city.

Intrigued by Colombine's success, the viceroy summons her to the palace and is completely captivated by her charms, just like Ramón. Camilla (the actress who plays Colombine) finds herself at the centre of a love triangle whose three sides are Felipe (the young officer who travelled with her from Europe and who shared a seat in the carriage with her during the long journey), the bullfighter (the popular idol) and the viceroy (the representative of absolute power on that side of the Atlantic). For a while Camilla seems to enjoy her triumph and the pleasure of riding in the carriage that the viceroy has given her. But the situation becomes unsustainable.

As a result of his weakness and his favours to the actress, the viceroy is threatened with being ousted by his courtiers. His passion is so overwhelming that he even considers renouncing his position to dedicate himself to a 'normal' life with his lover. The bullfighter is eaten up by jealousy and demands the exclusivity of Camilla's affections. After an expedition to the interior, the young officer Felipe has discovered the wisdom of the indigenous peoples and their integration with nature, proposing to Camilla that she abandon civilization and accompany him on his new adventure. Overwhelmed, Camilla decides to leave all three, giving the carriage to the bishop, renouncing her life 'outside' and accepting that it only has meaning inside the theatre.

La carrosse d'or resulted in one of the greatest commercial failures in Renoir's career. Nevertheless, in the words of Rohmer, it can be considered the 'open sesame' of all his oeuvre. 'The two extremes of his work, Art and Nature, Comedy and Life, are personified in two mirrors that, one in front of the other, perpetually reflect an image until they annul any demarcation between their two zones of influence' (237). The somewhat simplified treatment of the characters (in line with the homage to commedia dell'arte) allows Renoir to present his protagonists as representatives of basic conflicts. Camilla/Colombine is torn between the will to live and the obligation to represent. Life is identified with the free expression of feelings, but also with the sexual drive. Representation is what guarantees social existence. Felipe, the soldier, decides to abandon civilization in order to live with the indigenous people in harmony with nature. Ramón, the bullfighter, is accustomed, like Camilla, to representation and, although in permanent contact with nature (the fight with the animal and sex), knows that his pleasures depend on maintaining his social role. Finally, the viceroy is the most distant from nature, the antithesis of Felipe; for him Camilla represents an access to life.

In one of the last sequences of the film, Camilla, overwhelmed by her three suitors, asks herself where truth is; she believed there was a difference between the stage as the place of the lie and social life as the place of reality and truth. But she realizes this is not so: that there are lies everywhere and no truth anywhere, or that truth is something that does not correspond with what we thought was true, as well as that we cannot live without masks. 'I need to understand. I am absolutely sincere in life and on the stage. Then why do I triumph in the theatre and in life destroy everything I love? Where is truth, where does the theatre stop, where does life begin?' Yet truth does not have to do with taking off a mask, but with negotiating the masks that permit a more intense relationship, or a more just relationship, or a more supportive relationship in each moment. Ethics, moreover, probably has more to do with knowing which mask to put on than with removing a mask.

This reflection of Camilla in front of the viceroy is one of the few moments of seriousness that Renoir allows his character in the film, which is fashioned with the lightness typical of popular theatre. Shortly afterward, Camilla gives up being a lady to return to being an actress, since only by being an actress and representing the role of a servant can she also paradoxically aspire to be a lady and be sincere. Don Antonio, the troupe's impresario, explains it to her clearly: 'You are not made for what they call life, your place is among us, with the actors, acrobats, mime artists, clowns, tumblers. You will only find your happiness on the stage, each afternoon, for a brief two hours, practising your profession of actress: that is, forgetting yourself. Through the characters you embody you will perhaps discover the true Camilla.'

This speech by don Antonio is very similar to one by Danglard, the impresario of the Moulin Rouge in *French Cancan* (1954). When Nini, the washerwoman he has discovered and trained, is about to abandon him and the cabaret in order to live her own life, Danglard warns her: 'Do you think that it's important what you or I want? Only what they want is important. We are at the service of the audience. Do you know why it worries me to see you go? . . . It's because this profession loses a good soldier. I thought you were one of us. If this isn't so, then get out.' The audience in *French Cancan* is that of the celebrated Parisian cabaret. The audience in *La carrosse d'or* is colonial society in its entirety, the inhabitants of the imaginary city constructed by Renoir.

The defence of the profession that Renoir proposes in these two films dangerously coincides with a defence of the established social order. In fact, the end of *La carrosse d'or* parallels that of *La règle du jeu* (The Rules of the Game, 1939). In that film, the terrace of La Colinière is turned into a stage where the return to the social order is represented, based on the institutionalized lie, the acceptance of the position that corresponds to each person and the repression of feelings in public for the benefit of the preservation of power. The protagonist Christine faces the same problem as Camilla. She too falters and feels that 'the lie is a dress too heavy to bear'. Only a blow of reality, the accidental murder of Jurieux, will restore strength and false joy to everyone, allowing them to continue to represent in accordance with the established order. The affirmation of theatricality, where the actresses can be sincere, is at the same time the acceptance of a collective lie and of a situation of social injustice. Paradoxically, what is morally reassuring for the characters, is socially disquieting for society as a whole, 'for the audience'.

Before arriving at this moment (of a bitter pessimism masked by the joviality of the spectacle), the action revolving around Camilla reveals a way in which the incursion of artistic theatre in the theatre of reality can subvert the social system. This subversion begins with the representative function of Camilla, who surpasses the representation of her character. The people identify with the actress by means of the character; they do not identify with Colombine, a distant and simplified character, but with the actress whose life and truth consists of interpreting Colombine. Camilla is indistinguishable from Colombine. This is the key to this exercise of representation: Camilla is only loved because she represents Colombine, but it is not Colombine the people applaud, but Camilla.

From a psychological perspective, the identification of a person with their mask can be experienced as a condemnation. Hence the anguish of Camilla, who at one point would like to isolate herself, or the wish of the viceroy, who would like to abandon his position. In other cases the condemnation can be more severe. We could recall, for example, the anguish of Gatica 'el Mono' [the Monkey] at the end of his life, as depicted by Leonardo Favio in his masterful film. As much as he might try, Gatica is not able to free himself of his social role. His destiny resembles that of other great popular idols, such as Marilyn, Elvis or Maradona. How to revert to being just someone and being respected as just someone? Such figures experience the opposite of those people who attempt to negate themselves in the construction of their personalities and fail in the attempt, such as Norma Desmond (Gloria Swanson) in *Sunset Boulevard* (1950), recognized only by her loyal butler (and former director, Erich von Stroheim). For the former type of personalities, their destiny, forced by anguish, can be tragic. For the second type, their destiny is usually dramatic, or rather, agonizing. In Renoir's comedy the anguish, by contrast, is resolved with lightness.

Camilla's success is derived from the people identifying with her, because her character Colombine is a maid, a woman of the people; she makes jokes and treats herself nonchalantly, with humour, making light of herself. Like Harlequin, Colombine is 'one of us', 'a someone'. If Camilla represented the character Isabella in the 'commedia', or a tragic role like Antigone, she probably would not earn the same affection. She might receive admiration, or respect, but not the same affection, the one that converts Camilla/Colombine into a representative in the adjectival sense of representative, in the sense of representation of what 'we' (all of us as a people) are. Compared with her, the viceroy represents power, although not at all representative of his subjects.

In contrast, Camilla wins the favour of the city's inhabitants, who identify with her. They do not regard her as a white European foreigner who performs dances and songs unknown to them, but as a simple maid, who speaks their same language (even if it is French). Camilla's success furnishes her with representativeness. It is this very representativeness that the bullfighter and the viceroy dispute. Camilla could have chosen to be rich, by marrying the bullfighter, or powerful, by becoming the viceroy's mistress. She rejects both options, not for moral reasons, that is, not in a search for honesty or authenticity (Felipe's option), but for ethical reasons.

For a moment Camilla's decision has an egalitarian effect. Although the next day everyone returns to representing their roles and occupying different positions in the social hierarchy, the fact that Camilla can choose and did choose where to situate herself makes her once more a representative, but in this case one of individual freedom and of its potential. Camilla has not deluded herself that because she rides in the golden carriage she is the vicereine, but an actress; while riding in the carriage she did not cease to be representative of all the women (and men) of the dispossessed people who acclaimed her. They acclaim her because she is one of them, not for her to abandon them and sell out to wealth or power. Her political weapons are renunciation and defiance, combined with her refusal to abandon representation. One can represent (speak for others) without using power and influence for personal benefit. One can represent (embody the other) out of love of life. This is probably not the merit of Camilla, but of Renoir, who did not want to turn his character into a tragic heroine. Instead, he simply wanted the actress to unmask the powerful and reveal them as 'anyones', as men and women with weaknesses like everyone else. By means of accusation, defiance and representation Renoir, via Camilla, exposes the stage machinery, tricks and disguises, in order to declare the possibility of an egalitarian society hidden behind the pyramid of a theatrical society.

The principles of 'equality and fraternity' evoked by the film arise precisely within the context of one of the most hierarchized and theatrical societies in Western history. Richard Sennett analysed how in the great cities of the eighteenth century the social life of the dominant classes evolved following a theatre model. 'Playacting in the form of manners, conventions and ritual gestures is the very stuff out of which public relations are formed' (Sennett 1976: 29). Eighteenth-century society took this idea to the extreme, to the point of conceiving of itself as a stage (107).

In the eighteenth century, behaviour in the public realm was dominated by modes of theatricality. The existence of a public theatrical space permitted the preservation of intimacy: the expression and manifestation of intimate feelings or experiences was reserved for private space and excluded from public perception. Only off the stage could individuals be 'authentic'. To try to be 'authentic' on stage, that is, in the public space, not only implied unnecessarily exposing the most fragile dimension of the individual, it also constituted a threat for the maintenance of public life itself.

In accordance with these observations, Renoir introduces a double anachronism into his fiction. He does this deliberately, and perhaps even casually, since he simply wants to pay homage to theatre and Vivaldi, eluding political and postcolonial issues (which I will address below). The first anachronism is derived from the shifting of this theatrical society, exclusive to the European city, to an American colony (and, moreover, to a Spanish colony, not a French or British one). Such a shift produces bizarre situations. Renoir subtly highlights this strangeness by means of the amazed faces of the *cholos* awaiting the beginning of the performance, completely ignorant of what they are about to see.

A second anachronism arises from the moral problem that Camilla ponders, something inconceivable within the context of a society that accepted representation as inherent in social life. The incapacity of being sincere does not derive from the imposition of a social mask, but from the extension of theatricality to the private sphere. Such an extension, however, was not typical of eighteenth-century society, but rather was a modern phenomenon. According to Sennett's thesis, it was precisely the search for authenticity that produced the collapse of theatrical society and with it the elimination of the public realm, at the same time that the private sphere was abandoned. Camilla's ethical dilemma is actually that of a woman of the

1950s, in any case of an actress of that period, and not that of a common actress of the eighteenth century (and much less that of an Italian actress forcibly shifted to Peru). In reality, Renoir is presenting a contemporary issue within an ancient fable, by means of which he takes advantage of a model of social theatricality that had already disappeared.

Camilla's reflection seems more a reflection by Magnani, or a reflection by Renoir put into Magnani's mouth. The tone of this sequence differs entirely from the tone prevailing in the rest of the film, which is characterized by a 'joyful' acceptance of representation. The change of tone is so brief that it does not affect the plot and does not even end up being formulated as an ethical dilemma. Camilla considers abandoning representation for the benefit of a sincerity whose likelihood she herself doubts. Renoir too appears unwilling to abandon film production, judging by his career and by the continuity of this profound reflection in his other films.

Renoir choses to continue representing. Camilla choses to continue representing. Yet what both of them represent is a Colombine-Camilla doubly trapped in representation. Trapped in theatrical representation and in dramatic representation: in both she disappears as a person to become a public figure. As Sennett explains, the mechanisms that people employed to protect their intimacy in the public space, that is, the practice of social theatricality, in a strange way produced the elevation of actors to the special status of public figures (26). Obliged in a way to act, in order to succeed socially, when actors – as professionals in acting – succeeded in their sphere (the theatre) they were also guaranteed promotion to the highest levels of society. (Obviously this occurred principally with the great tragic actors; the success of a popular actress is only justified in a cinematographic fiction and in shifting the action from a European city to the colony).

The fable that Renoir stages could very well have been situated, following Sennett, in the nineteenth century (when, in fact, Mérimée wrote his novel). But in this case Renoir could not have played with commedia dell'arte nor have proposed such an ending to the film. Camilla's ethical problem, the problem of sincerity, could only have been contemplated in the twentieth century. In that century, however, the conception of the social person just as much as the conception of theatricality had changed enormously. Hazarding a double anachronism, Renoir recurs to a caricature of colonial eighteenth century society to ponder a contemporary issue. He uses alienation, in the Brechtian sense, but with a style that is more playful, tinged with ironic criticism, although with a dose of inevitable historical pessimism.

This pessimism contrasts, nevertheless, with an anthropological optimism, visible in the 'very human' treatment that Renoir bestows on his characters in this and other films, as well as in the concern for sincerity that affects all of them in a world they recognize as marked by the mask and the lie. This humanism of Renoir is in a certain sense itself anachronistic, not at all corresponding to the growing hegemony of the sociological perspective in the treatment of social issues. Indeed, an updating of the theatrical metaphor utilized by Renoir to describe colonial society would require using the frame analysis theory elaborated by Erving Goffman (1959), almost at the same time that the film was shot. However, the problem of sincerity would have been impossible to address with Goffman's micro-sociology. Sociology, including micro-sociology, does not admit ethical questions. And Camilla, a fictional character, a displaced and anachronistic one, would not have constituted an interesting case study at all.

5

What does 'represent' mean?

In languages derived from Latin the term 'representation' is polysemic. This polysemy endows the diverse concepts of 'representation' with a complexity that in some other languages are denoted by different words.

The first common meaning corresponds to that of 'mental representation'. I 'represent' or imagine to myself something that I am unfamiliar with, something that I have information about but have never seen, something that occurred in the past or that has not yet happened. That something can be an object, a situation, an experience. To represent, in this sense, is 'to bring clearly before the mind' (Merriam-Webster) with signs or symbols. In other words, imagining something that we cannot perceive, know or experience directly. This sense of 'representation' corresponds to one of the possible meanings of the German word 'Vorstellung', a term that Jacques Derrida, commenting on Heidegger, translated as 'the gesture which consists of placing, of causing to stand before one, of installing in front of oneself as available' (Derrida 1989: 106). Representation is a gesture of the subject in relation to the object; consequently, it is unilateral. It is also a mode of relation between the subject and the object in the absence of the latter. It is precisely the unilaterality and absence implied in 'representation' that provoked the criticism of a philosophy based on representation and not on presence, whose foundations reach back to Platonism and which has hegemonically dominated Western thinking since the Renaissance. Nonetheless, as Derrida notes, 'a criticism or a deconstruction of representation would remain feeble, vain, and irrelevant if it were to lead to some rehabilitation of immediacy' (108).

The second ordinary meaning corresponds to that of 'mimetic representation': to put something or someone (or oneself) in the place of another thing or person, or rather, from the point of view of the represented: to make present something or someone in another thing or person. A landscape or a face is made present through its pictorial or cinematographic representation; the pigments on the canvas, the printing on the paper or the electronic reproduction on the screen represent a concrete reality: the face of a person or the view of a landscape. The referent of the representation, that which is represented, can be absent or present, can be real or fictional. In many cases, 'mimetic representation' results from the materialization of a 'mental representation': that of the artist, of the witness, of the narrator, of who invents the represented object. In other cases, if the referent is unknown, the 'mimetic representation' serves to generate a 'mental representation' in the spectator. In both cases the corresponding German term is 'Darstellung'. In contrast to 'Vorstellung' it accentuates the existent mediation between the subject performing the gesture of placing something before perception and the subject perceiving this something placed before perception.

'Mimetic representation' can be understood as a 'making present', a 'presenting', a 'lending presence' to something or someone absent. But if that something or someone existed in the past, or is a fiction codified verbally or visually in the past, the prefix 're-' then acquires a temporal sense. 'Re-presentation' therefore also acquires the sense of 'making present', not only in the sense of 'lending presence', but of 'bringing to the present'. Nevertheless, representation is not always re-presentation, that is, it does not always imply repetition or renewing of something from the past, or of someone who actually or fictionally existed in the past. Sometimes representation is reproduction (copy) of something real (an object or event). Other times it is reconstruction (the result of a recollection) of something from the past. But in many cases, representation can be the materialization of images, ideas or imagined mental situations, without any correspondence to actual referents. In this case the prefix 're-' would make no sense, since there is no repetition but rather production. Henri Bergson noted this in 1910, proposing the use of the term 'presentation' 'to designate in a general way all that is purely and simply presented to intelligence' (Derrida 1989: 116). Two objections, however, can be raised that remain valid. First, can one impose a word on colloquial usage, as well as specialist usage, when another one – regardless of how ambiguous and imperfect it might be – functions effectively and its meaning is specified without much difficulty, thanks to the contexts of its use? Secondly, is not all representation, even that of known or remembered objects and situations, always a production of a signifier (of a painting, a text, a gesture) and therefore the presentation of the signifier itself, beyond representing another thing?

This new ambivalence of representation, its being at the same time reproduction and production, becomes much more evident in a specific modality of 'mimetic representation'. This occurs when what is represented is not an object, image or idea, but a person, a group of persons, a situation or an event involving persons. The actor or actress who represents another person attempts to place themselves in the place of that other person. In German, an actor or actress is for this reason called a 'Darsteller' and is the subject of a 'Darstellung' (placing before others). To distinguish it from the previous meaning, I will refer to this as 'dramatic representation' (being an other or pretending to be an other). The ambivalence observed in regard to 'mimetic representation' is highlighted when the subjective body of the actor resists any attempt towards transparency in the representation: the actor or actress cannot be erased to become the character, their presence cannot be eliminated for the benefit of the representation. This ambivalence generated a large part of the polemics on representation in the theatrical field that shook the twentieth century, among them some questions that directly affect the ethics of representation. Performance was proposed at that time as an alternative to the representation of roles or characters: the actor or actress presents themself on the stage with their own identity, without substituting their body for an other's. Yet this does not mean that theatres or artistic practices of presence in themselves, by renouncing dramatic representation, will lead to the end of all representation.

'Theatrical representation' refers to the staging of a dramatic work or of non-dramatic material that is presented after a dramaturgical elaboration. Representation, in turn, can refer to staging or to the moment of making the *mise en scène* present each evening. In the first sense, in regard to *mise en scène*, 'theatrical representation' is a mode of 'mimetic representation', to the extent that the *mise en scène* represents the dramatic text or the dramaturgical elaboration created by the author, the director, or the group of actors. In the second sense, as regards the actual execution of the *mise en scène*, 'theatrical representation' is closer to 'dramatic representation'. This occurs even though it does not represent an individual, but rather an action by means of a succession of situations, in which individuals act who represent other individuals (but who can also represent other things and whose presence is supplemented by a multiplicity of non-human signifiers). German has different terms for each of these meanings: 'Inszenierung' equates to *mise en scène*; 'Vorstellung', in a second sense, means 'theatrical representation'; 'Aufführung' refers to the theatrical event independent of the referent (dramatic text or theatrical script, if there is one). 'Representation' as well as 'performance' intersect in the term 'Aufführung', which is why it became a key concept of German theatre studies. In recent translations into Spanish it has been rendered as *'realización escénica'* (theatrical realization), a term that coincides with the first translation of 'performative utterances' as *'enunciados realizativos'* (productive utterances) (Sánchez 2014).

The two terms 'Vorstellung' (representation for spectators) and 'Aufführung' (realization in front of the spectators) cover the two dimensions of 'theatrical representation' that correspond to the ambiguity introduced by the prefix 're-' (reproduction / production) in the term 'representation'.

The intersection of 'mental representation' and 'mimetic representation' produces a new sense, that of 'being an image or symbol of something', by uniting the features or characteristics considered common to a set of things or persons, or defining for a group or a series of persons or things. This arises from the high degree of coincidence between how we represent something to ourselves, mentally or by imagination, and the realization of that imagining in an object, situation or person. In this case, there is no longer any correspondence between the represented individual or thing and the representing individual or thing; instead, only one individual entity (an object or person) represents a group by uniting common or identificatory characteristics. In a transcendent and identitary conception, the representative individuals were regarded as bearing the essence of a group. Yet what was called essence was nothing other than a collection of significative elements. A ceramic vase can be representative of the craftwork of a region or of a culture, therefore a person can be representative of a determined social group. 'Representativeness', in the sense of 'exemplariness', could be defined statistically if all the individuals were perceived under the same conditions; in practice, representativeness is constructed on the basis of the hierarchization of individuals in their social visibility.

Representativeness remains an aesthetic concept, while delegation (speaking for an other) is a legal or political concept. The former is situated in the realm of the imagination and observation, the latter in the realm of desire and action. 'Delegated representation' does not designate a being, but a doing. No one is a representative, but rather acts as a representative. That person can represent an individual, a group, a society or a nation. Yet this mode of 'representation' is not defined as a being (representative being), but as a doing (acting in representation). In a theocratic logic, God is the powers that be. In a despotic logic, the powers that be represent God. In a democratic logic, the powers that be represent the people. In the theocratic logic there is no representation, but presence. In the despotic logic the powers that be assume the privilege of representation and attempt to convince others that their representation is essential: they are representative of a transcendent authority, whose voice is heard solely through the representatives.

In a democratic logic the powers that be can only achieve such status through the delegation of the voices of many. When the representative acts against the interests of the represented person or people, than this person or these people have the right to revoke, to withdraw their delegation. This seems obvious when the delegation is individual, such as in the case of an agent, an attorney or an executor, but less so when the delegation is collective and the representative assumes an essential power that he or she does not deserve, since their representation is not an essence (being a representative) but a temporary condition (acting as a representative).

The representation of the interests and rights of a person, a family, a group, an organization, an institution, a nation or a territory, as the consequence of delegation of the will, corresponds to what in German is called 'Vertretung'. This sense should not be confused with the previous ones, although in general it is very common that this happens. This is, in fact, one of the great dangers of the ambiguity contained in our word 'representation'.

'Representation' is, consequently, a concept that is effective in four spheres: in the spheres of knowledge, of ethics, of aesthetics and of politics. However, the commonality of the term is not coincidental, while the transition from one function to another of the different representations is not a mere defect resulting from ambiguity or ignorance, but rather an intrinsic problem of any representation.

In *La Carrosse d'or* the director attempts to transmit his (mental) representation of a society, proceeding from the premise that such a society is constructed as a game of (dramatic) representations. The play within the film (mimetically) represents a fable, in which the characters act as though they were the protagonists of a (dramatic) representation. Theatrical representation and dramatic representation are confused not on the stage (although within the broadest framework everything takes place in the interior of a theatre), but on the social stage, where we would prefer that there is no representation (neither theatrical nor dramatic), but only affection and action. The outcome of such confusion is that Camilla, a professional of (dramatic) representation, is regarded as representative and consequently – now outside the theatre – as a representative (delegate). At the same time the legitimate representative (according to the social conventions of the era) appears solely preoccupied with the (dramatic) representation of his role, through which he aspires to compensate his lack of political representativeness.

Various concepts of representation are superimposed and occasionally confused. The actors had a mistaken (mental) representation of the place where they were going to perform (for them a theatre, in reality the courtyard of an inn). Camilla's lovers (mentally) represent to themselves a life that in her company is different, as though the transformation of reality would depend on her, a woman they know only as the performer of a fictional character. She, on the other hand, (mentally) represents to herself a life together with each one of her lovers, preferring to escape all of them. Her (mental) representation does not coincide with her real experience. In one case it contradicts experience; in another case it precedes experience in an idealized manner (at the cost of the efforts or sacrifice of another, in this case of the woman, Camilla); in a third case it serves to avoid an experience that forebodes dissatisfaction or pain.

The fact that her lovers' (mental) representations do not coincide with Camilla's exposes the unilateral dimension of all representation. Felipe imagines (represents to himself) an idyllic life together with Camilla, in harmony with nature, far from the ambitions and representations of the Old World. Yet this imagining of a life without representations, of a life of pure presence, is itself a representation. Camilla imagines that same life in a very different way: a life without theatre, travel, songs, entertainment, trapped in the middle of a jungle together with a man that she will probably have to take care of, since her relationship with reality is distinct and is based on a (mental) representation, not on a material relationship with persons and things.

A second sense of representation appears in the film's initial sequences. We are shown a theatre and in its interior a palace. By means of simply moving closer the director introduces us into a (mimetic) representation. We know that we are not before a realistic representation of reality, but an artificial representation of it. The (mimetic) representation of the action that takes place in the film does not adhere to the rules of realist narrative, but instead to those of a Baroque comedy.

This mimetic representation occurs, moreover, in the form of theatrical representation, in which the actors (Magnani, Lamont, Rioli) (dramatically) represent characters (Colombine, Don Antonio, the viceroy, Felipe …) following the instructions of the director (Renoir). The characters they interpret, however, are in turn immersed in another game of representation. The dramatic representation (Magnani represents Camilla) is doubled within the film (Camilla represents Colombine). Yet this not only occurs in the theatre, but also in the society represented in the theatre: Lamont represents Ferdinand, who represents the role of the viceroy, Rioli represents Ramón, who represents the role of the bullfighter, etc.

In addition, Camilla is doubly trapped in the representation, trapped in theatrical representation and in mimetic representation: in both she disappears as a person in order to become a public figure. But Camilla is trapped in her representativeness as well. Interpreting a character that is representative of the Italian people she becomes representative of the people in general. This representativeness surprises her. Camilla is representative of the people in the same manner that the golden carriage is representative of power. The same boat, therefore, transports the symbol of power and the symbol of the people. The bullfighter understands this immediately and he (mentally) represents himself as married to a woman who would bolster his popularity. The viceroy too understands this, he cannot miss the opportunity to unite in one display – Camilla riding in the carriage – the symbol of the people and the symbol of power.

Felipe tries in vain to free Camilla from this tangle of representations. He appears as one of the possible incarnations of Rousseau, in the latter's condemnation of theatre and in his nostalgia for natural goodness. But Rousseau was more complex in his thinking than Felipe. Camilla, in any case, is not willing to renounce representation, despite her momentary wavering. For Camilla, representation is life. With sound judgement she puts life before moral considerations, for moral judgement cannot condemn the individual to renounce their life or the happiness of living. Camilla is confronted with an ethical dilemma and choses life, going against morality. Camilla wants to continue being free, as a woman vis-à-vis the bullfighter, and as an artist vis-à-vis the viceroy. This is an ethical decision which nevertheless situates the question outside the sphere of morality. Camilla's choice of representation affirms her artistic potency, but also her political potency.

Here the last sense of representation emerges: the popular applause converts Camilla, without her desiring it nor the spectators (the people) directly intending it, into a potential representative (delegate) of the interests of the people. What is at stake in *La Carrosse d'or* is who represents the people better, the viceroy, the bullfighter, the officer or the actress? But according to which concept of representation? The viceroy is supposed to be the representative (delegate) of the law, to safeguard rights, to make decisions that affect the common good, but he should not be representative, nor (theatrically) represent his power. Felipe would seem to be destined to exercise a counter-power, with his denunciation of the theatricality of society and the corruption of customs, but he prefers instead to retire, to exit the stage. The bullfighter (dramatically) represents himself, having earned his popularity thanks to his virtuosity in a popular spectacle, yet such virtuosity does not grant him representativeness, but rather the right to (dramatically) represent his own character as a symbol of cultural identity. In contrast, Camilla does not represent herself; she represents Colombine, and through such a representation she becomes representative of the people; hers is not a representativeness that is merely aesthetic, it is a representativeness that is also emotional. Camilla and Ramón are representative in different senses: Ramón because he has assumed an imposed identity, Camilla because she is the catalyst of an identity until then silenced.

If Camilla chose the bullfighter, she would become, like him, a (dramatic) representative of herself and would lose her representativeness. If Camilla chose the viceroy, she would become a representative (delegate), but she could hardly continue to be truly representative of the people; her representation (delegation) would soon be exposed as a fraud. She rejects both and with this the legitimacy of moving from one representation to another. The same does not happen to her lovers. In particular to the viceroy, who in theory is the representative of rights, but cannot resist the temptation of also being representative of himself (representative of identity) and representative of the others (representative of emotions). In this sense then, the viceroy's behaviour is representative of a mode of performing politics, or rather, of exercising power, that continually resorts to theatricality.

6

Representation and alterity

The political potency of theatre, or rather of theatricality, stems from the ease with which the different concepts of representation (imagining, putting in the place of, speaking for others) are superimposed in a single practice. This potency can be realized for the benefit of the common good, or for its detriment and the seeking of individual interests. In this conflict of representations the taking of ethical decisions is unavoidable.

The transition from representation (mental, mimetic and theatrical) to representativeness is one of the key factors in the significance of the great dramatic roles; it also justified why the actors who interpreted them successfully (in the theatre in the nineteenth century and in film and television in the twentieth) could become public figures. Hamlet and Antigone are obviously not characters represented (theatrically) thousands of times because they represent (mimetically) a specific person, but because their drama is representative of a human experience that can be translated to the present. Of course, it is not that easy to represent (to make present) Hamlet or Antigone effectively, that is, to make the drama or tragedy present and not merely to represent (mimetically and theatrically) an exceptional fiction of the past.

A politician, a trade unionist or a leader of any type should neither have to be representative nor represent themselves as a politician, a trade unionist or a leader. It would suffice for them to responsibly carry out the task for which they have been chosen, in other words, to efficiently and honestly defend the interests of those they represent (as a delegate) and to carry out actions to achieve the proposed objectives. Neither should a public figure (whether a singer, an athlete or a fashion model) be representative of someone or something, since performing well what they do only qualifies them to (dramatically) represent themself. In no case does such a representation convert them into a representative (delegate) of the ideas or rights of those that applaud them for performing and not for producing (and much less for producing discourse).

Yet, can one just as emphatically affirm that the success of an intellectual (whether an actor, writer, musician or artist) does not qualify them to use their representativeness, or to exercise in some way the representation (delegation), which their readers or viewers implicitly place in them when they buy, applaud and disseminate their discourses? How can we distinguish the sole performing of their functions from the production of discourse, once we have accepted that verbal language does not monopolize the production of discourse and that image, movement and body – without use of the word – can be discursive means too?

These are some of the questions that Gayatri Chakravorty Spivak formulated in her essay 'Can the Subaltern Speak?' (1988), a foundational text of postcolonial studies. The subaltern woman (or subaltern man) is one who cannot speak. Her silence does not derive from a physical or intellectual incapacity, but from the lack of a possibility of speaking. Since the subaltern woman cannot speak, she has been excluded from representation, or has been the victim of perverse and appropriating representations. In traditional societies, subalternity has affected and affects women. It is precisely the case of the suicide of a young Indian woman, Bhuvaneswari Bhaduri, around which Spivak articulates her critique in the fourth part of the essay.

The critique starts from a questioning of the ideas formulated by Michel Foucault and Gilles Deleuze in their dialogue 'Les intellectuels et le pouvoir' (1972). Spivak questions the notion that subalterns do not need to be represented, as Deleuze suggests: 'There is no more representation; there's nothing but action – action of theory and action of practice which relate to each other as relays and form networks' (Spivak 1988: 275). According to Spivak, Deleuze has not paid enough attention to the polysemy of the term 'representation' and ignores the difference between the sense of representation as 'speak for', that is, delegated representation or 'Vertretung', and the sense of 're-presentation' as 'putting in the place of', in other words, the philosophic concept of 'representation' derived from mimetic (or dramatic) representation or 'Darstellung'.

In her critique of Foucault and Deleuze, who maintain the colonial subject intact, Spivak aligns herself with Derrida, who in addition to having dissected the concept of 'representation' – as discussed above – is for Spivak a thinker more sensitive to the question of the 'Third World'. The core of Spivak's argument rests on dismantling the idea of an oppressed and transparent subject. She finds the tools for this in *Der achtzehnte Brumaire des Louis Bonaparte* (1852), a text in which Karl Marx likewise insisted on the importance of the difference between 'darstellen' and 'vertreten'. The proletarian class, wrote Marx, is heterogenous. Such heterogeneity makes it unrepresentable, but not for this reason should it be deprived of political representation. There can be no re-presentation ('Darstellung'), but there must be representation ('Vertretung') (277).

Aesthetic representation cannot possess political effectiveness. For this reason, the fact that someone can be considered as representative of a people, a culture or a race does not grant them the right of representation. This is because such representation arises, as noted above, from an abstraction, usually inductive, idealized or manipulated, and not from the will of those who are to be politically represented and who cannot be deprived of their differences in a merely aesthetic operation. Homogenizing the representation of a people is an act of violence, as it negates their heterogeneity, deprives the individuals of subjectivity and transfers this subjectivity to an absolutized representation through an equivalence of re-presentation and delegation.

In the fourth part of her essay Spivak addresses the sacrifice of Bhuvaneswari Bhaduri, who attempted to send a message employing her own body. This seventeen-year old adolescent hanged herself in her father's flat in 1926. The fact that she was menstruating at the moment of her suicide excludes the possibility that she was trying to avoid the dishonour of an unwanted pregnancy. Later it became known that Bhaduri belonged to an armed group that fought for the independence of India. She had been tasked with a violent action, but incapable of carrying it out, she chose to commit suicide. Her suicide, nonetheless, was not a renunciation. She attempted to say something. That is why she waited for her period. Spivak's interpretation is that what the young woman wanted was to rewrite the ritual of 'sati', regarded as barbaric by British colonists, thus transforming her suicide into a political condemnation.

Bhaduri is mute in her death, not because her discourse is produced in her body, but because she did not find a space for speaking; her message reached no one. It is this lack of spaces of speaking that, according to Spivak, will continue to make necessary intellectuals' representation and commitment in the exercise of representation.

As well as defending representation as the delegated voice, Spivak's text also points to a revaluation of representation as performance, conceived as a mode of action and a mode of discourse. She understands representation as a necessary mediation for those who cannot articulate their discourse, since their discourse cannot be heard or understood. By means of learned gestures, dances, body ornaments, repetitive behaviours, rituals and liturgies, the subaltern woman can represent that which no one will hear. In this way they delegate to others the interpretation of such representations, and it is the responsibility of other women to give voice to these silent discourses, in spaces where such a voice can be heard, that is, where effective possibilities of speaking exist.

La Carrosse d'or would not resist a postcolonial reading. Nor would Jean Renoir deserve to be 'judged' according to postcolonial arguments. In his film, Peru and the indigenous Peruvians make up an undifferentiated landscape which the director did not want to enter (and with sound judgement, since, had he done so, he would have encountered problems that he probably would have been incapable of resolving). To more profoundly explore the practical consequences of Spivak's arguments it is necessary once more to enter a particular history and geography.

The representation of the subaltern woman was the predominant theme of a debate sparked by two of the most successful films in recent Peruvian cinema: *Madeinusa* (2006) and *La teta asustada* (The Milk of Sorrow, 2009), both directed by Claudia Llosa. The former was praised for opening up a space of representation in hegemonic cultural circles to the indigenous woman, for decades the victim of economic and cultural exclusion. She has also suffered from military and police violence, particularly vicious during the long years of conflict between Sendero Luminoso and government as well as paramilitary forces, responsible for thousands of rapes, abuses and assassinations, in many cases still unpunished. However, the film was also criticized for offering a stereotyped vision of indigenous men and women, of being party to colonial representations that served precisely to make violence of a racist nature tolerable.

In contrast to Renoir, Llosa does presume to represent the subaltern woman. She is, moreover, conscious that being Peruvian and a woman does not qualify her to represent a subjectivity that is alien to her. Although Peruvian, Llosa belongs to a cultural elite of European descent, and, as a matter of fact, the film is a Spanish-Peruvian co-production. Should she then accept the silence and avoid representation? She instead chose to accentuate the distance and construct a mythical and impenetrable society, in a way as distant perhaps from historical reality as the society represented by Renoir, yet assigning a leading role to the indigenous woman.

Madeinusa is an indigenous girl who lives with her father and sister in Manayaycuna, a small village in the Andes; her mother left the family some time ago, leaving behind only a memory and a pair of earrings. The film begins with an everyday chore for the girl, who has to circumscribe the house with poison to keep away the rats. The next day will inaugurate the Holy Time, the two days between the death and resurrection of Christ, in which sins do not exist, since God is dead and cannot see them. Precisely on that Maundy Thursday is when Salvador, a young engineer from Lima on a business trip, sees himself suddenly obliged to spend the night in Manayaycuna. Don Cayo, the mayor and father of Madeinusa, decides to provide him with accommodation, but also to keep him locked inside, in order to prevent him from witnessing the ancestral festivities.

The film then develops as an ethnological fiction, the construction of a new syncretism partially made up of various elements of the festivities: the election of Madeinusa as representative of the Virgin Mary from among the girls of the village, the clock in the centre of the square, the procession, the celebration of the death of God, the cutting of ties, the dances, the masks, the fireworks. The ritual acts subsequently alternate with the carnivalesque excesses, although in this case divine blindness grants the sinners absolute immunity.

Since God cannot see, Madeinusa decides to steal the heart of the engineer from Lima and convince him to take her away. He succumbs to the temptation of the young Lady of Sorrows. Don Cayo, who was waiting for the Holy Time to rob his daughter of her virginity, is disappointed when he discovers that the *gringo* has preceded him. Salvador does not intercede to prevent the incest: he looks at Madeinusa with distance, with disdain, even with repulsion. There is no love story here between Salvador and Madeinusa. The only thing that matters to the girl is to follow her mother's path and free herself from the oppression of the village and the family; the engineer is nothing more than a means to this end.

Don Cayo and Chale, the sister, try to prevent Madeinusa's escape. Chale ties her pants and cuts off her plait; the father locks her in the attic holding all of the gifts from the village to the Virgin Mary. But she is able to escape and Salvador agrees to take her with him. Just when the happy end seems imminent, she remembers the earrings and decides to return to find them. She discovers that her drunk father has destroyed them with his teeth in an attack of melancholy, before falling asleep. The destruction of the emotional link with her mother incites a rage in Madeinusa that the rape had not provoked; in vengeance she laces the chicken broth with rat poison and gives it to her father. The Holy Time is finished, God has recovered His sight of the sins of mortals, but this does not seem to disturb Madeinusa.

When Salvador arrives he finds the father dying. Again he does not intercede. Madeinusa tries to get close to him, but he rejects her. The sister immediately accuses the *gringo* of having murdered her father. Madeinusa confirms the accusation. The last shot shows El Mudo's lorry, the same one that brought the engineer to the village. This time it carries Madeinusa as a passenger, who combs the long hair of her doll. She says she is going to Lima and smiles.

Even though Madeinusa is the protagonist of the film, and despite Llosa filming her in extreme close-ups, identification with her is avoided at all times. The distance does not function as alienation, as a means of exposing the fiction, since the fiction is precisely what holds up the film. This distance is instead the way in which Llosa internally stages her caution. Salvador represents the external gaze on the Andean inhabitants and the internal colonialism of a society that perpetuates racial separation. His respect for the indigenes is not able to overcome an internalized disdain that turns into physical repulsion and is resolved only through compassion. The staging of this caution turns disturbing in the animalization of Manayaycuna's inhabitants: the rats are present from the beginning, the alternation of the shots of the woman's eye and that of the cow, also at the beginning, determines the perception of life in the village. Llosa depicts an inaccessible humanity, which is rendered physically through an absence of feelings, focused (in Madeinusa's family) on the absent figure of the mother.

La teta asustada (2009) attempts to go even further and consequently the risks are multiplied. On the one hand, there is a direct reference to the real suffering of Peruvian countrywomen and to the unhealed wounds that the dirty war inscribed on their bodies. Fausta is not as distant as Madeinusa, she is not an indigene in a remote village, but an inhabitant of Lima's suburbs, and her drama is as understandable as her desire to bury her mother in the village where they were both born. Nevertheless, the fiction created to represent the wound, the potato that blocks Fausta's vagina and represents her malady, that of the 'frightened teat', is much less potent than the fiction of the Holy Time that articulated the previous film: it transforms collective grief into an individual anecdote.

The background never made explicit for the film (and also of *Madeinusa*) is the suffering caused by corruption and racism during the last two decades of the twentieth century in Peru. The Commission on Truth and Reconciliation, which carried out an extensive investigation of the twenty years of armed conflict, documented more than 69,000 mortal victims, the majority of them indigenous peasants. How to approach such pain? The film resorts to an interpolated character, the pianist. In search of inspiration she asks Fausta to sing some songs; Fausta agrees so as to acquire the pearls that will allow her to transport her mother's body to the village. But after the pianist triumphs before Lima's high society with the melody that Fausta has invented, the pianist spurns the young woman, with the same repugnance that Salvador looked down on Madeinusa, as though the interchange (sexual or musical) with an indigenous woman had stained them and only distance could restore their condition of white 'civilized' citizens.

The pianist does not offer Fausta her theatre so that Fausta can sing her songs. She does not even go on stage to represent Fausta. She simply appropriates her melodies for her own benefit. The negation of representation leads to a new dispossession and a new silencing. The fact that this sequence occupies a central place in the film indicates Llosa's concern with the problem, but does not resolve it. In fact, Fausta's ailment, and above all the memory of her pain as victim, are diluted in a new ethno-landscape, more artificial and grotesque than that fabricated for *Madeinusa*.

In this case filmic representation, the *mise en scène* of the action, is what clearly impedes the intention of (delegated) representation, prevents it from acquiring the necessary power for the victim to find an effective way of speaking. Are aesthetic representation and representation as delegation thus irreconcilable? Is mimetic representation always an obstacle to the representation of who strives to give voice? Do representations exist in which fiction intensifies and does not usurp or silence the voice of those women who are represented?

Taken to an extreme, ethical caution can lead to the cancellation of the ethical relationship itself. This consequence is inverse to that described by Badiou in his criticism of the idea of alterity inspired by Lévinas. Respect for the rights of the Other conceals, underneath the principles of tolerance and the acceptance of difference, a homogenizing and neo-colonial desire that, according to Badiou, is summed up in the formula 'become like me and I will respect your difference' (Badiou 2001: 25). Others are recognized as subjects of an ethical relation as long as their differences with us are not so irreconcilable with our ideas, morality and aesthetic criteria that they horrify us. Claudia Llosa endeavours to avoid the colonizing gaze on her protagonist, but her caution reaches such an extreme that it makes an ethical relationship between Salvador and Madeinusa impossible. It obliges the spectators to similarly situate themselves outside, before an alien humanity that could be understood – and herein lies the risk – as a non-humanity. This 'non-humanity' is precisely the condition of subalternity revealed by Spivak's critique and her Indian colleagues: aesthetic representation does not suffice, in this case another type of representation is urgently needed.

Miguel Rubio Zapata collaborated with Claudia Llosa in the construction of the ethnographic fiction that serves as the basis for the film. For forty years the members of the Grupo Cultural Yuyachkani (Yuyachkani Cultural Group) directed by Rubio studied the rituals, dances, masks and music of Peru, incorporating them in their theatre work, which also included other literary sources as well as sophisticated techniques of gestural training. His knowledge of popular Andean culture allowed Rubio to productively collaborate with Llosa's team in the construction of the invented ritual. In the transition from theatre to film the fiction acquired greater effectiveness in generating a self-enclosed fiction. Nevertheless, it lost the representative (enunciative) force that their previous works had possessed.

Yuyachkani began their work at a time (the early 1970s) when the priority of Latin American theatre was to serve as a space of speaking and less one of aesthetic representation. Mimetic representation was a means necessary for representation in terms of delegation. This initial approach evolved during the ensuing years, in which distance and caution emerged, but never to the point of making Yuyachkani give up representation nor its responsibility as intellectuals and artists in a country afflicted by political corruption and armed violence.

Of the many works by Yuyachkani, two stand out as particularly relevant in the context of this discussion: *Antígona* (2000) and *Rosa Cuchillo* (2001). The former was premiered in the Casa de Yuyachkani in Lima in February 2000, when Fujimori was still in power. In this solo work the actress Teresa Ralli played the different characters of Sophocles' tragedy, freely adapted by José Watanabe, a Peruvian poet of the generation of the 1970s. Antigone's rebellion, a character made 'universal', who represents civil disobedience and defiance in the face of unjust power, seemed necessary in Peruvian theatre prior to the publication of the Montesinos videos and the fall of the authoritarian government, under which the activities of the dirty war and the massacres of peasants had continued and in some cases even increased. Many bodies of innocent victims still remained to be buried. For this reason, during the preparation of *Antígona*, Teresa Ralli and Miguel Rubio met with women, the mothers and sisters of the missing, in work sessions. 'Seeing and listening to the Peruvian *antigonas* in our studio, entering into a dialogue with the everyday reality of their struggle to find the bodies of their husbands and brothers in order to bury them … gave Teresa the foundation of physical presence that, without knowing it very well, we had been looking for' (Rubio Zapata 2006: 61). The representativeness of the character of Antigone allowed the actress a dialogue with the women who in the present share the same fate as Antigone. It is precisely this dialogue that lends representative legitimacy to the actress, who otherwise would have been condemned to a merely aesthetic representation.

The concurrence of the aesthetic and enunciative impact of this representation became evident in the performances realized in marginal neighbourhoods, in particular in Sicuani (Cuzco), Abancay (Apurímac), Huanta (Ayacucho), Trujillo (La Libertad) and Chimbote (Ancash), in the presence of victims and in support of the awareness campaign for the Commission on Truth and Reconciliation. Representation here plainly revealed itself as a tool for communication, in this case, as a tool for accompanying the victims and for creating community.

On 13 November 2000, Alberto Fujimori left Peru for Brunei to attend the APEC summit, but instead of returning to Peru diverted his route and went to Japan, from where he sent a fax resigning as president. The process of transition was initiated shortly afterwards. On 4 June 2001, the actor Augusto Casafranca was present, together with thousands of family members, victims and activists from human rights organizations, in Lima's Plaza de Armas square, waiting for the president of the transition government to sign the decree creating the Commission on Truth and Reconciliation of Peru.

Augusto Casafranca, however, was present as a citizen and also as the actor/representative of Alfonso Cánepa, whom he had lent his body and his voice. In Julio Ortega's *Adiós Ayacucho* (Goodbye Ayacucho), Alfonso Cánepa, a peasant activist who was tortured and buried incomplete in a common grave, decides to travel to Lima to ask the president to help him find the rest of his remains. The novel served as the basis for the creation of a solo theatre piece with the same title that Yuyachkani premiered in 1990. Eleven years later, Alfonso Cánepa was once again present in Lima with a demand that was shared by thousands of victims.

The actors of Yuyachkani, who had renounced the art of dramatic representation to develop techniques of gestural and musical performance, discovered that their work on the body empowered them now for a mode of representation much more urgent than mimetic representation.

> If our actors had searched for another body inside their body before, this time they had to lend their own body, because presences invaded our theatre that searched for their own body, now specific, material, stripped of all metaphor... Thus our actors, who had had presence as their centre, decided to work on the absence in themselves, to evoke the bodies of the absent.
>
> 32–3

Rosa Cuchillo was premiered in November 2001, after the election of Alejandro Toledo as president and the opening of the Commission's investigations. In contrast to *Antígona*, *Rosa Cuchillo* was conceived to be represented in the popular markets of the Andean villages. By means of a scenic ritual, charged with elements that Yuyachkani had found in the traditions of these same villages over the course of years, it served to accompany the process of mourning and healing.

The actress Ana Correa embodied a character from a story by Óscar Colchado Lucio, Rosa Huanta, who after dying continues to search for her son, armed with the same knife that she used while young to defend herself from rapists while sleeping. She is accompanied by her dog Huayra, also dead, victim of a puma that killed it to steal a sheep. Rosa and Huayra travel the other worlds, the World Below, 'Uqhu Pacha', and the World Above, 'Hanaq Pacha', before returning to our world, 'Kay Pacha', in a search to balance life and, through dance, recover memory and with it harmony.

As in *Antígona*, *Rosa Cuchillo* owes as much to fiction as to the real testimony of the victims. In this case, Ana Correa's encounter with Angélica Mendoza, known as Mamá Angélica, the mother of Arquímedes Ascarza Mendoza, who was kidnapped and 'disappeared' in Ayacucho on 12 July 1983, was decisive. Her words and her attitude significantly influenced the theatre piece.

In the public performances put on by Yuyachkani during the holding of sessions of the Commission on Truth and Reconciliation in Huamanga and Huanta (Ayacucho), Huancayo (Junín), Huanuco, Lima, Huancavelica and Puno, the double representation became effective: the individuality of the actress diminished with the manifestation of the character; what resulted from the representation was the sensitive presence of an ordinary woman. A woman of the people, previously not invested with any type of representation, was transformed into representative of a situation of pain, mourning and demands for justice. Rosa Cuchillo represents a communal pain. The possibility of this representation does not lie in a specific quality of the individual actress that performs, nor in the fictional character that serves to elaborate the action, nor in the articulation of the artistic elements used in the *mise en scène*, but primarily in the actress's capacity to empty herself of personality, thanks to which the spectators' emotions are diverted towards the common: the actress lets herself be inhabited by an external force, which subsequently is transformed into a collective force.

Ana Correa lends her body to Rosa Cuchillo in order to transform herself into a space of speaking, symbolic of a discourse until now silenced. Yet this is not an exercise of mourning, but of accompaniment. Rosa Cuchillo does not appropriate the voice of the victims, who speak with their own voice in the audiences; she accompanies them and labours to fortify a collective agency. Although a fictional character, the pain and hope she represents are real, as real as that of the women whom she accompanies and whom she momentarily represents, without supplanting them.

7

Frauds

Under what conditions is an exercise of representation with emotional implications and political will ethically acceptable?

A first response could be the following. A representation of the happiness or the pain of the Other is potentially mobilising when it enables the actor and the spectator to be moved by the represented happiness or pain, as common experiences that are particularly and contingently realized (that is, what provoked such experiences must not necessarily have happened this way and, therefore, decisions made by external agents could have altered them). In contrast, a representation is paralysing when it produces an effect of particularized empathy, resolved in a relationship of mental sympathy between the individual spectator and the individual character, the latter apparently marked by a destiny that will never affect the spectator.

Let us assume that, together with the will to produce a theatrical work with artistic value, the intention of those who engage in a production is to make visible an experience that is representative of a social and political problem, one that political authorities tend to marginalize and is not generally known socially. Making an individual case visible can contribute to depicting a human dimension that is inaccessible to the majority of potential spectators of the work, by means of compassion stimulating changes in social and political attitudes. The objective of the representation is to arouse compassion, to the point that compassion mobilizes me.

> Compassion … is above all a levelling movement of an unbalanced situation, the refusal of using my absolute virtual power, by means of which *I re-establish an equality de iure or de core where there is a legal inequality.* True compassion is naturally not satisfied with emotionally re-establishing the shattered equality; its impulse is rather to re-establish the equality in practice as well, by means of that immediate intervention that the linguist [Todorov] called 'morality of sympathy'. It translates into the decision, when I cannot save the victim, to share their fate.
>
> Alba Rico 2007: 1015

Compassion does not have to be a self-satisfied emotion; it can possess an emotional and reactive dimension. Without reaching the extreme described by Todorov, compassion can arouse – and in fact has aroused and arouses – the desire to work for the benefit of those who suffer, even at the cost of relinquishing one's own well-being, leisure time, or physical or psychological integrity.

According to Santiago Alba Rico, compassion requires imagination. In order to act in relation to a problem or an injustice, I need to imagine the experience of those who are affected by that problem or injustice. Imagination (or mental representation) faces two enemies: fantasy and horror. Fantasy produces parallel worlds, in some cases employing elements or structures from this world, yet without any link to actual reality. Horror is derived from the vision or the announcement of an undesired experience, whose representation we resist. Fantasy and horror are contrary to compassion, since we are confronted with dehumanized human figures. Fantasy encloses representation in itself and distances it from reality. Horror is alien to representation (it is not unrepresentable, but not represented). The majority of commercial films operate in the realm of fantasy. Horror functions as its negative pole, leading us to being content with fantasy, even if we regard it as fantasy.

The resistance of imagination against fantasy constitutes one of the key ethical issues in artistic practice, but also in political practice. Given the power of the fantasy industry in conditioning and moulding imagination, it would be possible to conceive of forms of compassion that do not resort to representation, but are rather directly activated through emotion. Nevertheless, even if one assumes the intermediary condition of representation in the arousing of compassion, for representation to be mobilizing it has to affect me, and affect me in a way that cannot be devoured by the representation itself. Yet if the experience resulting from a certain social or political situation is depicted in a *mise en scène* that encloses representation in itself, my capacity of representation becomes domesticated, becomes diverted, and my feelings controlled by the very apparatus of representation. What affects me are not only the experiences of the represented person and the reality that conditions or determines them, but also the way in which that person is represented and the effects planned by those who have designed the representation. The representation is justified in the visualization of a marginalized reality, but what it also visualizes is the execution of the representation itself.

This is a risk consubstantial with what I have called 'practices of the real', which have grown in recent years as theatres of the real have been well received by festivals and institutions eager for novelty and attracted by the convenience of expanding their audience and cultivating their social standing. That which arose from being affected and from political commitment has degenerated into a formal category or into a mere stylistic attribute. It allows, moreover, fake artists to invade the contexts of new theatre with a minimum of technical or fictional effort.

The degradation of the practices of the real shares some traits with what in the 1970s was denounced as 'porno-misery'. It is a phenomenon that affected Latin American film after the rise of neorealism at the end of the 1950s and the success of Third Film in the 1960s. Social inequality and the proliferation of marginalization in Latin American societies compelled directors to pay attention to these realities. This produced some of the great films of Latin American cinema: *Los olvidados* (The Forgotten, 1950) by Luis Buñuel, *El chacal de Nahueltoro* (The Jackal of Nahueltoro, 1969) by Miguel Litin and *La Raulito* (Little Raoul, 1974) by Lautaro Murúa. Neorealism, which spread through Latin America in the second half of the 1950s, encouraged the presence of non-professional actors on the screen. Third Film continued the New Latin American Film tendency presented at the Festival de Viña del Mar (1967); as formulated by Octavio Getino and Fernando Solanas (1969), it influenced filmmakers' commitment to social and political reality. Still, the representation of misery was seen by certain producers as a business opportunity: the representation dispensed with commitment and became sensationalism. This is how 'porno-misery' cinema grew as a profitable genre for the precarious Latin American film industries.

The success of 'porno-misery' was contested by two young Colombian filmmakers, Carlos Mayolo and Luis Ospina, who made *Agarrando pueblo* (The Vampires of Poverty) in 1978. This is a meta-cinematographic work, in which the directors portray themselves in the process of 'grabbing' images of street children and marginalized persons, demonstrating the tricks of staging that many contemporary directors resort to in their allegedly documentary productions. *Agarrando pueblo* is a 'fake documentary' that denounces the fraud and the cynicism of social documentaries that convert poverty into spectacle. To this end, Ospina and Mayolo do not hesitate to act the part of such cynical filmmakers themselves: they reveal the manipulation of shots, the purchasing of behaviour and performances in exchange for money, the preparation of scripts for false interviews, including the use of elements of theatrical staging such as costuming, make-up, lighting and rehearsals. Reality does not matter as much as the illustration of prejudices and clichés, some with high culture pretensions (in one sequence, for example, Lévi-Strauss is cited).

The satire reaches it extreme when an alleged intruder spontaneously interrupts the meticulously prepared filming of the supposed members of a family paid to represent the inhabitants of an impoverished home. The man turns out to be the assumed owner of the house, from whom the producer tries to buy his calm and silence. But the man lowers his trousers and cleans his arse with the money, afterwards kicking out the entire film team with a knife in hand. This interruption too has obviously been prepared in advance. In the final discussion, Mayolo and Ospina enter the frame to speak with the actor, Luis Alfonso Londoño. They ask him his opinion of filmmakers who dedicate themselves to 'grabbing the people' and about the meaning of the film. The 'actor' dsplays great wisdom in his political and artistic position. 'What I like is to confuse, while what you want is to be unconfused,' he claims, before declaring that what he likes best about the film is its satire and obscenity. 'No one was going to imagine that I would have the pleasure of stripping naked and cleaning myself with bills. As I said, I am the only person lucky enough to have cleaned myself with bills, not dirty ones, but ones just out of the bank.'

This attitude is contrary to that of filmmakers who 'grab the people' (as the Spanish title literally translates), who are only concerned with money, at the expense of stealing the image and the word of the people. 'I go behind the document,' affirms Luis Alfonso. Yet he has just acted in front of the camera – a brilliant performance, by the way, absolutely plausible and much more difficult than that asked of the young couple of fake paupers, who simply had to stand immobile and repeat the words of the script. He gets angry, laughs, takes off his clothes, gesticulates, jumps, dances, plays physically with the film as though he were trained for it.

There is nothing wrong with acting, with 'pretending,' provided it helps to contribute to the production of what Luis Alfonso Londoño calls a 'document'. In *Agarrando pueblo* this is achieved by exposing the cinematographic apparatus of the construction of 'reality'. The problem does not lie in the manipulation, but in the concealing of the procedures of manipulation. An artist, as Rabih Mroué notes, can manipulate the spectators, as long as this manipulation is part of the critical game and does not pursue spurious or purely lucrative aims. Orson Welles, who began his career by deceiving the masses of US-American listeners (*War of the Worlds,* 1938), returned in *F. for Fake* (1974) to the idea of the hoax and of falsification as a mode of resistance, against an art market based on 'authenticity' as much as against a film industry based on the accepted lie. The tale of Elmyr's hoax, the painter of fakes, is interspersed with the story of other great falsifications, including a series of portraits of Oda Kojar painted by Picasso and subsequently copied by her grandfather, as well as that of the film itself, presented by Welles with a fake trailer.

Falsification and fraud, practiced by artists sometimes in a playful manner and other times in a cynical one, are procedures for condemning the concealment of the invisible manipulation in approaches ostensibly naïve about the reality of others. As a film anthropologist, Jean Rouch was very conscious of the falsification inherent in any attempt at documentary recording, which is why he chose very early on to explicitly introduce fiction into his works. In his *Petit à petit* (Little by Little, 1971) the Nigerien businessman Damouré practises an inverse ethnology in Paris, treating the surprised Parisians in the same way that anthropologists have treated his people in Niger. The Parisians, less accustomed to this than the Nigeriens, reveal themselves to be cooperative and sincere. They are not contaminated by the effects of anthropological expeditions and humanitarian aid organizations, nor sufficiently infected by the simulative perversion of television.

Some years afterwards, the Brazilian director Sandra Kogut carried out a new exercise of inverse ethnography in France, but in this case the 'tribe' she observed was already contaminated. *Adieu Monde ou l'histoire de Pierre et Claire* (Goodbye World, or the Story of Pierre and Claire, 1997) is an ironic documentary about the inhabitants of a remote village in the Pyrenees. Accustomed for many years to the cameras of ethnographers, television reporters and perhaps even a few indirect disciples of Jean Rouch, they reveal themselves to be actors experienced in the representation of themselves, familiar with all the tricks of filming. They show the director the best spots to place the camera and which camera angles result in the best perspectives. Seeing that it was impossible to film spontaneously, Kogut decided to film the meta-fiction. She proposed the story of Pierre and Claire to the inhabitants as a relational object: the versions and interpretations that they provided of the story would enable each one of them to be known better, beyond the character they assumed. At the end of the documentary, one of the inhabitants hands over a script to the director, explaining that 'if you had come to see me at the beginning you wouldn't have wasted your time and your film. This is the story of Pierrine and Claire.' One villager imagines that Pierre and Claire travelled to Brazil and had a daughter, who is the director. Another claims that the fiction is reality and vice versa. A shepherd, the most taciturn one, raises his injured finger and states that this is true, it was not prepared for the film. Some things are fake and others are true: they are all necessary for creating a world. Theatricality can contribute to illuminating the reality muddled by documentalist inflation; fiction serves to recover the real in a community accustomed to representation; it restores the condition of spectators to the 'actors', to make them persons once more and, in this way, to mutually recover listening.

Fraudulent representation can have two readings as well as diverse practical consequences. A first reading highlights the implosion of representation, questioned from inside itself by means of irony or *mise en abyme*. This is the neo-Baroque option, visible in many artistic proposals of the 1980s, but which has also influenced media culture in a more general manner. It constituted one of the weakest and most criticized dimensions of postmodern culture, since it fell into a pleasurable abandon in a representation without referentiality (even if this pleasure was derived from a certain expression of meaninglessness, impotence or anguish).

A second reading instead points to an active practice of representation as a tool. This option rests upon the following: once the critique of representation has exposed its fraudulent uses, furthermore, when it has been demonstrated that to a certain extent all representation contains an inescapable nucleus of falsity or fraud, the actors and spectators of any aesthetic representation, or the active or passive subjects of any political representation, 'deduct' this nucleus from the representation and can concentrate their attention on the discourses and intentions. In other words, representation can be regarded as a game, but a game that can be played seriously, as it has real practical consequences.

This is not a cynical option, since it proceeds from the premise that everyone, educated in decades of media representations, is familiar with the rules of the game. For this reason, a person who acts, or who exercises the function of representative, does not do so and exploit the ignorance of the deceits of representation or the unawareness of its risks. Rather, they act or exercise their function aware of their condition as a temporary actor in a game, which is only sustained thanks to the consensus of actors and spectators, of the representatives and the represented. It is then when political representation can take place in modes of theatrical representation without turning into fraud. That is to say, it is precisely the awareness that any representation in a hyper-mediatized society is in itself a fraud that allows the use of aesthetic representation, in terms of a consensual game, as a means of social or political representation.

8

Body and representation

The search for reality can require taking the path of representation, in forms such as film within film or meta-theatricality. The theatre work of Angélica Liddell demonstrates how a commitment to the real can be compatible with a determined wager on representation. It also shows how the meta-dramatic exercise does not lead to a perverse Baroqueness, but rather to a use of the Baroque that permits an honest relationship with others (the non-professional actors invited onto the stage) and with the reality in which the work aims to symbolically intervene.

Perro muerto en tintorería: los fuertes (Dead Dog in a Dry Cleaner's: The Strong, 2007) was co-produced by Atra Bilis, the company founded by Angélica Liddell and Sindo Puche in 1993, and the Centro Dramático Nacional (CDN, National Drama Centre) of Spain; it was premiered at the Teatro Valle-Inclán in Madrid, the CDN space supposedly dedicated to 'new dramaturgies'. Liddell, an artist who until then had performed in off venues in Madrid and whose work bluntly denounced the institutions of family, education, culture and politics, received the commission of premiering a new production at the CDN on account of her growing reputation as a theatre artist. Rejecting the offer would have been in keeping with her position against the system, but not accepting it would have meant missing an opportunity to present the themes and experiences that have affected her and driven the production of her previous works in a larger forum, with greater cultural and media resonance. *Y los peces salieron a combatir contra los hombres* (And the Fish Came Out to Fight Against the Men, 2003) expressed the indignation over the dozens of deaths of sub-Saharan migrants during their attempts to cross the Strait of Gibraltar to reach the Spanish coast, in contrast with the attitude not simply indifferent but even complicit and reactive of society and political authorities. *Y cómo no se pudrió Blancanieves* (And Since Snow White Did Not Rot, 2005) addressed the violence of invisible wars, the horrible experience of child soldiers, specifically that of a girl soldier, in which Angélica projected her own personal experience. In order to take these experiences to the CDN, Angélica Liddell had to start from an exercise of humility: she would not present herself as the renowned author and virtuosic actress who takes by the hand the migrant woman whom Europe has denied entry. No, she would present herself as part of that system that transforms the migrant woman into a marginal body, but which also transforms the actors into whores, fools or dogs (Liddell 2008: 169).

Angélica transformed the Teatro Valle-Inclán into a dry cleaner's, the place where the marginalized clean the clothes of the whores who serve the powerful. On one side there is an enormous reproduction of Jean-Honoré Fragonard's *L'Escarpolette* (The Swing, 1767); it represents the ideal and pleasurable life, based on hypocrisy and concealment, and far from the terrible reality that unfolds outside the garden that Europe would like to be. The young woman courted by her lover and immortalized by the painter constitutes the negative of the actress-dog. Only by renouncing privilege can the dramatist-actress ethically claim to speak for those left outside the painting, even inviting them to enter it.

The actors present themselves as 'dogs', duplicated in puppets visible in various places around the stage that reproduce their bodies, but shrunken, discoloured, immobile. Like dogs, the actors occupy the same social position as the whores: they are tolerated because they are despised; they are objects of gratification, without their dedication to their art entitling them to the rights of citizenship and much less of property on which the system rests. The bodies of the whores are bodies for hire; whom do they belong to? Whom do the bodies of the actors belong to? In themselves they lack value, they only acquire it in confrontation with the audience, with the gaze that represents power. The actors are exposed bodies. Occasionally they exhibit their nakedness, in violent poses. Other times they protect themselves with strange costumes, or with the jerseys of the sports teams that maintain our citizens entertained and nurture the hopes of non-citizens. Life in this apocalyptic Europe is a competition in which there is no place for compassion, for love, for tenderness. Whoever falls behind can be considered alien, can be considered an enemy, and whoever is considered an enemy must be eliminated by the State. The enemies are no longer citizens, they are no longer human beings; consequently, it is immaterial if they are alive or dead. Their corpses are not the remains of a conscious existence, but merely the refuse of a necessary battle.

The actor-dog is also a fool. As an exposed and despised body, the fool can say whatever they want during the performance, because although they address the audience, throw their hypocrisy, their deceit, their crimes, in the spectators' faces, these remain protected in the darkness, for they know that at any moment they can leave the performance. Angélica plays with this, not conceding the spectators the right of reply, not illuminating the theatre when she accuses them, not allowing them to breathe. She tries to take control of the spectators symbolically; she achieves this temporarily during the three hours that the performance lasts, and then abandons them to their fate.

The theatre is the site of lies, the site of marginalization. The theatre is also a dry cleaner's: without wanting to, and in order to eat, the actors contribute to washing the consciences of those who have accepted killing so that their security is guaranteed. What Angélica proposes is confronting the spectators with the recycling of their waste. When Baron de Saint-Julien tries to look under the skirts of his lover, he discovers what he did not expect: filth, pain, death. His pleasure, like that of all those depicted in that gallant painting, is a guilty pleasure. The spectator would like to have the strength of that actress-director who identifies herself with a dog, who is able to challenge 120 people, challenge the Centro Dramático Nacional, challenge Europe and bear all of the pain that such a challenge provokes in a fragile body, in a body punished by the experience of so much ignored death, of so many corpses that only she identifies as bodies with the same rights as hers.

In his chapter 'The Simulacrum and Its Double: the Threat of Raw Bodies', Alba Rico denounces the categorizing of migrants as non-citizens, as bodies deprived of rights. He does this by reflecting on the contrast between the enlarged image of a perfect body on a billboard and the real body of a young Ecuadorian prostitute leaning on a wall beside the billboard. The almost naked body of the prematurely aged prostitute appears especially troubling when competing with the model of incorruptible beauty. The real body sabotages the pleasure offered by the image of the body, but it also sabotages the promise of happiness with which the advertising fantasy contributes to the subjugation and modelling of subjectivities.

> What bothers us about migrants, ultimately, is that *they have not overcome the body,* that mortal remnant. Bodies, as the philosopher Gunther Anders suggests, are old compared with our machines, which are much more perfect, faster and predictable ... But bodies are old too, or above all, in the hegemonic circulation of goods, whose accelerated renewal marks the rhythm of the life cycles and imprints on our bodies the guilt of an excessive duration. ... Poverty, illness and crime, in contrast to their opposites, *possess body.*
>
> Alba Rico 2007: 205

European citizens are instructed to look after their bodies with a 'balanced' diet, to practise physical exercise and diverse bodily techniques, to maximize hygienic precautions, consume chemical supplements and, when necessary, subject themselves to surgical interventions that correct the deviations of nature. When we take care of our bodies, what we seek in reality is to rid ourselves of the body: being as young as possible (even at the price of relinquishing experience in many cases), avoiding pain as much as possible (even at the price of relinquishing pleasure in many cases), shunning ugliness as much as possible (even at the price of masking ourselves in many cases). The goal is to maintain oneself as long as possible in the circuit of competition and in the chain of consumption. The European citizen prefers the image of the body, prefers that their body be an image, an image not troubled by the shadows of ugliness, pain or death. In a certain sense, the European citizen who looks after their body strongly resembles the virtuoso: by looking after their body so much, they end up negating it.

In contrast, the migrants do not have a right to an image. They are bodies. They are allowed in as long as they are bodies. Physical labour is reserved for them, in which they are above all bodies: manual workers, cleaners, carers. Yet, '[w]hat is a body? A degraded image … The limit and failure of globalization … The result of a subtraction that subtracts precisely that which protects and dignifies our bodies … The process … by virtue of which the body is excluded from humanity' (3499).

Being excluded from the image, migrants are also excluded from rights. Hannah Arendt had warned about the paradox of human rights, which protect not humans, but those that are a bit more than human, since those who are only human, only human bodies, are not any different from other bodies. This is what Giorgio Agamben theorized under the concept of 'naked life'.

'Why do we not allow migrants to enter Europe?' asks Alba Rico. 'Why do we oblige them to enter as bodies?' (3535).

In the last part of the piece, Angélica Liddell invited a young migrant woman, Nasima, onto the stage. In contrast to the actors, she did not come on stage masked, but exhibiting her identity. Unlike what happens in reality, she did not enter the theatre as a body, as the actors had done, but as a subject of rights. The young Muslim began her intervention with a paraphrase from *The Social Contract* by Jean-Jacques Rousseau ('The preservation of the State is incompatible with the preservation of the enemy') and continued by denouncing the hypocrisy of Europeans and their betrayal of the humanist ideas that had been expressed by Enlightenment thinkers:

> Now, … tell me, what is Europe? …
> In Europe feelings and desires are sold and bought.
> Europe has massacred bread and love.
> In Europe nobody offers anything
> without expecting something in return …
> That is why we have to go out and kill in the streets of Europe, we have to
>   kill to be innocent.

> We have to kill the people of Europe, in order not to shoot the unarmed
> and starving Africans
> that jump over the fences built in Europe.
>
> Liddell 2008: 231–3

Nasima does not invite compassion, but rather prepares for action. Liddell follows Jean Genet and Heiner Müller in their alignment with those excluded from representation. This Nasima recalls the Ophelia in *Die Hamletmaschine* (The Hamlet Machine, 1977). Yet a truth inhabits her body that does not necessarily inhabit Müller's character. Does this constitute a justification of terrorism? A theatre piece can hardly encourage acts of terrorism. Yet we have to be very naïve or arrogant to be surprised when those who are obliged to be present as mere bodies, deprived of representation, prefer – as Alba Rico points out – to identify themselves as Muslims, Chechens, or Afghans and 'be' enemies, even 'terrorists', rather than simply '*naked others*' (Alba Rico 2007: 3523).

Nasima, defiant, attacks the preconceptions with which enlightened Europe constructs Others, migrants, and the hypocritical negation of real citizenship that such representations share: 'It is easier to see bloodied bodies of Muslims than bloodied bodies of Europeans or US-Americans. That is why I am a cliché. You need many corpses, you need five years of uninterrupted violence to become a cliché.... Thanks to the million deaths now I have become a cliché and Europe can die of boredom.' (Liddell 2008: 234). The cliché is the result of ignorance, of superficial repetition, of laziness, cowardness, hypocrisy, cruelty.

Nasima was the only live actress in the piece. Nevertheless, she was outside the game, outside representation. How can a Muslim woman with a veil, who pronounces the Spanish phrases badly and wears an absurd Barça jersey, the symptom of a pampered colonialism, how can that woman have a right to representation? No, she does not have it, not beyond the cliché. That is to say, she does not have a right to citizenship; she has to accept working in the dry cleaner's, hidden between the piles of dirty clothes of the customers and whores, or otherwise make herself visible and become an enemy of the State, who can kill her according to the social contract signed by all of the citizens with rights. Yet Angélica gave her a chair next to her dog actors, her dead actors, and also offered her the privilege of the swing, the swing that was the symbol of pleasure of Europeans, of the hope of Europeans, and which now served Nasima so that she could dream.

> Life can continue normally thanks to exoticism. Thanks to exoticism you
> colonized us. Thanks to exoticism you enslaved us. Thanks to exoticism

you annihilate us. Thanks to exoticism you deport us when we are very poor. Or you imprison us in places called 'internment centres'. The first crime committed against us is poverty. Economy is one of the forms of crime. Economy is one of the forms of racism.

235

While Nasima climbed onto the swing that hung from the gridiron and balanced herself on it, usurping the place reserved for European citizenry in the old painting constantly visible on the other side of the stage, at the back of the stage Angélica wrote with indomitable energy on the wall: 'Is there some son of a bitch who wants to kill me?' There were none in the theatre. Outside, there are many. But they are cowards. They prefer that others do the dirty work. The social contract has trained citizens in cowardice. Their murderous drive pulses sluggishly underneath the hypocrisy. They try to hide the bodies under the images, ignore the corpses on which those images feed.

9

Ethics of the body

The title of this chapter coincides with that of a book, a collection of conversations in which the playwright and actor Eduardo Pavlovsky outlines his ideas on art and experience. After working as a psychoanalyst in the 1970s, Pavlovsky became internationally known with his play *El señor Galíndez* (Mr Galíndez), premiered on 18 January 1973 at the Teatro Payró in Buenos Aires and later performed in numerous cities in Argentina and Europe. The work explored the 'banality of evil' in the everyday routine of a torturer, played by Pavlovsky himself, and his assistants. This was not a realistic play, but a synthetic work, in which psychoanalytic research on the pathology of the torturer was fused with a denunciation of torture as an institution.

Hannah Arendt formulated her concept of the banality of evil after attending the trial of Adolf Eichmann in Jerusalem. This bureaucrat had strived to carry out his task as efficiently as possible, even though he knew that this task would result in the internment, suffering and death of thousands of people. Arendt was able to imagine the victims' suffering as much as Eichmann's reasoning by simply listening and writing. But to imagine the torturer, who practises evil face to face, skin to skin, with the victim, and who is able to banalize their actions, Pavlovsky had to put his own body on stage.

Torture already existed in Argentina – and in all of Latin America – in 1973, as Pavlovsky and Hugo Kogan (who directed the play) noted in their foreword to the 1974 edition of the play. Yet it was the military junta that, having assumed power after the coup d'état on 24 March 1976, institutionalized it as a tool of political repression in Argentina. Shortly after the premiere of *Telarañas* (Cobwebs, 1977), Pavlovsky had to go into exile in Uruguay, Brazil and ultimately Spain. There he worked for several years before he decided to 'unexile himself' in 1981 and join Teatro Abierto (Open Theatre), a resistance movement organized at the beginning of the 1980s by committed intellectuals with creative and militant biographies in the previous decades, including Griselda Gambaro, Carlos Gorostiza, Roberto Cosa, Ricardo Monti, Osvaldo Dragún and Mauricio Kartún. In 1983 he premiered *El señor Laforgue* (Mr Laforgue), followed by the plays *Paso de dos* (Pas de Deux, 1990) and *Rojos globos rojos* (Red Balloons Red, 1994), among others.

The ethics of the body is not exclusive to theatre practice. In fact, the reflection on ethics carried out by Pavlovsky draws from his experience as an actor and as a psychoanalyst. Pavlovsky recalls that one of the motivations that led to the foundation in 1981 of Plataforma (an organization of leftist psychoanalysts who strove to inscribe their practice in historical-social reality and in the political debate of the time) was the realization of an antiauthoritarian ethics that would help generate new subjectivities. 'The ethics of group therapy requires accepting that the small truths we arrive at in the sessions are sometimes produced by the group, not the ones the coordinator thinks they have' (Pavlovsky 2001: 141). Pavlovsky calls this 'ethics of the act', since it does not arise from theoretical reflection but is instead realized in practice, in the taking of everyday decisions and in the commitment of each individual in relation to social and political reality:

> This, for me, is ethics: not saying just anything according to how circumstances demand … One can, with certain things, be flexible and say 'I was wrong'. But there are certain things when one cannot say 'I was wrong' and undergo a total, radical ideological change. What no one can do is look the other way … In *Rojos globos rojos* El Cardenal states it clearly: 'How beautiful it is to say the same thing every day in this country and not go wandering from one side to the other.' This is the only ethics I can speak of: the ethics of the act. Of the irrevocable commitment. I know no other. For this reason I also think that Teatro Abierto was an act of ethical enunciation. It put its body on the line.
>
> 141–2

Pavlovsky already knew what it meant to 'put his body on the line'. During the performances of *El señor Galíndez* there was an attempt to plant a bomb in the Teatro Payró. 'In the ethics of the act there is always danger. That is the risk. This has always been so. We didn't invent it' (141).

Rojos globos rojos is a work constructed as a sum of fragments, mounted on the body of El Cardenal, a role interpreted by Pavlovsky. The word only has significance when it is an act, and the act necessitates presence. Pavlovsky's theatre is an 'eminently physical' one (107). The playwright offers his body as an actor, but without any exhibitionist desire. In contrast to the widespread belief in the exhibitionist tendencies of actors, Pavlovsky discovered in the 'poor theatre' of Jerzy Grotowsky a model of the anti-exhibitionist actor, 'a person who offers themself with a maximum degree of nakedness, devoid of feigned facial expressions and gestures' (73). This led to the idea of 'theatre as a place of showing, not of exhibiting, of nakedness before one's own emotional states' (ibid.).

The theatrical performance, in Pavlovksy's practice, is very far from the aseptic execution of the virtuoso: it is afflicted by risks. Real risks, derived from the political commitment assumed at each moment. But also personal risks, derived from the degree of involvement of the author-actor in the embodiment of the ideas and experiences: 'For me theatre was and is a continuous discovery of myself ... when the most personal things are raised to an aesthetic level, what is mine is no longer mine. Now it is not only personal, but also belongs to a specific social-historical context' (23).

This 'what is mine is no longer mine' once more recalls the process of transformation of the actor into 'someone', it is the process we have identified in Camilla-Colombine and in Rosa Cuchillo. The actor empties themself of themself, to become not a character with a defined identity, but 'someone'. When this is done not just out of virtuosity, but rather to make a silenced discourse heard, then this sacrifice acquires an ethical dimension. Ethics only exists in relation, in relation with others, and in this case the others are as much the spectators as those who gain representation in the actor's emptying of themself.

Yet what kind of emptying is Pavlovsky talking about? Without a doubt, one very different from the emptying of Grotowsky, one instead located at an intermediate point between the sacrificial emptying of Artaud and the subjective emptying of Brecht. We can recognize it in some works of body art or in some recent stage works. However, it only becomes effective when one reaches the point at which privacy is indeed interrupted and a certain erasure of personal identity is achieved, when the actor puts themself in the condition of being a specific 'someone', not an abstract 'anyone', but some man or woman.

In contrast to what happened in Peru, Colombia, Guatemala, El Salvador or Mexico, where the indigene populations were the most repressed, anyone could be regarded as an enemy during the years of neoliberal military repression in the Southern Cone. In fact, numerous artists and intellectuals of the middle class were arrested, tortured and in many cases 'disappeared' or murdered. In those years, the idea was not to put one's body on the side of the actual or potential victim: the idea was to put one's own body at risk. Being or not being an artist was irrelevant. Some of the most powerful acts of resistance of those years were carried out by persons who were not artists, who were 'ordinary' persons. Among them, the courage of the Madres de la Plaza de Mayo continues to move us; 'they put their bodies on the line' at the risk of sharing – as occurred in some cases – the same fate as their sons and daughters.

In Argentina, the violence unleashed by the Triple A (Argentine Anti-Communist Alliance) against leftist militants, students and intellectuals in previous years was institutionalized under the government of the military junta. Following models practised in Brazil, Chile, Bolivia, Paraguay and Uruguay, the junta chose to direct the repression through a 'parallel terrorist state', benefitting from international consulting, especially from French officers who had participated in the war in Argelia. Those considered as subversive were not detained, but kidnapped, not subject to trials or jailed, but 'disappeared'. This produced a legal void and total despair among the victims as well as their families. Relatives of the 'disappeared' began in the first months to try to ascertain the whereabouts of their children, partners or siblings. They failed in their searches, but in the course of wandering from ministerial offices to military vicariates, some of the mothers got to know each other and decided to convene in order to make their claims visible.

Their first gathering took place on 30 April 1977 and went almost unnoticed. Yet little by little, despite the silence of the media and the fear that gripped Argentine society, the group of mothers grew and gained public presence. The government, annoyed by the defiant presence of the mothers, ordered the police to break up the group. In response to the order from the police 'to move on', Azucena Villaflor suggested complying, and the mothers, instead of remaining grouped together, began to circle the Plaza de Mayo square. Later on they identified themselves with nails on their lapel and a white headscarf, which would become a scarf embroidered with the names of the disappeared son or daughter. 'The crazy women', as they were called by the military officers, grew into a threat (Gorini 2006). The army infiltrated agents into the group and a few months later several mothers were kidnapped and disappeared, among them Azucena Villafor.

Despite the initial response, the mothers maintained their struggle and internationalized it. As the years went by they lost hope of recuperating their missing relatives, but they refused to recognize death. That their relatives were dead was something that the same people who publicly denied knowledge of the matter were obliged to declare. And they did not declare it. Justice was likewise not administered when Raúl Alfonsín assumed the presidency after the end of the military dictatorship. Far from responding to the mothers' demands of investigating the disappearances and crimes by a bilateral commission, Alfonsín delegated the task to a commission of experts, CONADEP, headed by the writer Ernesto Sábato, who elaborated a disappointing report titled 'Nunca más' (Never Again) (CONADEP 1984). The 'Sábato Report' began with the following statement: 'During the 1970s Argentina was convulsed by a terror that came from both the extreme right and the extreme left, a phenomenon that has occurred in many countries.' Despite this condemnation of state terrorism, this first sentence introduces an inacceptable justification of the crimes that were committed, not to combat 'leftist terrorism', but to annihilate all the militants and potential militants on the left as well as their families. A little while later, the laws 'Punto Final' (End Point) and 'Obediencia Debida' (Law of Due Obedience) were passed.

The mothers became activists without wanting to. Their activism was that of 'ordinary' people. In retrospect, their actions have been interpreted from the perspective of the logic of representation. Yet the representation in their actions was a means for action and not an end in itself. In activist practice the aesthetic dimension fulfils a subsidiary function. For this reason, there is no difference in activism between artists and non-artists.

10

'Putting the body on the line'

'Poner el cuerpo' – literally 'putting the body', and by implication, 'on the line' – is one of the principles that guide the practices of contemporary resistance, but also one of the potent ideas employed in the recuperation of Latin American conceptual practices of the 1960s and 1970s. In contrast to what occurred in Europe and North America, conceptualism in the Latin America of those decades did not coincide with a peaceful postmodernism, but with societies governed by dictatorial regimes and/or subject to states of violence. Latin American conceptual art was *by nature* a political art. Action art, and in particular body art, was a high-risk practice, not because artists voluntarily practised violence on their bodies, but because of the vulnerability of those same bodies when facing the apparatus of repression and control. The exhibition *Perder la forma humana* (Losing the Human Form, 2012), curated by the group Conceptualismos del Sur, offered an inventory of – as well as several proposals for – historiographic readings of those years, when artistic practice necessarily coincided with activism and gender activism could operate not only in the sphere of micropolitics, but directly in that of macropolitics. Activism also penetrated the artistic and literary practices of artists and writers who refused, as Pavlovsky remarked, to 'look the other way', even if they did not conceive of their production in these terms.

Under the heading 'artistic activism', the curators suggest the following:

By 'artistic activism' we refer to those modes of production of aesthetic forms and of relationality that put social action before the traditional call for the autonomy of art ... artistic activism 'is' not, nor ceases to 'be', art. It is legible, or not, as art depending on the frame and the place from where one tries to make something legible ... 'being' an artist is not regarded as the essence of subjects, but as a function ... If artistic activism succeeds in abolishing the distance between object and subject, this is because it demands nothing less than the practice of 'putting the body on the line'.

Expósito, Vindel y Vidal 2012: 49

Activism is one of the ways of returning experience to art, as John Dewey proposed in 1930, not with the intention that artistic practice integrate itself in everyday or extraordinary experience, but instead assuming the commitment of intervening in the changing of experience by means of social and political transformation. Art does not exist as a noun, but as an adjective. What is artistic belongs to aesthetic representations, but it can also belong to social or political action. The activist subject may or may not be an artist, but the artist who choses an activist practice does this knowing that, in that practice, they are no different from the rest, they are one among many. What is more, the realization of this practice deprives the activist subject of the protections of representation, because even when producing representations, they are obliged to 'put the body on the line'.

'Putting the body on the line' is an ethical decision that opens up political action. 'Putting the body on the line' is an act of freedom. The action is social as long as it is an experience and not merely living something. The action is political as well if the experience occurs or intervenes in the public sphere, not reduced to either an event nor a representation of an experience. The impact of the political action is usually not direct, but rather symbolic. Whether this symbolism is or is not artistic does not matter, but depends on the function assigned it at each moment.

'Putting the body on the line' implies being willing to make a personal sacrifice for the benefit of a group, an idea or a project of coexistence. 'Putting the body on the line' has a ceremonial dimension, that can be realized as a festive celebration of life (in a demonstration, a dance, a collective action), but it can also be realized painfully, even tragically, putting at risk one's own fate, freedom or even life. The artists who worked with their body in the 1970s in some cases engaged in practices that put at risk their physical integrity or at least implied a suffering that was not imposed externally. Personal sacrifice was intrinsic to actions that condemned the sterility of welfare states and indifference towards the suffering of others. The sacrifice could also be understood as the only way an individual action achieved enough symbolic resonance to signify or represent the pain of others. In the performing and visual practices of those years in Latin America the real or symbolic sacrifice assumed by actors or artists in the realization of their practices did not exhaust all of the risks. Nevertheless, the sacrifice (regardless of the manner in which it was practised) was understood as one of the possible ways of justifying the representation of other people's pain, not as dramatic representation, but as the mimetic or synthetic representation of that pain.

Fascism only acknowledges the athletic body, that which can swell the ranks of military forces or contribute to the machinery of production.

Fascism negates the subjective body. Subjectivity only occurs in the social body, the body that is superimposed on the state. The fascism that ravaged Latin America in the 1970s was not designed by fugitive Nazis from Europe (although some contributed to it), but rather in the offices of the 'most democratic country in the world'.

Fascism surged in South America in the 1960s and 1970s with unusual force. Indigenous people and peasants were the victims of a new genocide, many thousands of activists and sympathizers of social and political movements were sacrificed as 'enemies of the homeland' to the dictates of the hemispheric Empire. The Doctrine of National Security, devised by the US-American administration during the highpoint of the Cold War to combat foreign imperialism (that of the USSR) on the continent, was furnished with powerful military tools: the SOA (School of the Americas) in Panama trained the repressive cadres of Latin American military forces, while the Chicago Boys instructed business people, economists and politicians. General Pinochet was one of the most eager adherents in applying such doctrines. After overthrowing and murdering the elected president, Salvador Allende, on 11 September 1973, Pinochet headed one of the most sinister regimes in Latin America – sinister not because of the number of victims (the dictatorship in Argentina was much more bloody, while the 'dirty wars' in Peru, Colombia or Guatemala took many more lives), but because of the concurrence of normality and surveillance, liberalism and repression, progress and torture, religiosity and death. During the first months of the regime, the 'shock doctrine' was applied with a fervour characteristic of devout followers. Its effects lasted for so long that by the time the majority of neighbouring countries had made the transition to 'formal democracies', Chile still maintained its dictatorial regime. Only the imminent collapse of the Socialist bloc drove Pinochet to step down from power after the plebiscite of 1988, though keeping control of the military and turning Chile not only into a 'formal democracy', but into a 'supervised democracy' until 1997, ruled by his constitution, introduced in 1980, until today.

Among the artists who 'put their bodies on the line' in public spaces inhabited by militarized or repressed bodies are Pedro Lemebel and Francisco Casas, who used the name 'Las Yeguas del Apocalipsis' (The Mares of the Apocalypsis) to present their works. Their actions took place during the last months of the Pinochet government and especially in the years following the plebiscite, under the governments of the 'Concertación' (Coalition of Parties for Democracy). These actions were doubly significant, since leftist political activism and gender activism coincided in them, a coincidence more than problematic for a society where leftist bodies too had been normatively disciplined.

Pedro Lemebel, whom Roberto Bolaño called 'the greatest poet' of his generation, stood out for defending his political freedom with the same determination as his freedom of gender (Bolaño 2004b: 76). He explained this in his *Manifiesto*:

I am not Pasolini asking for explanations
I am not Ginsberg expelled from Cuba
I am not a fag disguised as a poet
I do not need a disguise
Here is my face
I speak for my difference

In addition to praising the name, Bolaño was surprised in his review of Las Yeguas by the 'miracle' of its survival:

Who were las Yeguas? They were, foremost, two poor homosexuals, which in a homophobic and hierarchized country (where being poor is a shame, but being poor and an artist is a crime) almost constituted an invitation to be shot at, in all senses of the word. A good part of the honour of the real Republic and of the republic of letters was saved by las Yeguas.

Bolaño 2004b: 76

On 8 October 1988 Lemebel and Casas rode naked on a mare into the university campus of Las Encinas. The work was titled *Refundación de la Universidad de Chile* (Re-Foundation of the University of Chile), referring to the foundational 'entry' of Pedro Valdivia in Santiago to declare the city the capital of Chile. Two naked bodies replaced an armed body, a mare replaced a horse, two homosexual bodies replaced a horseman, two vulnerable bodies replaced the conquistador, two united bodies replaced a single isolated one, two sexual bodies entered the asexual space of knowledge. The action performed by Lemebel and Casas draws its impact from its subversion of a normalized representation: that of the virile horseman, the conquistador and father of the homeland, who protects and suppresses bodies as much as knowledge. This is not a direct action, but rather a representation that challenges dominant representations; it is a dissident representation, by means of which the repressive regime is confronted, at the same time proposing opening the university towards the social sphere and relocating knowledge in desire and in the body.

On 12 October 1989 (the anniversary of Columbus' landing in Guanahaní), Las Yeguas subverted another foundational myth with their work *La conquista de América* (The Conquest of America). Lemebel and Casas danced the *cueca* (the Chilean national dance) on a map of South America covered with shards of glass from broken bottles of Coca-Cola. The action was performed in front of the Commission of Human Rights, after the plebiscite was held, but before Pinochet had abandoned the presidency of the Republic. The work was once again a representation, in this case of the suffering caused by the dual colonization: the European, 500 years beforehand, and the neoliberal, both with the support of arms. The injuries on the dancers' feet represented the pain inflicted by the dictatorial regime; the blood that stained the map that both of them trod represented the risk of infection with AIDS and the new stigmatization of homosexuality as a consequence of the epidemic. There is nothing original in this action: The *cueca* had been used beforehand by groups of women, who in demonstrations of resistance danced alone in mourning for their missing husbands or children; the shards of glass already belonged to the history of action art, just like the blood. Yet the action realized by the two homosexual artists shocked (and in some cases outraged) those present, while its evocation continues to be strongly upsetting.

Lemebel and Casas offered an action of accompaniment. But in contrast to those carried out by Yuyachkani a few years later, they accompanied not only the victims, but all of Chilean society. Their accompaniment, moreover, did not engage in representativeness, but rather in critically questioning the contemporary marginalizations and injustices that continued to be concealed underneath official commemoration.

One can observe parallels between this work by Las Yeguas and certain actions of 'pain' practised by conceptual artists of the previous decade. Gina Pane similarly injured the soles of her feet in *Action Escalade non-anesthésiée* (Unanaesthetized Escalation Action, 1971). The work (titled an 'action' by Pane) was realized in the artist's Paris studio in the spring of 1971, without an audience (thus avoiding theatricality), but with the presence of the photographer Françoise Masson. This was therefore an unrepeatable action, but destined to be a representation (in the photographic reproduction). Pane's work was a representation in other senses as well. It literally represented a climb (the aim of the action was not to reach the top rung, but to represent a climb). It metaphorically represented a paradoxical experience: every ascent involves suffering, all progress involves cruelty. Allegorically, it represented the violence and the pain caused by the Cold War, specifically by the Vietnam war. In this sense, the artist assumed the function of representing (of speaking for) those far away and deprived of access to the communication media in the West. Finally, the work could be considered representative of a way of doing art in the 1970s, of social awareness and of political discontent.

The fact that we can regard an individual artistic practice as representative of a context or of an awareness indicates that singularity can only be constructed in the plural; singularity is all the more valued, moreover, when it incorporates the expression of collective experiences, behaviours, emotions or desires, even though in many cases these are repressed, silenced or made invisible.

For Gina Pane (though not all artists of her generation believed this), the documentation was consubstantial with the work. As was representation. The repetition of the movement (in the climb, but also in the realization of the injuries) and the repeated image (to record the movement) were necessary for the significant action to exist. Lemebel and Casas, in contrast, did not worry about documenting their actions. In fact, what was performative for Casas at the moment was not so much the actions, but the life he shared with Lemebel within the social and artistic context of the Chilean transition. In contrast to Pane's action, theirs was not representative of anything, it did not intend to rob the widows of their *cueca*, nor the 'disappeared' victims of their struggle. It did represent, certainly, communion in pain and a will for life from singularities in a tense relationship with their territory.

During the government of Patricio Aylwin, Las Yeguas presented their last joint action, *Tu dolor dice: Minado* (Your Pain Says: Mined, 1993). This was a painful criticism of the impunity of those responsible for crimes against humanity, once the Retting report was published by the Commission on Truth and Reconciliation on the Victims of the Dictatorship. A recording of a previous action, *Homenaje a Sebastián Acevedo* (Homage to Sebastián Acevedo, 1991), a miner who set himself on fire in the Plaza de Armas square in Concepción in protest against the disappearance of his two children, was projected on the wall of the former torture centre in Belgrado Street in the centre of Santiago. Lemebel and Casas laid on a floor of coal, covered by quicklime, while one heard series of names of cities and of identification documents, both of them referring to forced 'disappearances'. Later, inside the house, Las Yeguas occupied an entire space in a basement with glasses full of water; at the back of the stage, separated from the spectators, they recited – as in a litany – the names of the victims mentioned in the report.

An ethical decision activates representation, in which one puts the body on the line. Representation is a medium of symbolic action, a medium of subversion, but also a vital and revitalizing experience. For this reason subversive representation resists reproduction, not ontologically but ethically.

11

Hell

Unlike Lemebel, Bolaño did not live in Chile during the years of the dictatorship. He had moved with his family to Mexico in 1968. He did return for a few months when he turned twenty, to visit relatives and experience what would be the last days of the socialist government. After the coup d'état took place he was arrested. 'They were about to kill me,' B. informs his father in *Últimos atardeceres en la tierra* (Last Evenings on Earth, Bolaño 2001: 59). Freed by the intercession of a soldier friend, he left Chile and did not return until the 1990s.

Aside from this trip in his youth, Bolaño did not directly 'put his body on the line', as did Lemebel, in the streets and public spaces of Santiago, Mexico City or Barcelona. Yet few other writers have literally risked their body as much in their writing. In some of his novels, such as *Estrella distante* (Distant Star, 1996) or *Nocturno de Chile* (By Night in Chile, 2000), the horror of the dictatorship is depicted with a subtlety that shows its perversion. Bolaño did not stand out, nevertheless, as an author of militant prose. His militancy was expressed in his almost inhuman dedication to a literary labour in which he believed passionately. Literature did not entice him to works of fantasy, on the contrary, it committed him to a struggle with words, so that these words would gnaw at reality, would sweat or bleed with it. 'Putting the body on the line' in his case meant not being intimidated by colossal narrative plans, dedicating himself instead to the production of a 'torrential' prose, full of encyclopaedic lists, brutal realities, incredible adjectives and vast digressions that no one asked for, but which he believed necessary to justify his narrative choices, to justify his own creative task. 'Putting the body on the line' also implies a mode of relation – primarily physical – with his characters, who at the same time can seem tender and grotesque, brilliant and clumsy, generous and ridiculous. They are participants in an uninhibited, often brutal, sexuality, balanced in their behaviour between poetry and sweaty skin, between beauty and impulses, between aesthetic pleasure and the violence of the flesh. His novels' characters experience pleasure and suffering without sublimation, without compassion for themselves – like the author, who presents himself as one more among them.

Although all of this was already evident in his previous novels, in particular in *Los detectives salvajes* (The Savage Detectives, 1998), Bolaño achieved a maximum of dedication in his posthumously published work *2666* (Bolano 2004a), a novel of over 1000 pages, written in a race against a terminal disease, stealing days and hours from it to finish the work. *2666* is a novel replete with deaths that breathes life, a novel driven by death that teems with love of life. This love explains the excess, which is not arrogance, but rather the submission to a necessity, to something that emerges from the words, but also from the characters' bodies. These appear and disappear, sometimes repeatedly, as though the narrative flow makes them surface here and there, or the desert wind unearths them for moments by removing the sand, sometimes only for an instant, sometimes long enough to show their lives.

The novel begins with the hunt for an absent body, that of Archimboldi. The search for the body unleashes a storm that brings up hundreds of bodies, some alive, many others dead. Structured in five parts (at one point Bolaño considered publishing the text as five separate novels), the narrative is supported by a series of coincidences triggered by Archimboldi's travels, the four critics who study his work, the professor who guides them through Santa Teresa, the journalist who for the sake of love saves the professor's daughter from certain death, the deaths of women who did not find a saviour in Santa Teresa, the death of the purported executioner and nephew of the aged writer, and all of the persons who during the years of the narrative passed through the desert of Sonora, a sort of centripetal grave in which all the narrative lines – as in *Los detectives salvajes* – ultimately disappear.

'The Part about the Crimes' is undoubtedly the most disturbing section of the novel. It reports the murders of women and girls in Santa Teresa between 1993 and 1997. Ninety reports, brutal and precise, are detailed in little over 300 pages. In each one of them the victim is identified, when possible, her wounds are described, the violence she was subject to is reconstructed and her life in the city is succinctly recuperated. Bolaño decides to look horror directly in the face, something that cannot be represented because it eludes the imagination.

Santa Teresa is a fictional city in the state of Sonora where Bolaño restores the reality of Ciudad Juárez in the state of Chihuahua. There is no attempt to construct a parallel world, as in the 'landmark' novels of Latin American literature (from Cortázar to García Márquez), but to create the conditions for 'imagining', that is, for representing, the pain and the injustice. The names are fictitious, but the reality and the experiences behind those names are real.

On 12 May 1993 the body of a young unidentified woman was found in the hills of Cerro Bola, the victim of torture and sexual violence, with signs of death by strangulation. She was the first of a series of twenty-five women discovered dead that year in Ciudad Juárez, a third of them with signs of sexual violence. In the following years the numbers increased, among the victims were numerous girls as young as twelve. The criminal police and the authorities in the state were utterly negligent during the first five years, delaying the investigations of the missing, ignoring the pattern of gender violence, blaming the victims, humiliating the families, destroying or faking evidence and accusing false culprits.

The majority of murdered women and girls were workers or students, humble girls and women, in some cases mothers, members of tremendously vulnerable families without the means to demand their rights from politicians and the justice system. The humiliation that all of them suffered before dying, in addition to the physical violence, was an indication of the contempt of their kidnappers towards the victims, a contempt that extended to how the police treated the corpses, like those of prostitutes: from their point of view, bodies with utilitarian value when alive, worthless when dead.

Yet the women were not prostitutes. Many of them worked for the 'maquiladora' industry; the rest owed their employment or their presence in the city to this industry. The *maquiladoras* (assembly plants) were set up in northern Mexico when the federal government launched a plan in the 1970s to industrialize the border region. Numerous transnational corporations installed themselves near the border to combine the advantages of low wages and good transport connections. The economic growth and permissibility attracted the drug-trafficking mafias too – another major transnational business. The signing of the North American Free Trade Agreement in 1994 propelled the expansion of the *maquiladoras*, but also of internal migration, the unplanned growth of nearby cities, the extreme inequality in their social structure, the situations of exploitation of young labourers and corruption.

There existed, therefore, a political, social and economic responsibility that neither the state government nor the corporations were willing to assume. It was easier to support unqualified agents in their regard of the women as prostitutes. In this way the crimes were not classified as 'femicides'. In response to the demands from international associations and organizations, the federal authorities continued to maintain for years that these were scattered episodes within the framework of the widespread violence that plagued the state of Chihuahua and other northern states. They attributed this violence to the expansion of the drug trafficking mafias as well as to the poverty and destructuring of many families, which caused a rise in domestic violence. This hypothesis, unacceptable for the families, was contradicted by numerous reports and judicially refuted by various courts.

In 1998 the Comisión Nacional de Derechos Humanos (National Commission on Human Rights, CNDH) concluded that state authorities were guilty of 'negligent omission' and issued Recommendation 44/98, which was rejected by the municipal and state governments. Nonetheless, neither the CNDH recommendation, nor the report by the Special Rapporteur of the UN, nor the appointment of a special public prosecutor for the investigation of homicides of women (FEIHM), had any effect. The murders and disappearances continued in the following years, in the face of the passivity and – according to families and human rights organizations – the complicity of the police and judicial authorities. The violence against the women was exacerbated by the harassment of the families and human rights activists, as well as illegal arrests and assassinations carried out by the police against alleged suspects, their families and representatives.

A few days after Bolaño's death in a Barcelona hospital, Amnesty International presented its report 'Mexico. Intolerable Killings. Ten Years of Abductions and Murders in Ciudad Juárez and Chihuahua' (Amnistía Internacional 2003). Even though the errors and the negligence of the police and judicial bodies made it very difficult to establish an exact number, the report estimated that 370 women had been murdered in Ciudad Juárez between 1993 and 2003, of which a third were also victims of sexual violence. This figure has to be augmented with the number of missing women, which according to non-governmental organizations, could double the number of murders during this period. The majority of victims were young women or adolescents, workers in the maquiladoras, service workers and students, with very limited financial resources, in many cases forced to make long commutes to their workplace or school. The girls and women were kidnapped, held captive for hours or various days, subject to physical and psychological violence, humiliation, mutilation and ultimately murdered, generally by strangulation. Although some arrests were made, it is extremely doubtful that those responsible were caught. The solving of common crimes (of domestic violence or in the context of prostitution) concealed the absolute impunity of those responsible for the femicide.

During the trial held in the Inter-American Court of Human Rights in Chile for the eight victims discovered in December 2001 in a former cotton field, the representatives of the State insisted in proposing contextual explanations for the crimes, even claiming as an explanation the changes in traditional roles in the family as a result of the labour activity of the women. Even taking into account the report by CEDAW (The Convention on the Elimination of all Forms of Discrimination Against Women) presented by the State, according to which the homicides were related to a 'a culture of discrimination against women based on the erroneous conception of their inferiority', the Court did not hesitate to categorize the crimes as the 'homicide of women for reasons of gender, also known as femicide' (CIDH: para. 143 on p. 42). The sentence also cites the report by the special prosecutor, who denounced 'the lack of technical and scientific capabilities as well as the training ... of the members of the criminal police'. In addition, the report criticized that 'the state governments did not introduce public policies directed at furnishing the prosecutor's office of this state with the infrastructure, work processes and specialized personnel that would allow it to carry out the investigations of the homicides of women within a reasonably acceptable range of assurance' (147 and 149). In its conclusions the Court established that

> the inefficient response and the indifferent attitudes documented in regards to the investigation of said crimes ... seem to have allowed violence against women to continue in Ciudad Juárez. The Court states that until 2005 the majority of crimes continue to be unsolved, with the homicides that present characteristics of sexual violence the ones with the highest levels of impunity.
>
> 164

Bolaño pays tribute to the women, restoring the dignity robbed from them by their aggressors and by those who ignored the injustices committed against them. But he does not achieve this by reconstructing any of their lives, as would be usual in a conventional narrative. He imposed on himself the discipline of rewriting the ninety stories about the found bodies and their respective forensic reports. And he imposes his reading on the reader. These are horrifying reports, especially when they detail the real suffering of girls and young women and the real acts deliberately perpetrated by criminals. It is not necessary to reconstruct the personal life of the young women to be able to imagine the pain that was endured, the collapse of their life expectations, the experience of a horror whose existence they could have never imagined. Around each one of these moments of horror, which become infinite during the reading, he describes the lives of the visible inhabitants of Santa Teresa: that of detective Juan de Dios Martínez and his lover, the director of a psychiatric clinic; of Harry Magaña, the *gringo* policeman who on his own account investigates the murder of a girl from his village and ends up dead himself, in an announced death narrated live; that of Klaus Haas, the German computer expert who is unfoundedly blamed for the crimes and who ultimately accuses the possible culprits, the sons of millionaires and drug traffickers; that of Lalo Cura, a young man descended from a chain of rapes, hired as a killer and later as a policeman, apparently the only one interested in observing the clues and making logical deductions, although without any desire to be a hero; that of Sergio, the journalist from Mexico City reluctantly covering the murders; and that of Azucena Esquivel Plata, the PRI congresswoman searching for her missing friend, Kelly Rivera, and who seems willing to mobilize the federal apparatus.

Despite its centripetal power, the 'Part about the Crimes' does not constitute the axis of the fiction, which revolves around the character of Archimboldi, his acquaintances, his critics and their acquaintances. The lives cut short of the women and girls of Santa Teresa have their obverse in the very long, in some ways 'fairy tale', life of Archimboldi, who fashions himself into a writer during the First World War, in the shadow of Ivanov (behind which is concealed Mikhail Bulgakov) and hardened by the pain of so many men and women dying before his eyes, without death being able to trap him. His 'excess of experience' compensates the 'scarcity of experience' of his critics, in the same way that the heroism or glamour of certain characters compensates the mediocrity or sordidness of the lives of others. Sex, evil, death, the randomness of existence, generosity and the details of imagination or creativity that distinguish these humans are recurring themes in all of these stories.

Why resort to real pain?

Perhaps because the speed at which information circulates in contemporary society makes it impossible for fiction to retreat into itself. Or perhaps because the real pain on the other side of the screens demands of the artist a responsibility that they cannot assume from mere fiction. Perhaps because the impunity and the evil affected him in such a way that the recuperation of the pain in Ciudad Juárez imposed itself as a necessity in the creation of Santa Teresa. Perhaps because the dead women are victims and – without desiring it – representatives of so many other victims who 'by chance' have suffered the sentence of an unimaginable evil. Perhaps because the unimaginable evil that unfolded in Ciudad Juárez is the representation of evil, not in the shape of a devil, but in the shape of an out-of-control industrialization, of a neoliberalism without scruples, of a systemic corruption of power and its agents, of a looking the other way of a middle class that relinquishes its capacity of speaking for the benefits of security and consumption. Perhaps because they were accidental representatives of life, because they were 'ordinary' women in a world where you have to be someone, be the owner of something or at least of your own name, in order to have a right to life.

12

Document and monument

The reader of *2666* is left in no doubt about the ethical decision and the aesthetic necessity that justify the use of the real pain of the women of Ciudad Juárez in the representation that Bolaño elaborates and situates in the imaginary city of Santa Teresa. For the reader of these pages who has not gone through the experience of reading *2666*, doubt could arise – and has often been formulated – about the legitimacy of utilizing and representing the pain of others for aesthetic, literary or academic ends. Does representing the pain caused by evil not constitute an intolerable aestheticization, which can even result in prolonging the crime itself? Why not act against evil, instead of representing it or representing the pain of the victims? Does representation, at the same time that it contests the silencing of the crimes, not also amplify their symbolic potency?

Susan Sontag addressed a similar issue in her book *Regarding the Pain of Others* (2003), in which she analyses the effects of the reproduction of war photographs that provide testimony of horror and probes the legitimacy of their use. Sontag does not question the legitimacy of the act of photographing the horror, since she assumes that the photographer is there to capture reality and that reality should be made known. She examines the reproduction of the photographs and the contexts in which they are reproduced, as well as the representations that the photographs materialize. What is the point of looking at images of horror, of corpses, of mutilated or gravely injured bodies? The first response is the most common one: the representation of horror activates memory and prevents the repetition of criminal acts. This would correspond to the effectiveness of bringing individuals to trial for war crimes or crimes against humanity, including those trials that do not end in punishment, such as those organized by Truth Commissions. The re-presentation of the crimes is meant to affect bodies and symbolically project a representation contrary to that of the crimes. Restitution and prevention likewise justify the museums of memory, even if Sontag mistrusts the existence of what is termed 'collective memory': Memory is always individual memory, so that such museums do not serve any use if they do not affect people individually and ultimately condition their political decisions.

Yet, in a second moment, Sontag becomes more forceful in her reply: there are images of horror that should only be seen by those who do something to alleviate or avoid the repetition of the pain they represent (Sontag 2003: 42). When we merely contemplate the horror we can feel affected, but this effect is emotional and passive, it does not lead to action and is therefore useless. Sontag explicitly rejects the exhibition of war photographs in artistic contexts.

Bertolt Brecht faced similar issues during the making of his *Kriegsfibel* (War Primer, 1955), which reproduces images of horror published ten years before in the press. In contrast to Sontag, he did regard it necessary to republish these images, arguing that 'whoever forgets the past cannot escape it' (Didi-Huberman 2008: 34). Yet Brecht waited ten years, since his goal was not to confront the horror, nor even to make the cruelty of the war comprehensible, but rather 'to teach how to read images'. In accordance with his theory of alienation, Brecht opted for distance, accompanying the images with epigrams. Only the passage of time and the poetic elaboration resulting from the montage of image and poetry made taking positions possible, in relation to that part of history that we never wanted to look at again.

War photography is regarded as documenting horror, reproducing crude fragments of reality. Yet a long tradition of the composition and modification of such images also exists, converting the documents into constructed representations or stories, which in many cases support stories dictated by de facto interests or powers. This contribution of photography to hegemonic narratives, that is, to the construction of official fictions, is completed with a second fictional exercise, which consists of always depicting the victims and aggressors as 'Others': as barbarians, savages, Communists, Muslims, prostitutes, humble women, poor girls. On the pages of newspapers and magazines, or on the screens of television or digital devices, the victims are always 'Others' who live in alien lands, even if these territories are situated in our cities or neighbourhoods. The effect of terrorist attacks is to shatter that security of the image or screen. But when the victims are citizens 'on this side' of the image, the means of representation are much more prudent. Why does the corpse or wounded body of a Bosnian Muslim, a Gaza Palestinian, or a worker in Ciudad Juárez offer less resistance to representation than that of an inhabitant of New York, London or Madrid? Why should the corpse of a prostitute be more contemptible than that of a worker?

Sontag wrote her essay in the wake of the attacks of 11 September in New York. Her reflections, however, cannot be disconnected from her experience in Sarajevo during the Serbian siege of the city in 1993. The siege of Sarajevo began on 5 April 1992 and lasted until 29 February 1996, taking the lives of more than 12,000 people and leaving another 50,000 injured as a result of bombings, military attacks and snipers. Sontag was one of the first internationally renowned intellectuals who went to the city in solidarity with its inhabitants. Her response to the question of why she went to Sarajevo already implicitly included what she would later write about the representation of the pain of others: 'I have to say that I had never thought of going to Sarajevo, because I did not know what I could do. What can you do in Sarajevo if you are not a journalist or work for a humanitarian organization?' (Sontag 1993). 'Incited' by her son David Rieff, who was writing a book on the war in Bosnia, Sontag finally travelled to Sarajevo and after two weeks there found the reason for a second trip: to put on a play, Samuel Beckett's *Waiting for Godot*. From then on, Sontag in turn 'incited' other intellectuals to be present in the city.

If the moral caution cited by Sontag in *Regarding the Pain of Others* was based on the perverse consequences of the aestheticization and fictionalization of the representations of horror in war photographs, the explanation she gave for her involvement in the war in Sarajevo alluded specifically to aesthetics, fiction and representation. It is precisely that involvement in a real situation that legitimizes fiction and representation in a context of violence and urgency, such as Sontag experienced in 1993 when she staged Beckett.

Sontag's reflections are occupied exclusively with the exhibition and distribution of the images, not with their production, since she understands that the photographer is obliged to record what happens before their camera. But in the case of the arts of representation, of literature, painting, theatre and film, horror cannot be recorded so directly; it requires representation, a process of construction and composition, in a certain manner the reconstruction of the real as fiction.

We have to think that an artistic practice made of the pain and suffering of others would arise from being affected, not from self-interest. If I decide to represent or artistically intervene in a situation it is because it affects me and because I do not find any other manner of action other than my writing, performing or doing. It is an action that involves me. Such action has nothing to do with self-interest, since self-interest implies distance in regard to what I observe as an object; it likewise implies the expectance of gain, no matter if that gain is not strictly economic (although the accumulation of experience or knowledge can be rewarded economically, before or afterwards). Since the action arises from an affect and is realized with involvement, the action (writing, performance, art work) is in itself an ethical act, in which the artist commits themself in their physical and subjective integrity, in their own life.

The representation of experiences of horror or the intervention in a situation in which they are produced requires a sacrifice from the artist. The sacrifice is not an end in itself, but a necessity derived from a desire of representation. Yet why assume a sacrifice based on representation? Would it not be preferable to avoid the representation? Might the sacrifice of the artist (as has so often been denounced in regard to the body art of the 1970s) turn into an exhibitionist exercise, which in no way helps to stop or repair injustice?

Roberto Bolaño decided that the unpunished femicide and the guilt of the State in which he had formed himself as a writer called for his work of fiction. Furthermore, the use of that pain for a narrative work demanded a maximum of commitment from him. *2666* has monumental dimensions, because in a certain sense it is a monument. But *2666* is not a memorial, it is a symbolic gift from the author to his characters, including the young women of Santa Teresa, a gift that does not return life, but which accompanies the action of relatives and activists in defence of human rights and which transports occurrences that the Mexican State strove to make invisible or minimize to a place of literary centrality.

We are so accustomed to monuments always serving official history that we forget the possibility that monuments can also serve to support other actions. Bolaño dared to produce this type of dissident monument. As a dissident monument, it is not at all static or permanent; it is so penetrated by life that only life maintains it upright. Life is not a happy fantasy, life is joy and boredom, sordidness and beauty, hope and death, contemplation and flux, laughter and awkwardness, banality and pleasure, experience and apathy. The monumental tension is countered by a vital tension; hence the imperfection that he himself alluded to. Bolaño could have concluded his literary career (and his own existence) with a perfect novel. He could have constructed a brief story about the life of one of the victims, of a family, of a detective. His literary mastery would surely have produced a – formally and politically – impeccable work. Nevertheless, he chose instead the difficult option and avoided a virtuosic representation. Virtuosity is unacceptable when what is being represented is a matter of life or death.

'Throwing the body into the fight', the principle that guided Pasolini, becomes effective once again. As in Pasolini, words remain very close to bodies, to emotions, to desire. This is the justification for representation not retreating to literary monumentality. It is also what stimulates excess and formal rebellion. The ethics of representation is manifested here very clearly as a challenge against the dominant morality, as the last action of a 'savage' writer who takes the side of those who suffer, even at the cost of his own 'respectability', even at the cost of not achieving narrative perfection, even at the cost of his own survival.

13

Representation and sacrifice

Angélica Liddell too erected a monument to the women of Ciudad Juárez, to those dead and those alive, with the same desire for commitment and with the same requisite imperfection as Bolaño. *La casa de la fuerza* (The House of Strength, 2009) is Liddell's theatrical production with the longest running time in her entire artistic career, five hours and half, during which Angélica accompanies the audience on a journey from intimate pain to collective tragedy. It is a work in which the performers (the professional and the non-professional) do not pretend: they show us what they know how to do and they reveal their skills and limitations. The actresses occupy the stage, recite the words they have to say and put their bodies at the disposal of the action, without concealing anything. The *mariachis* (traditional Mexican folk music groups) offer their music as accompaniment when Angélica asks for it and leave when they have finished. As do the cellist Pau de Nut, the girl who speaks the words of the prologue and Juan Carlos Heredia, the champion 'Strongman', who at the end of the show puts on his display of strength. All of them can pretend to be better actors, Angélica can arrange the stage so that the pieces function more harmoniously, she can avoid the interruptions in the rhythm, can cover up the defects in acting or in the form. She does not do so, because *La casa de la fuerza* is at the same time a vindication of fragility and, symbolically, of the women who the 'force' tortured, raped and murdered. For this reason, the monument erected by Angélica is, paradoxically, a fragile monument, where – as with Bolaño – there is no room for perfection and much less for virtuosity. For this reason too, Angélica advises her actresses to work with the mistake, 'like athletes when they lift weights until they are at the point of bursting. On stage, working with the mistake means working without modesty' (Liddell 2009a).

The prologue anticipates the vulnerability: a six-year old girl comes on stage and says: 'No mountain, no forest, no desert can deliver us from the harm that others prepare for us.' Then she climbs on a small airplane and exits the stage. This opens a triptych that presents three dimensions of loneliness and violence. The first part is an ensemble section performed by three women, Getsemaní San Marcos, Lola Jiménez and Angélica herself, dressed in costumes that recall the period costumes for Anton Chekhov's *Three Sisters,* but transposed to an indefinite space that could be a poor *cantina* of the mid-twentieth century. The women lament their abandon, accompany each other in their loneliness, drink beer, sing *rancheras* (Mexican country songs) of spite (traversed by pain, but also by macho ideology) with the *mariachis*, they dare and entertain each other with real electric shocks, talk about action films, expose their breasts, their desolate beauty and finally they devote themselves to the exercise of strength.

The second part recovers a previous work titled 'Venice'. Accompanied by Pau de Nut, it narrates the story of Angélica's failed love affair (a passion lived out in public with an artist who shortly afterwards left her and scorned her) and her despondency in a Venice hotel. There the obsession over the failed relationship and personal messages intersected with the news of the destruction and death caused by the Israeli bombing of Gaza in January 2009. In order to exorcise her pain, Angélica offered free sex online. In her diary from those days those three experiences are superimposed. On stage, Pau de Nut performs Vivaldi, while she repeats the words she had heard a waiter say in a restaurant in Venice, words with which she had tried in vain to move the man she loved and who only responded to her love with scorn: 'Tiramisú means lift me up'. After reading from the diary, Liddell cuts her arms and legs with a razor. The cuts formed part of the public and theatrical relationship with her lover. But they were also the necessary consequence of Angélica's work on her own experience of pain and her search for beauty in sacrifice: 'Blood has an aesthetic potency that is brutal, brutal ... I use it pictorially. To reveal the internal I begin with the surface. When you choose strength, blood and self-confession, ultimately you are talking about fragility' (ibid.).

The cuts had first appeared in the presentation of *Actos de desobediencia* (Acts of Disobedience, 2008) and continued in her succeeding works: *Anfaegtelse* (2008) and *Te haré invencible con mi derrota, Jackie* (I Will Make You Invincible with My Defeat, Jackie 2009), works in which love was presented as inseparable from sacrifice and that prepared the immense fresco of *La casa de la fuerza*. In the latter, Angélica not only cuts herself, she also summons a nurse on stage, who extracts several centilitres of blood from her and her two actresses, with which they subsequently draw a heart on their white shirts. In one of the letters that Liddell received from her lover after their separation, he reproaches her for a type of narcissism in her psychological anguish, 'because what is important is humanity ... Asking for love is an act of egoism and of pride ... You haven't been raped in Ciudad Juárez. Then accept it. To suffer they have to rape or shoot you, like that, in a plan of humanity.'

Afterwards the long sequence of physical work begins, a transposition to the stage of the decision that provided the title for the work:

On 2 October 2009, the day of my birthday, I felt terrible because of the passage of time ... I had practically stopped reading and writing. I had begun to develop a rejection of intelligence, of art, culture, thought ... That same day, I signed up for a gym ... I discovered that physical exhaustion helped me to support the spiritual collapse ... *La Casa de la Fuerza* is ... the place where we are not loved, where we do exercises of non-feelings to compensate the excess of feelings. It is the place of humiliation and of frustration.

Liddell 2009a

For more than an hour the three actresses attempt to de-subjectivize themselves by means of physical work. The key is provided by another reference to Chekhov's *Three Sisters*. 'We must work', repeats Irina during the entire play. Work appears to her as an escape from the melancholy she blames on bourgeois idleness. Liddell recreates a brief scene from Chekhov's play, to then dedicate herself to the effort of lifting weights, carrying ten heavy sofas from one side of the stage to another and emptying sacks of coal in the centre of the stage, before she attempts to move it with shovels. Useless work, sterile strength; an inversion of the biblical sense of work: one does not suffer working in order to survive or to produce, but rather one survives working, without producing, to avoid pain. The actresses voluntarily degrade themselves to the condition of bodies without image, to the condition of bodies without representation, constructing the metaphor of a humanity that has relinquished its responsibility of action and thinking. This would be so if the actresses were women in a neutral space, if the metaphor would enclose itself. But the actresses' work also serves for the construction of theatrical representation, and the theatrical representation is then depicted as action and as thought. The work claimed as salvation is, consequently, not the physical work in itself, but the work on representation, by means of which desperation is turned into thought. But for individual suffering to effectively mutate into action there must be a shift towards the collective. That is when the actresses clamour: 'Let's go to Mexico, please, let's go to Mexico!'

Angélica had been invited to Mexico to give a workshop and present a piece at the Transversales festival in Mexico City and Pachuca. The presence of violence in everyday life and the persistence of femicide in Ciudad Juárez profoundly affected the artist, who felt the imperative – as Bolaño had felt it years before – to put her work at the service of the expression of pain and of the representation of injustice. 'Sensibility always moves from the personal to the collective' (Liddell 2009b). Other works by Angélica (*Y los peces salieron a combatir contra los hombres* [And the Fish Came Out to Fight Against the Men] and *Y cómo no se pudrió ... Blancanieves* [And Since Snow White ...

Did Not Rot]) had followed the same process. In an interview before the presentation of *La casa de la fuerza* at the Avignon festival she explained it in the following manner: 'When I speak of my pain, I relate it with a collective pain. It is not simply a matter of compassion: to put yourself in the place of another, act in a way that the pain of the other seems as real to us as our own pain.' (Liddell 2008: 157).

Three Mexican actresses, Cynthia Aguirre, Perla Bonilla and María Sánchez, now occupy the stage. They inform the audience of the femicide in Ciudad Juárez and relate their own experiences. They are not victims, they are professional actresses, but they come from Chihuahua; for them, the pain of the victims is not information, but a reality that affects them. The six actresses join together in a kind of healing ritual – they create a female universe of solidarity and care, which only the cellist, Pau de Nut, responsible for making the beauty of music present, has access to. The work concludes with the sequence featuring Juan Carlos Heredia, a man almost two metres tall and weighing 173 kilos, who repeatedly responds to the poems the actresses give him with, 'To love so much, to live so alone'. Afterwards he puts on his exhibition: he turns over a car full of flowers and performs some of the numbers from the exhibitions and competitions of his discipline. Strength again becomes mere spectacle, beauty and tenderness silently close the stage.

In this work Angélica fulfilled the condition of sacrifice. 'Perhaps one can only be ethical from a position of suffering', she had written a year before. 'The poet, the artist, carries on their imperfect shoulders of a fool the weight of millions of humiliations' (Liddell 2008: 157). To make this burden visible, Angélica transferred to the theatrical representation the practices of self-injury and physical resistance that many artists had carried out as actions in the 1970s and which were transformed into spectacle in the subsequent years. Of these practices she maintains an aesthetic fascination for the injured body (present in the work of Acconci and Stelarc), for the emotion of recuperating artistic figures from the past (as in Burden and Abramović), for the manifestation of the female condition and the vulnerability of the body (as in Ono and Pane) and for the conversion of one's own body into a resonance chamber of violence silenced (and in some cases perpetuated) by hegemonic powers. The realization of these practices in a medium of representation always entails the risk of spectacularization and, consequently, of the annulment of its affective and critical potential, but it also augments its ritual potency and collective dimension. Angélica Liddell's work no longer presupposes, as for example Pane's does, a direct relation between the individual woman artist and the anonymous group of victims; such a relation is mediated by the collectivity of the stage itself and the theatrical event. This mediation is relevant, since it prevents narcissistic tendencies and a disproportionate inflating of artistic egos.

Sacrifice, in itself, does not dispute representation; rather, it challenges the spectator as spectator, claims their intellectual and emotional participation. As in ancestral ritual forms, pain or injury are not means of negating the body, but means of integration, by which the individual recognizes themself in their materiality or in the community. On the one hand, pain is a reminder of our corporeal condition and with it of our finiteness. Pain makes us bodies. Being bodies, we are mortal. But being bodies, we are also alive. The experience of pain is a necessary condition for wanting to live, since there is no life without body, no life beyond the corporeal condition. Yet pain also constitutes the strongest nexus with the rest of living beings: since the experience of pain is not transferable, the recognition that my suffering has also been lived by others close to me unites us in a community around the sacred. The sacred is not so because of its transcendent or mysterious condition, but because of the impossibility of translation. Pain, in the sense of the sacred, can only be known by means of repetition in experience. It is repetition, in the form of ritual, that creates community.

The sacred is not concealed inside boxes covered in precious metals and encrusted with jewels, with the objective of enclosing a transcendent immateriality in them. The sacred is not materialized ephemerally in bread or wine, the sacred inhabits the body of human beings as social beings, as beings that recognize in the bodies of others experiences that are untransferable but repeatable. The sacred enables the consciousness of mortality not to act against life.

In a drawing from 1946 Antonin Artaud imagined the 'theatre of cruelty' as a series of deformed bodies, enclosed in coffins, pierced by hieroglyphics and organic figures (or more precisely, organic movements fragilely coagulated for their depiction on paper). The cruelty arises from the insurrection of the body against the domination of language, from the insurrection of the flesh against the domination of appearance. The theatre of cruelty is a theatre in which bodies makes themselves evident: mortal bodies, linguistic bodies, sexualized bodies. In Rodez, away from the stage, Artaud furiously devoted himself to the task of pouring a sacred corporeality over his notebooks.

In his struggle with the pencils to make them capture his body, Artaud admired the skill of Vincent Van Gogh, the only painter he claimed who had been able to free faces from the death that they always 'carry in themselves'. The theatre of cruelty was realized in *Van Gogh le suicidé de la societé* (Van Gogh, the Man Suicided by Society, 1947) through the transformation of the painter's body into the stage ('the field of action') of the conflict: 'The problem of the predominance of flesh over spirit, or of body over flesh' (Artaud 1976b:

487). The body had already been proposed as the site of action and representation in a previous work, 'The Conquest of Mexico'. In that case it was the body of Montezuma that was transformed into a stage for the conflict between magic (incorporated spirit) and technology (materialist rationality). After being interned in psychiatric institutions for nine years, Artaud recognized himself not in the face of the Aztec emperor, but in the 'insane' painter. For only in 'insanity' did the medicine (and culture) of the epoch explain that someone could burn their hand for love (after being rejected by his cousin in Etten) or cut off his ear in rage (after an argument with Gauguin). Van Gogh was the object and victim of psychiatry due to these acts and to other behaviour, just like hundreds of women in those same years who were classified as 'hysterics'.

Pain was for Van Gogh a manifestation of life, a means of knowledge and an inalienable experience for the artist: 'I would never do away with suffering,' he wrote to Theo, quoting Millet, in 1885, 'for it is often that which makes artists express themselves most vigorously' (Van Gogh 2014). The physical pain, which the artist worked with as a means of communion and communication with nature and society, was countered by the psychic pain that medicine – as an institution of 'organized crime' (Artaud 1976b: 483) – provoked in the so-called patient. The objective was to neutralize his singularity and return him to the vegetative life, to rob him of the ethical responsibility with which he had identified his artistic activity and even his very existence.

'I have chosen the realm of pain', wrote Artaud in *Fragments d'un journal d'enfer* (Fragments of a Diary from Hell, 1926) (Artaud 1976a: 96). Pain is the source of life. Pain is the affirmation of life. For physical pain, like pleasure, is an experience that is radically immanent. Physical pain is life when that experience is freed of transcendent justifications and accepted as a condition of corporeality, that is, of life itself. The philosopher Santiago López Petit thus sees in Artaud's work a clear example of resistance against powerlessness and of an affirmation of life, what he terms a 'wanting to live'. Artaud's struggle against 'organized crime' and its medical arm, psychiatry, is an example of how an individual can rebel against the crushing of subjectivity under the immensity of overpowering social apparatuses, before which one feels impotent.

There is no alternative for those who attempt to hurt themselves but to protect them from themselves, to immobilize them, to deactivate them socially and physically. Consequently, at the end of *Pour en finir avec le jugement de Dieu* (To Have Done With the Judgement of God, 1947), Artaud rebelled with vehement fury against any immobilization, but also against any violence: 'and it was then / that I exploded everything / because my body /can never be touched.' (Artaud 2004: 1652). Against the intent to domesticate he responded with maximum exposition, with an expansive exposition, even if such expansion implied self-destruction.

The theatre of Angélica Liddell updates a resistance based on 'un-power' (López Petit 2010) into a 'pain towards life,' realizing on stage what Artaud could only realize by drawing in his notebooks during his internment. The exhibition of one's own life and the 'exhibitionist' showing of infantile traumata make it very easy for those who, today as well, want to explain and neutralize such work with pain by applying protocols of psychiatric diagnosis. Yet such explanations forget that pain experienced and represented on stage is, like that of Artaud, a 'pain towards life' and not a pain against it. It is not theatrical representation that neutralizes pain, just as the visual representation in the Rodez notebooks did not neutralize it. It is psychiatry that attempts to domesticate these experiences recorded on paper, as symptomatic of certain psychological disorders, thus with no chance of affecting the sane. It is the cultural apparatus that tries to domesticate the experiences represented on stage as representative of a type of art long superseded, based on the elaboration of traumas and the metamorphizing of distant suffering.

The emotional suffering, physical exertion and real injuries in *La casa de la fuerza* accompanied each night the performance in which the crimes were made present. Although the Mexican actresses denounced the impunity as well as the responsibility of the Mexican State, the work's discourse insisted on the continuity of the gender violence: 'In the same way that jokes about Jews culminate in Auschwitz, the routines of contempt for woman culminate in femicide.' (Liddell 2009a). Theatre intervenes in this chain with a symbolic potential undeniably much more limited than television or film. Its efficacy is not political in a direct sense, but rather ethical. Angélica's goal is to practise a radical humanism, via the recognition of the body of the other woman in my own. That Other is an unknown woman from a far-off place, radically different in her individual body and in her biographical experience, but identical with me in rights and affects. The action art of the 1970s pointed in some cases in this direction, but in a more abstract way, without an explicit affirmation of alterity and of the singularity of the bodies that were excluded from representation. The representative relation is no longer established synthetically or symbolically (between the individual body and the collective body), but mimetically (between body and body) and therefore affectively.

Angélica Liddell took to an extreme the ethics (and the aesthetics) of sacrifice by means of the physical punishments that she herself and – to a lesser extent – her actresses inflicted on themselves (electric shocks, cuts, lacerations, forced labour etc.) and through the moving story of moral pain caused by amorous scorn and the subsequent experience of loneliness in Venice. The physical and moral pain serves to create the field of exhibition, in which the pain of others is revived or repeated in an effort to represent (for comprehension) with representing (for delegation) the suffering of the Palestinians massacred in Gaza or the women raped and murdered in Ciudad Juárez.

What is new in this piece, however, is the explicit insertion of an ethics of care. This was already evident in previous works, in particular in the relationship maintained with Nasima in *Perro muerto en tintorería: los fuertes*. This care is the compensation for the performance, but also the affirmation of a space of autonomy, which the enemies (the psychiatrists, the immigration police, the racists) cannot enter. The stage as autonomous space serves as the site for symbolic restitution.

Angélica Liddell wanted to symbolically introduce an ethics of care in restitution for the pain suffered by the women who did not have any such tools to protect themselves from torture and male violence in Ciudad Juárez. She did this from a distance of many kilometres and some years. Representation, by retrieving and bringing to the present the silenced pain of the women and their families, was not incompatible but rather convergent with the creation of a space of sisterhood on the stage, deliberately incorporated by means of friendly words, soft contacts, caresses, looks of understanding and complicity.

Angélica, who turned her renunciation of motherhood into a political position and a theme of representation in *Lesiones incompatibles con la vida* (Injuries Incompatible with Life, 2003), proposes installing a community of care, a sisterhood with the five actresses, but also with the mariachis, with the cellist, and above all – what is most surprising – with the strongman, with whom poems are interchanged, who is taken by the hand and finally covered in flowers. In this way, a space of humanism is staked out in which the participants ephemerally but concretely find refuge, as participants but also as symbolic representatives of those who were denied humanity, a space of caresses, of tender words, of shared repose, of delight in the joy and pleasure and also of solidarity in moments of suffering.

The practice of care is not incompatible with the expression of rage and the demand for justice. An articulation on stage is realized in this manner of those two concepts of morality identified by Carol Gilligan (1982) in her book *In a Different Voice*. Various psychological studies with boys and girls, adolescents and youths have demonstrated that sex and gender are determining factors in the formation of the concept of morality and subsequently of justice, as a consequence of diverse educational experiences and models of affective or familial relations. According to these studies, boys conceive morality as based on laws and obligations, which governs an individualistic society, composed of solitary egos, in which action is awarded. Girls, in contrast, conceive morality as based on responsibility and on empathy, in a connective and multilateral society, in which any decision has to be considered taking into account the duration and evolution of relations. The former leads to an ethics of rights and justice, the latter to an ethics of well-being and care. Processes of autonomy and experiences of maturity act to correct this difference, but without eliminating it. This results in the idea that women develop a morality that differs from that of men, from which a deficient sense of justice is postulated. Gilligan's book refutes this false assumption, with the goal – among others – of seeing the ethics of care and the ethics of law as different, but without any subordinate relation. She advocates an articulated elaboration of both of these conceptions, for the premise of 'equality' that operates in the ethics of justice is as important as the premise of 'non-violence' that operates in the ethics of care.

The ethics of care is not based solely on the recognition of the face associated with language; it rests on the recognition of the subjective body. It is the ethics of care that is projected outwards. Reality is not idealized, one is conscious of the existence of violence, of injustice, of inequalities. The concrete realization of a humanistic relation is set against this inhuman reality. Care melts away social masks, it is realized as a relation between different bodies that recognize each other in the equivalence of suffering. Care momentarily suspends identities and physical distances, operating at the level of emotion. The woman-director ceases to be a director, the Mexican actress ceases to be Mexican and an actress, the strongman ceases to be strong (and could be a boy), for all of them are affected in the same manner by the blows and caresses, by the humiliations and the poetry.

Angélica provides an ethical response to a reality that affects her, putting her experience at the service of representation. Not the experience of a moment or of a process, but the experience of an artistic creation that demonstrates the continuing commitment to the manifestation of others' pain and of a life dedicated to creation. In the continuity of vital experience and artistic production, Angélica Liddell's practice could serve as a precise example of the definition that Bakhtin proposed of the 'ethical act': 'I act, i.e., perform acts, with my whole life, and every particular act and lived experience is a constituent moment of my life – of the continuous performing of acts' (Bakhtin 1924: 3). The ethical act for Bakhtin does not correspond to a moment, to an isolated decision, rather, it is identified with the totality of life. From this point of view, there is no doubting the coherence between Angélica Liddell's way of life (which she makes public herself via her writings in a variety of media) and her artistic productions. Nevertheless, the application of Bakhtin's definition to a theatre professional poses a problem: Is this life for representation a real life? This is the same question that the character in Renoir's film asked herself, before accepting the continuity of the comedy. Angélica herself seems to provide a similar answer when she affirms: 'On stage I have strength, in life none. When you know me, you see I am weak' (Liddell 2009a). Yet, if strength is on the stage, if, in a certain manner, the true life, as Artaud claimed, takes place on the stage and not in reality, would this not create an inversion of the relation between ethics and aesthetics?

This is the abyss that artists who dedicate their existence to their creative production inevitably face: their dedication can drag the existence of those others, with whom the artists expresses their solidarity in the representation, towards the realm of aesthetics. Only a thin line separates appropriation from ethical responsibility. Those who have witnessed *La casa de la fuerza* and cried during its performance will have no doubt about the author's honesty, in the same way that readers of *2666* will not doubt its author's commitment. Yet these works, being non-hegemonic monuments, cannot be regarded as anti-hegemonic models. For they are 'ethical acts', or moments of an 'ethical act', hardly divisible from the subjective singularities that realized them, nor from the individual decisions that, in their imperfection, invest them with coherence.

14

Fiction and pain

One of the traditional figures in political art is that of the fool. The fool is that incomplete body that accompanies power and treats important matters playfully. In order to fulfil their task, the fool has to relinquish the care and respect of themselves and be pure alterity. Only by being pure alterity can the fool put their body on the line, risking punishment or loss of life; only by being pure alterity can the fool laugh at themself, mistreat themself, at the same time as they laugh at others, denounce and accuse.

Bakhtin reminds us that fools were not like theatre actors, who slip out of a role when they leave the stage,

> but remained fools and clowns always and wherever they made their appearance. As such they represented a certain form of life, which was real and ideal at the same time. They stood on the borderline between life and art, in a peculiar mid-zone as it were; they were neither eccentrics nor dolts, neither were they comic actors.
>
> Bakhtin 1941: 8

The fool does not transform themself, they simply mask themself. This mask frees them to do and say what without a mask would constitute a crime. The mask (wig, helmet, robe, or extravagant accessories) safeguards the fool. When the fool performs an action that requires the intervention of other persons, these are simply quoted, without the need of incorporating them. This allows the fool's body, for example, to contradict the character, to make it grotesque, to sublimate it. Brecht searched among the fools for a model for his epic theatre, in fact copying some of their techniques in his performances. Yet a true fool would never have been willing to interpret a text that conditioned their individual liberty, not even one by Brecht. For we are not talking merely about psychological transformation, but about mimetic transformation in general.

The fool is always themself and in the performance does not assume a distance, but rather appears simultaneously in their personal and in their political condition. Consequently, the fool does not transform themself, the fool is always a fool, on and off the stage the fool is forced to live their life as an 'ethical act'. It might seem surprising that those incomplete bodies, readily disposed to obscenity and to performing immoral gestures, should appear as examples of ethical behaviour. Even more surprising is that they are capable of intervening politically, putting their body and their life at risk, but not their ethical coherence.

In contrast to the majority of people, the fool does not engage in politics in their leisure time. In contrast to the professional politician, the fool does not relinquish their individual freedom while they work, because – as occurs with the professional politician – the fool is not obliged to represent a role nor follow a script. The fool is free when they work, that is, when they perform their role before others. Precisely because the fool has poured their personality into alterity, when the fool represents, when they perform their role in accordance with their techniques and tricks, the fool can also act, can perform an action with effective and even immediate consequences. Ethics and politics coincide in their doing, which manifests itself at the same time as performance (representation) and (effective) action.

The fool, furthermore, codifies a gesture of resistance belonging to the theatricality of the oppressed: pretend to be foolish or insane in order to be able to say the truth without being condemned to punishment or sure death, or to do what they want when they do not have the necessary power. 'Play fool, to catch wise,' asserted slaves in Jamaica (Scott 1990: 3). In many cases this was the only course of action available to peasants, servants, children or women.

Angélica Liddell appropriated this figure in *Perro muerto en tintorería*, identifying it with that of the 'bloody actor'. They coincide in the poverty, exposure and naked corporeality that equates them with animals as much as with the immigrant workers lacking citizenship rights. Angélica's fool arises from her renouncing the privileges of her status as a celebrated theatre artist (invited to present her work in a national theatre) and from her desire to be an actress on the stage, a body among bodies, a woman among women. Hers is a tragic fool, who carries out her mission by means of sacrifice:

> How strange that the fool is regarded as a fool by those who are true fools. The true cretins despise the fake cretin. Yet the fool evades the sensation of servility by mocking those who hire them and those who pay to see them, by doing their job well the fool mocks all of them, making art ... Deep down, the fool is a spectator too, but a demanding spectator. The fool expands the stage to the world where all of society acts.
>
> Liddell 2008: 157

Indeed, it is outside the delimited space of the theatre, in the open space of social theatricality, where the fool exposes themself with the greatest risk. The shifting of the fool's mockery to the public sphere transforms their representation into direct action. Jesusa Rodríguez left political cabaret to take her theatrical practice to the streets and squares, where she acted in the company of people active in denouncing injustice or defending their rights. The members of the group Etcétera made their theatrical doings productive in political actions against impunity. The clown Leo Bassi did not hesitate to take his mockery to the houses of the powerful or dare the worldly power of the church by founding his own church in Lavapiés, a poor neighbourhood of Madrid. Both Jesusa Rodríguez and Leo Bassi utilized television with political aims, either producing their own series (Rodríguez) or intervening in programmes with mass audiences (Bassi). With the excuse of making people laugh at monstrosity or excess, something in principle inoffensive by the logic of the media, they were able to communicate with persons and groups who, given the poverty of means of the fool as well as of the viewers, would never have been able to listen to the 'truths' proclaimed in the cabaret, in the theatre, in actions and urban tours or in the small church in Lavapiés.

Bassi and Rodríguez play the fool to situate their message in the media. Yet this is a procedure that any citizen can employ. The fake fool or the fake lunatic turns into a wise fool, in the sense explained above, when they do not act merely to resist or in their own interest, but when they act from a place of alterity: In order to speak what has been silenced, to claim justice, to deflate dogmas by means of humour or to incite actions via accusation. The fool's truth is not situated in the sphere of knowledge, but in that of ethics. The fool's truth is what affects human relations and political decisions. It is a truth more related to the consensus of justice than the consensus of knowledge. In many cases, the fool's truth is that of common sense, or of common intelligence, that which challenges the territory staked out by experts and specialists who impose their judgement.

Among the characters created or recreated by Bolaño in *2666* is one of an exceptional woman, Florita Almada. This fake clairvoyant condemns the crimes on television, becoming the celebrated spokeswoman for the missing women, to the dismay of the victim's associations. Florita Almada is a woman, and being a woman in Chihuahua – according to the sexist mentality admitted by the Mexican State itself – means to be burdened with the stigma of incompleteness. Nevertheless, though related with her sex for these reasons, Florita is not a fool in the strict sense, but a person who decides to act the role of clairvoyant in her own life, who abandons her personality to become alterity, to understand others and help them, even if for this she has to play the fool and make everyone believe that she has powers of divination, that her visions come upon her while she loses control of herself and enters a trance.

The story of Florita is a commonplace one, like almost all of the stories that Bolaño narrates in this part of the book. She is an ordinary woman, a woman from the *barrio*, one more survivor in the rootless societies of northern Mexico. Her appearance on television does not take place on a channel with a mass audience, but on a local one watched only by a few viewers. Her action will not be decisive; nevertheless, it is one more action among the many that occurred for years, without any repercussions on the investigations or on the punishment of the guilty.

For the authorities, as well as for any educated person, Florita can only be an idiot or a fraudster, someone respected only by those who are even more stupid or ignorant than she is, or someone who deceives those she considers more stupid or ignorant. Florita is that type of person looked down upon by power as much as by the intelligentsia, like clowns, who can only amuse children or those like children, but who cannot offer their opinion about more complex or complicated issues. Yet Florita, who might seem an idiot, is not so. In fact, one could say she is a fake clairvoyant, because she does not *believe* in divination, but *knows* the uses of divination. Her knowledge is encyclopaedic, but her encyclopaedism does not transform her into an idiot, like Bouvard and Pécuchet. She uses divination, superstition or clairvoyance as modes of communication accepted by her neighbours, in order to supply them with information or practical advice with a certain amount of scientific foundation. They visit her with problems affecting their souls and leave with physiological remedies, which they transform into miracles and voodoo. Bolaño ensures that the reader knows that Florita Almada is not a fraudster, but that she also does not believe in her art. She is a pragmatic woman and even a wise one, who deceives in order to do good and not for her own benefit. Thus, when Florita enters into a trance on television to denounce the murders of the young women in Santa Teresa, the reader suspects that her trance is a performance, put on to make her accusation more acceptable and lend it greater resonance.

> Then she glanced at Reinaldo, who was fidgeting in his chair, and began to talk about her latest vision. She said she had seen dead women and dead girls. A desert. An oasis. Like in films about the French Foreign Legion and the Arabs. A city. She said that in this city they killed little girls ... I don't censor myself, ladies, especially not at times like this. It's Santa Teresa! It's Santa Teresa! I see it clearly now. Women are being killed there. They're killing my daughters. My daughters! My daughters! She screamed as she threw an imaginary shawl over her head ... The

police do nothing, she said after a few seconds, in a different voice, deeper and more masculine, the fucking police do nothing, they just watch, but what are they watching? What are they watching? ... don't touch me, you coldhearted wretches! Don't worry about me! Haven't you understood what I've said? Then she got up, turned toward the audience, went to Reinaldo and asked him what had happened, and a moment later she apologized, gazing straight at the camera.

435–7

The ease with which Florita recovers from the trance and the final look at the camera serve as indications chosen by Bolaño to make evident that his character is not insane, but someone who acts to transmit a message, someone who does not care if she appears crazy when she denounces on public media the crimes that very few are talking about. Obviously, for the victims' associations, who worked each day in extremely hostile conditions, the television appearance seemed like frivolous opportunism. Yet is this television appearance not also a way of opening up a space for those who indeed have the capacity for action?

Florita Almada utilizes her status as a medium to say on television what no one dares say without risking reprisals. Only by acting the fool can Florita remain unharmed; not only this, but her appearance has such an impact that she is invited onto channels with larger audiences. Florita's gain as a clairvoyant is also a gain for the visibility of her accusation. She uses theatricality the same way that Bolaño uses narration: Both of them are affected by reality and appropriate it in an exercise of representation that is solely justified by its excess. The excess is not an indication of arrogance, but of excessive commitment, a translation of a corporeality that recognizes in itself its physical limits, but does not accept moral limits. One discerns the humility of the fool and not the arrogance of the diva behind the performances of Florita and Bolaño; humour erases any transcendent dimensions and prevents the ego from swelling.

One could question – inside the fiction – whether the spectacle of a clairvoyant might not be the best way to show a series of crimes of such magnitude, as if such a spectacle were a means of denunciation or self-promotion. Similarly, one could ask – outside the fiction – whether fiction itself is compatible with the pain contained in the material on which that fiction is erected, and if such a construction functions as a means of symbolic projection or instead constitutes an improper appropriation. This is not about considering the legitimacy of reproduction, as Susan Sontag did in relation to war photography, but of fictional elaboration. Why add imagination to a reality that speaks for itself? Or in harsher terms: What is the point of the 'lie' popularly attributed to all fiction in a confrontation with such serious facts and such painful experiences?

Retrieving Alba Rico's proposal, one could answer that only imagination opens up the gates of compassion, of that compassion which enables empathy from a distance and which can be transformed into action. Yet fiction does not result simply from adding imagination to reality. Fiction can also be conceived as a possible reality.

Paul Ricoeur identified 'fiction' as one of the meanings of the concept of 'mimesis', about which he had previously issued the following warning:

> If we continue to translate mimesis by 'imitation' we have to understand something completely contrary to a copy of some preexisting reality and speak instead of a creative imitation. And if we translate mimesis by 'representation'... we must not understand by this word some redoubling of presence, as we could still do for Platonic *mimesis*, but the break that opens the space for fiction.
>
> Ricoeur 1983: 45

'Mimesis', in Ricoeur's conception, is the representation that opens up fiction. This is so because it returns representation to the time of the occurrence or the duration of lived experiences. 'Mimesis' is the embodied representation, in which the materiality or organicity of the representers and the temporality of their act of representing inevitably operate in this embodiment. Yet 'mimesis' as symbolic text (novel, performance, historical narration, film, documentary film, photographic narration etc.) owes its efficacy to the coherence with other modes of 'mimesis' that antedate and post-date the production of the text. Such coherence is not based on the verisimilitude or the material fidelity to the facts represented, but in the structuring of time, common to life, to narrative and to the reception or subsequent appropriation of the text: 'Time becomes human to the extent that it is articulated through a narrative mode, and narrative attains its full meaning when it becomes a condition of temporal existence' (ibid. 52). Fiction, consequently, is the way in which narrative re-articulates the facts of life or of history, maintaining a temporal structure coherent with them and in continuity with the ways in which this new reality will be received and reused. Fiction understood this way is not the invention of new realities, it is not the creation of 'lies' or fantasies, but the imagination of a reality that exists in time and thus, because it exists in time, it is human.

Avoiding the suspension and the reification of experience can be one of the reasons that moves artists, or 'storytellers', to fill out the fiction intrinsic to all 'mimesis', loading it with imagination or even with an unreality that contrastingly accentuates the complexity of experience, restoring to the facts the temporality lost in the trace or in the document. This is fiction that works with reality, not a fiction that utilizes reality to construct an intermediate world or a parallel world (the usual options in the literature and cinema of the last two decades). It is possible to situate this tension in texts or films that superimpose fiction and testimony, composition and document. Marguerite Duras and Alain Resnais did so when confronting the pain caused by the Second World War – and still alive – in *Hiroshima, mon amour* (1959). Resnais, who with the assistance of Chris Marker had realized one of the most unsettling documentary films on the Nazi extermination, *Nuit et Brouillard* (Night and Fog, 1955), believed it necessary to reinforce the fictional dimension even more, in order to confront the destruction and the prolonged suffering brought about by the explosion of the nuclear bomb over Hiroshima. To this end, he turned to Marguerite Duras, who suggested approaching the reality of destruction and death through the intimacy of two lovers: a young French actress who has travelled to Hiroshima to make a film about peace and a Japanese architect employed in the reconstruction of the city. Reality reaches the lovers in their isolation and infiltrates through channels that seemed impossible, between the skins fused in an embrace. The individual trauma of the actress is superimposed on the collective trauma of the city's inhabitants and of the Japanese in general. The return of the intense love experienced years ago with a German officer in the small town of Nevers during the military occupation of France makes painfully tangible the sentiment of loss. It resonates in each of the documentary images, in each of the faces and bodies of the survivors, in the silenced memory of the streets and ruins that will never be rebuilt. Life continues, with the pain and memory, and the music, sounds and images contribute to forging a representation that makes remembering tolerable and hope possible.

15

Fabrications

If the emptying of the actor, the radical shedding of their personality, has been accepted by numerous artists as a necessary condition for representing the Other, the disappearance of the author could be understood as a way of approaching representation when there is no direct embodiment. Instead, stories are constructed arising from the need to understand an occurrence, from the reactivating of indignation, the bringing to the present of an experience or the sharing of a loss. Authors can attempt to disappear inside their stories. But they can also disappear behind false names, camouflaging themselves within real or imaginary groups, or transforming their real name into a fiction indistinguishable from others. The Lebanese artists Walid Raad, Lina Majdalanie and Rabih Mroué have employed some of these strategies in the course of their production, in an attempt to address the political confusion and armed violence that conditioned their experience of youth and the beginnings of their artistic production in Beirut.

Their biographies run parallel to the history of Israeli colonial aggression and of civil wars. The Six Day War took place from 5 to 10 June 1967, burying Nasser's pan-Arab dream that had been supported by Hussein in Jordan and Salah Jadid in Syria, and saw the annexation of the Sinai, the West Bank and the Golan Heights by Israel. The activity of the PLO in Amman during the following three years generated numerous political, social and military conflicts. Nasser's death accelerated the definitive rupture and after Black September many Palestinians again fled to the West Bank and Lebanon, where the PLO leaders settled. Lebanon then became the centre of the conflict in the Middle East. In 1975 a civil war erupted that pitted the Maronite Christian community against the Muslim one, provoking (or justifying) the intervention first of the Arab League, and then of Syria and Israel. The civil war lasted, with assorted actors, until 1990, with the violence increasing between 1980 and 1982, when the capital was occupied by a succession of international forces. It reached a turning point with the Sabra and Shatila massacre, where thousands of Palestinian refugees were murdered, raped and mutilated by the Maronite Phalange militia, with the complicity of the Israeli occupation authorities, in vengeance for the Damour massacre of 1976, perpetrated by PLO militias, which in turn avenged previous attacks against their people. Although that same year Israel retreated from Beirut, which had been completely destroyed by the fighting, the occupation of the country's south continued until 2000, ten years after the civil conflict ended. The Amal and Hezbollah guerrillas persisted in the violence against the occupation, parallel to individual episodes carried out by these militias and diverse national and international agents in the rest of the country, among them the assassination of the former prime minister Rafiq Hariri, presumably on order of the Syrian government. In July 2006, a new conflict between the Israeli army and Hezbollah, with the intervention of Iran and Syria, resulted in the bombing of infrastructure and towns all over the country and a new refugee crisis.

The ruins of this last destruction is what Joana Hadjithomas and Khalil Joreige wanted to portray in the film *Je veux voir* (2008), featuring Catherine Deneuve and Rabih Mroué. Catherine Deneuve's 'I want to see' echoes the protagonist's necessity to see in *Hiroshima, mon amour*. And the scepticism of the Japanese architect as regards the capacity of his lover to understand echoes Rabih's renunciation, who until then had never wanted to return to his home town to see the consequences of the bombing, 'partly because everyone was there taking photos'. Does this direct vision allow a knowledge or an understanding not supplied by the images recorded, nor by the stories read, by others? Probably not. Yet the operation reveals the 'fabrication' inherent in the historical narration based on documentary images as much as in direct experience conveyed as memory.

The idea of 'fabrication' occupied a central place in the reflections that Rabih Mroué himself wrote about the work *Three Posters* (2000), made in collaboration with Elias Khoury and premiered at the Ayloul Festival in Beirut. The piece is based on a document found on a shelf in the offices of the Communist Party of Lebanon (CPL), a VHS tape that contained the testament of Jamal el Sati. Sati was a cadre in the CPL who had enrolled in the National Resistance Front (NRF), formed after the Israeli occupation of Beirut and the Sabra and Shatila massacres. Before embarking on a suicide attack against an Israeli army barracks in southern Lebanon, Sati recorded his testament on camera. He did it three times, as Rabih explained in the work, to ensure better control of the image and words that would identify him as a martyr for posterity.

Mroué believed that his work was based on a double process of fabrication: The fabrication of the actor and the fabrication of the martyr. The actor fabricates themself as a 'blank body' (Mroué 2013: 423). The martyr fabricates themself as an actor without a body. That actor, whose professional work consists in emptying their body in order to make it available for the memory, words, fantasies and movements of others, is challenged when the words they have to say are 'I am a martyr', when what they have to embody is the verification of their own death and disappearance. The actor did not intend to deceive anyone: The audience in Beirut knew who he was, the representation of the recording of the testament was revealed as such (it was not actually a video tape but recorded live in an room adjoining that in which the audience sat). But when the actor began to read real facts about himself, the information ruptured the fiction and questioned the fabrication of the martyr. The martyr had been fabricated years before. In *Mann ist mann* (1926) Bertolt Brecht showed how the techniques of montage that served to construct fiction could also serve to dismantle and construct a man. The video was used by the NRF (and subsequently many other armed groups) to offer the final montage of the process of fabrication of a martyr. The aim is to transform an individual's body into a representation of itself, in which 'of itself' has moreover been replaced by a collective identity: the identity of the suicide militant who gives up their desire for life in order to achieve the objectives the Party has decreed as beneficial for the liberation of the people. By renouncing their freedom and sublimating their emotions to the ideals of resistance, the martyr is transformed into an actor, an actor who renounces their personality to interpret a character. But since the physical representation (the suicide previously determined by the leaders) will be invisible, the martyr acts in front of the camera beforehand, in a representation without a body, in a representation in which the martyr abandons their body to transform it into word and image.

The fabrication of the martyr is questioned by the fabrication of the actor in a manner much more incisive than how history itself questions it. In fact, even though the document exists and was broadcast on television in 1986, doubts have been raised that Sati's suicide ever took place. This suspicion about the truth of the facts inspires one of Mroué's most interesting reflections:

> What happened? We will never know. But, and this is most important, we know that the body of the fighter will never be found. He has disappeared and even today, no one can say with certainty what became of him. But the factual details of this story are not ultimately important for what it really points to, like Jamal el Sati's video, are the questions of truth and its mediation.... For, after all, Jamal's repetitions humble us in our own artistic enterprise: They ask how an artwork can be constructed that aims to be critical of the notion of 'truth', a work that claims to convey 'truth' without any editing, while itself being a 'fabrication of truth'.
>
> 309–10

Rabih Mroué exposed in this work the limits of a documentary theatre understood as a construction based on the truth of documents, showing how the documents, including those produced in extreme situations, at the limits of what has been called the 'last truth', are always a fabrication or the result of a process of fabrication. The revelation of the martyr as actor can cast a shadow over the labour of the professional actor, but at the same time it provides the actor with the freedom to continue with the fabrication of truths.

The recourse to fiction or 'fabrication' offered some Lebanese artists a way of responding to the dissatisfaction produced by the official history of the civil wars and the lack of documents on which this history was built. The aim was not to create an alternative history, but to question the linearity of a history based on events and facts that are merely external. How should one tell such a complex story, listen to the reason that is present on all sides, separate reason from cruelty, understand without justifying and represent without betraying the memory of dozens of thousands of deaths, hundreds of thousands of displaced persons, with the wounds still open and the traces still visible in the streets of the cities and along the roads of the entire country? How should one tell that story using only verifiable and quantifiable facts? History does not do justice to experience. But neither does the trivial account of the victims' lives. What knowledge do the photographs of a destroyed place contribute? Or the exhibition of the victims' faces? An exhaustive investigation of the remains can serve to determine procedures and responsibilities, yet this knowledge does not necessarily facilitate comprehension or much less the restitution of experience. What fiction contributes is an indication of everything that the official histories leave out.

Historical work in the Middle East faces a serious problem: The destruction of archives and documents as a consequence of war and bombardment. If history as such does not always achieve a just balance between what it relates and what it leaves out, how much less if its stories lack sufficient documentary foundations? Fiction is inherent, much more evidently than in other cases, in so-called 'official history'. The first option for complementing or rebalancing history could be the recourse to memory or to the construction of counter-memories.

In the fiction of the Lebanese artists studied here the historian's obsession with sources makes no sense: What is crucial is not that the documents are originals, but that they supply the necessary mediation for restoring a reality made up not only of facts, but also of experiences. Walid Raad refers to Freud's analysis of hysteria and the latter's discovery that those subjects who have suffered a traumatic experience remember what they have lived very differently from how it actually occurred. This remembrance combines memory and fantasy, both based on imagination, in order to produce a reality in which the traumatized subject lives. It is no use 'awakening' the subject, because imagination has effectively shaped a reality. The Atlas Group dedicated itself to the production of 'hysterical documents', symptoms of a collective memory marked by the trauma of fifteen years of civil wars. The 'hysterical documents' are not the production of an individual, but rather the attempt to reconstruct those traces that the destruction of archives and the death of individuals had erased or that conventional history has ignored (Didi-Huberman 2002: 82).

In Walid Raad's work, as in Aby Warburg's *Atlas Mnemosyne,* documents are regarded as symptoms, since the goal is not to narrate a story, but to confront a lived past. Nevertheless, the fictional construction of documents produces the fictional construction of the body of the historian and of the rest of the authors. Raad's presence in the theatre of his presentations does not have the function of giving a body to the story, but rather of sustaining the fiction itself. The body is a signalled absence. Paradoxically, in the search for a history compatible with life, what appear are ghosts.

16

Dis/appearances

The origin of the term 'phantasm' reaches back to Plato's thought and does not refer to the idea of a 'ghost' (or apparition of a person), but to the idea of a 'reflection' of a person or thing on a crystalline surface. 'Phantasm' acquires a more precise sense in Aristotle's texts, who employed it to refer to mental images ('phantasmata'), defining them as the traces of actual impressions, preserved and transformed in the soul ('psyche') similar to how they are preserved (and transformed) in a painting or on a wax tablet. 'Phantasmata' fulfilled a crucial function in the theory of memory as much as in the theory of thought. These 'phantasmata', however, only make themselves present in the 'phantasia', that is, in the imagination. Imagination, thought and memory thus appear connected in a fluid movement around the concept of 'phantasma', which can be translated as 'mental representation', but which in the strict sense is not the image of something absent, but rather the presence (or return to presence) of that thing.

Precisely because 'phantasm' cannot be translated simply as 'representation', that *image that makes itself present* – or rather, that *sensorial presence* to which the term refers – can be deceiving, can leap from imagination to reality, appear as a body or become a ghost. The ghost as apparition does not represent the absent person, since in the imagination of who sees the person, or in the culture that brings them to life, the ghost *is* the person – even if a person deprived of body, a person constituted as an image, in many cases with the aid of water, vapour (from fog or sea mist) or ice. As the ghost does not represent, it escapes the categories of truth and falsity. Nothing is deducted from and nothing is added to a fiction by saying it is true or false. Experimental science, with its standards of refutation, or secular justice, with its laws, are defenceless against phantasms. In turn, the greatest enemy of a ghost is its reduction to a mere image. The ghost, a presence without body, cannot resist the positivity of images deprived of presence. The virtuality of the ghost was the exception in a world made up of physical images and of bodies inseparable from the sensorial dimension. The possibility of perceiving images independent of bodies has created a virtual reality in which there is no place for the ghosts of yesterday. Ghosts seem condemned to dissolve themselves on the surface of a reality that has become image. For ghosts – beings without bodies – need bodies to continue the possibility of their existence.

The Argentinian writer Adolfo Bioy Casares imagined a fantastic story of ghosts that at the same time announced the impossibility of them in the age of the simulacrum. *The Invention of Morel* (1940) narrates the experiences of a fugitive, who after arriving on a desert island is surprised by the presence of a group of people he believes to be 'tourists'. Crouched in the marshes, he observes the movements of the intruders and spies on their conversations. He identifies the scientist Morel and the young woman Faustine, whose beauty captivates him. Once he has overcome his fear that the tourists will report him to the police, the fugitive decides to initiate contact with them, yet they do not seem to notice his presence. Intrigued by such behaviour, he returns to the abandoned building, the 'Museum', where he spent his first days on the island and discovers in its basement the machine that explains the strange 'life' of the strangers. Morel has designed and built a sophisticated apparatus for recording and audio-visual reproduction that allows him to superimpose on the material reality of the island a virtual reality, eternally repeated, that preserves certain moments of his own life in the company of Faustine and other persons. The fugitive realizes that, without knowing it, he has lived with mechanical ghosts. Infuriated with Morel, but incurably infatuated with Faustine, the fugitive decides to manipulate the film and infiltrate himself into the apparatus, in the hope that some other witness will give life to his own image, thus enabling him to encounter the image of the loved one.

The ghosts on the island are fake phantasms, since they lack presence; they are therefore mere representations. In contrast to pre-technological phantasms, the tourists do not generate themselves as an image, neither are they produced by the body that observes them, but by an external apparatus that does not lend them presence and much less a *soul*. The ghosts exist only to the extent that the body that observes them ignores the mechanical apparatus and puts its own body at the disposal of their life. It is in this unknown body (that of a future visitor to the island) in which the fugitive trusts for the realization of his love for Faustine. Morel's invention is an apparatus of continuance independent of the body, but one that only functions effectively when it affects a body and thanks to the intervention of that body.

As a narrative, *The Invention of Morel* is itself a fantasy that, being immune to any criticism of falsification, offers the reader a game and a problem, inviting reflection on the false life of representations and the incompatibility between the virtual image and the ghost. The island on which Morel's invention is eternally repeated is also a theatre without bodies, a theatre of absences, a theatre that – as visionaries dreamed at the beginning of the twentieth century – does not need actors to devote itself to vision. In contrast to dramatic theatre, where the characters seem to be able to live over and over in the performers' bodies, in the theatre of absence what is foregrounded is disappearance itself. The apparitions represent disappearance. The animated forms represent death. They are not ghosts, however, since they lack memory and because who observes them is oblivious to the memory they should preserve.

Rabih Mroué and Lina Majdalanie decided to exacerbate the absence inherent to all practice of theatrical representation, as a means of situating themselves in a cultural context affected by the traumas of civil war and the threats that hover over those individuals who refuse to renounce their individuality. 'It seems to me that there are two kinds of image: the one that confirms the presence and the one that affirms the absence. For me, if I use images in my work, it is to prove our absence' (Mroué 2013: 105). Mroué and Majdalanie's theatre is not one of ghosts, but of bodies in search of fleeing bodies. One could say that, in many of their works, Rabih and Lina, trained as dramatic actors, strive in vain to put themselves at the service of ghosts who refuse to transform themselves into characters. Interruptions and repetitions are symptoms of a memory that resists remembering. Consequently, the difficulty of recovering the faces or the figures of the bodies to be represented lies in the proscription of the individual (as well as the representation of the individual) in a society where the only body recognized is the collective body.

These questions were addressed by Mroué and Majdalanie in their work *Who is Afraid of Representation?* (2005). The actors took up a formidable challenge. Lina was to represent a series of artists who had based their practice on the prohibition of representation. Paradoxically, those artists whose work could not be represented had been catalogued in a book compiled by Amelia Jones and Tracey Warr titled *The Artist's Body* (Warr 2000). Rabih, in turn, was to represent the little-known author of a multiple crime, Hassan Ma'moun, executioner and victim at the same time, subject and object of a pain difficult to access for the actor, even if he put into practice all of his techniques of emptying. The artists and the murderer were absences whose presence was doubly negated, due to the prohibition on representation and to the respect for alterity. Representing a work of performance art could be considered a betrayal of the 'truth' that claims 'Performance's only life is in the present ... Performance's being, like the ontology of the subjectivity proposed here, becomes itself through disappearance.' (Phelan 1993: 146).

If the truth of a work of action art is solely manifested in disappearance, any representation is an attack against memory: Remembrance, in the form of the reactivation of that work, works in the direction of its oblivion, of the oblivion of the true experience that can only exist in the present. However, are the published photographs and stories not already tools of remembering?

In order to subvert the prohibition of representation, Lina recurred to orality. To avoid that her presence could be regarded as imposture and raise suspicions of an attempt at supplanting the body of the artist in its unrecoverable present, Lina avoided a direct relation with the audience. She communicated with them through closed circuit video that – like the book – transmitted an image of her, but – like the book – manifested her absence. Rabih, in contrast, did represent the role of Hassan Ma'moun in front of the audience. But if he could do so without reservation, it was because he represented not only a murderer, but also a dead man. Hassan's voice reached the audience through Rabih's body, as though he not only lent Hassan his body but also the capacity for fabrication that he has perfected over the years. Like Sati, Ma'moun was an actor, and it was the actor, who repeated again and again his story, modifying it in search of the best image, whom Rabih represented. Lina could not physically represent the artists, since they are individual persons, who by working with their body have linked their practice with the work of subjectivity. But she could represent – orally – their works. Does the story not respect the unrepeatability of the action much more than the image? In particular, when who represents them inhabits a region where images are regarded suspiciously, individual subjectivity as sinful, and action art is a rare practice?

In the second part of the work, Lina Majdalanie adopted poses in front of the camera that remained frozen on the screen, accumulating like ghosts, while she repeatedly returned to continue narrating the stories of her artists. Lina's body became an electronic spectre, not a live one, as Bioy Casares imagined, but a mute and immobile spectre. She multiplied her body until the images of it equalled the number of cadavers accumulated in the office by Hassan Ma'moun. The images accentuated the absence and again provoked the implosion of the performance.

The theatre of absences emerged in an extreme manner in works such as *Looking for a Missing Employee* (2003) and *33 rounds et quelques secondes* (2012). The former investigated the disappearance of an employee of the Ministry of the Treasury, Rafaat Suleiman, and the unsuccessful investigations by the police, incapable of finding him in a country where 'everybody knows everybody'. Rabih occupied a seat among the audience, while the image of his face and the image of his hands was projected in closed circuit video on stage on two screens; a third screen showed the annotations taken by an assistant on a notepad. The missing employee was evoked on the two-dimensional screen by newspaper clippings, photographs, manuscripts and diagrams, which supplied incomplete information and which, like in other works by Mroué and Majdalanie, supported contradictory stories about the fate of the civil servant. Only at the end was it revealed that the employee did not disappear socially, but rather physically, his body dissolved in acid after being murdered.

Rafaat Suleiman is not a ghost, but the name of a citizen of Lebanon who was denied life as well as memory. The fictional work of Rabih Mroué serves in this case to return to Suleiman his phantasmatic condition, to restore his presence and allow him, like Hamlet's ghost, to claim his vengeance. Yet Mroué does not lend him his body. That would be too easy, too conciliatory: After all, Suleiman was 'disappeared' physically and his social disappearance was helped by the state's corruption. For this reason, Rabih prefers to disappear as actor-author too, to reduce himself to a non-phantasmatic image, a virtual image, delegating to the members of the audience the necessary corporeality, so that both images can become ghosts and in this manner recuperate the condition of persons. In fact, when the performance finishes, Rabih's face remains fixed on the screen, looking attentively at the room, impassive (like Bioy Casares' Faustine) before the reaction of the spectators and their progressive disappearance.

The apparatus created for *33 rounds* radicalized absence even more, since no actor was present on the stage during the performance, not even in a mediated form. The audience was confronted with a set that reproduced the home of a well-known Lebanese theatre director. The information about his identity, as well as about his recent suicide, was supplied by a *mise en scène* made up of news flashes, advertisements, music and messages. They arrived and were reproduced in the various devices their owner had not bothered to turn off: answering machine, television, fax machine, mobile phone, computer. By means of a staging constructed out of television broadcasts, songs, recorded voices, SMSs, emails, Facebook pages and faxes (amplified or projected on a screen at the back of the stage), the audience became aware of the circumstances surrounding the director's death, as well as the reactions of his relatives and acquaintances. The same devices that in other countries had served to propagate the Arab revolutions during the spring of 2011 here served to represent the death, both socially and politically unproductive, of an artist for whom life, for strictly private reasons, had become unbearable.

The theatre was turned into an installation to represent absence. A receptacle of messages without an addressee, attempts at dialogues now impossible. The artist himself was not represented: Only his death was represented. As well as the absence of a body that would have been needed to participate, together with other bodies, in a revolution that never took place in Lebanon.

Technically, these two works could be performed in the absence of their authors. They could function as installations, where everything, as in *The Invention of Morel*, has been previously recorded. Nevertheless, the ethics of representation demands presence. As a matter of fact, *Looking for a Missing Employee* was performed on one occasion without Rabih Mroué and Hatem

Imam travelling physically to the performance venue. This happened, as one of the set designers, Samar Maakaron, explains, in Shizuoka, Japan. Rabih and Hatem were trapped in Beirut due to the closing of the airport and had to participate from a distance, via three internet connections (Maakaron 2008). The physical absence of the actors did not change the set-up of the presentation, which would have been changed, however, if they had renounced co-temporality and opted for a pre-recorded presentation.

17

Presences

Technological devices require a new concept of absence, no longer defined in physical-spatial terms, but in affective-temporal ones. For presence to occur in a performance situation of this kind, there must be an affective implication (whether ethical or political) on the part of the actor-author in the representation that takes places in a determined time. Or the actor-author can decide to share the same time as the bodies of the spectators invited to attend (or activate) the functioning of such an apparatus.

The telematic presence of Rabih Mroué and Hatem Imam in Japan does not differ very much from the telematic presences we are accustomed to in our everyday life. In reality, a great part of our daily communication is transmitted through devices, even when the distance between interlocutors is only a few metres. Leaving aside unidirectional communications (advertising, music videos, broadcasts produced by organized media), the majority of such communications are generated in the social sphere (whether labour, private or everyday). Very few of these communications are framed in political action, much less in a relationship of intimacy. What stands out in the telematic presentation by Mroué and Imam, therefore, is not so much the use of the device itself, nor the realization of co-temporality, but the intensity that the specific realization can generate. In this case, the intensity arises from two factors: the aesthetic experience that the work proposes and the prohibition produced by the absence, which necessitated the use of the internet.

The journalist and filmmaker Mohamed al-Atassi had to resort to Skype to make his second film on the Syrian dissident Riad el Turk in 2012, a few months after the revolution and when the repression exercised by Bashar al-Assad's government initiated a lasting conflict. The first film, *Ibn al'Amm* (2001), is a documentary on the life of the secretary-general of the Syrian Communist Party (Political Bureau) between 1973 and 2005, who spent more than two decades in the prisons of Hafez al-Assad, father of the current president. His call for democratic reforms and opposition to the support that the Syrian government gave to the Maronite Christians during the first years of the Lebanese civil war provoked his arrest on 28 October 1980. During the greater part of the eighteen years that his imprisonment lasted, despite never being tried, Riad al-Turk survived incommunicado in a cell without windows.

His only intellectual and physical entertainment was the temporary compositions he made on the floor or on a sheet with black lentils that he extracted over months from the soup he was fed. Riad al-Turk was freed in 1998, but after the death of Hafez al-Assad and the refusal of his son Bashar to introduce democratic reforms, his participation in the Damascus Spring (2000) sent him once more to prison for another fifteen months. Five years later, he promoted the transformation of his party into the Syrian Democratic People's Party and since then has abstained from politics.

In the first film Mohamed al-Atassi asks Riad al-Turk to recreate in front of the camera some of the compositions with lentils to which he dedicated his hours in prison. There is nothing extraordinary in these drawings, except for the visualization of a routine repeated thousands of times, a survival strategy that years afterwards, before the camera, ultimately acquires a symbolic dimension. Conscious of this, the elderly hand of the politician skilfully arranges the grains on the white sheet until he has composed the word 'freedom'.

'Freedom' is what the activists and citizens who participated in the Syrian revolution of 2011, with its epicentre in the city of Homs, once more shouted. The repression of this cry by Bashar al Assad's army made it impossible for Mohamed al-Atassi to travel from Beirut, where he resides, to Damascus, where Riad al-Turk lives. *Ibn al'Amm Online* (2012) conveys the testimony of the Syrian leader at the same time that it documents the apparatus of communication and filming. What in another moment and in another context could be regarded as a mechanism of Baroque representation, functions in this film as the manifestation of the violence exercised by the regime and the unstoppable commitment of those who fight for democracy. It is the armed repression that prevents the trip and imposes the telematic communication; it is the ethical and political responsibility of the director and, above all, of the elderly politician, that compels both of them to use any medium available to give testimony and mobilize action.

During the presentation of the IX Edition of the Jerusalem Show (2011), it was likewise necessary to resort to Skype to enable a round table with the participation of Palestinian writers and former political prisoners. The situation arose in the context of a proposal by the Italian artist Beatrice Catanzaro. During a stay in Nablus, involved in a cultural project with the women of that city, she discovered a section of the municipal library preserving the books that used to circulate in Israeli jails from the 1960s on and were consequently read by Palestinian political prisoners. The books tell a particular, personal and political story: in the magazines used to cover them, in the underlinings and annotations, in the messages concealed between their pages. Beatrice suggested that this section of the library travel to Jerusalem, to rescue from oblivion that experience and that epoch of political resistance, then led by leftist organizations. What better place to house it than in another library, in this case a private collection belonging to the Khalidi family that includes valuable manuscripts, some of them more than ten centuries old? The goal was to contrast two memories: the memory of a millennial culture in the legacy of a formerly well-off family, now dispossessed and politically neutralized, for whom books are an asset in themselves, and the memory of activist resistance, in the struggle and punishment of bodies that rebelled, for whom books and language have always been a tool. In order for the books to remain tools and to avoid the aestheticization of the project, professor Esmail Nashif was invited to organize a series of conversations with former prisoners and political militants, titled 'A Needle in the Binding'. But since the majority of participants in the conversations organized by Esmail live in the West Bank and do not have authorization to travel to Jerusalem, the talks were conducted via Skype, in connection with the International Academy of Art Palestine in Ramallah. The bodies that were detained for years continued unable to travel, in contrast to the books (and only because the books were old and disconnected to the bodies that wrote them).

The apparatus of communication is facilitator and violent at the same time. Facilitator, since it allows communication where physical barriers imposed by the powers that be obstruct it. Violent, since it necessitates accepting representation, a situation of observation and recording superimposed on communication itself in the form of a double screen. This representation has nothing to do with play. The women of Ramallah would have liked to travel to East Jerusalem, while Riad al-Turk would have preferred to meet with Mohamed al-Atasi in Damascus. Telecommunication was the only way of making the discourse possible. Decades ago it would have been inconceivable – at most a landline telephone could have been used, and before that an exchange of letters. The means of communication permits a co-temporality of persons separated by distance for different reasons, in this case by repression and by occupation. Yet co-temporality implies the acceptance of representation.

It would be ethically reproachable to apply aesthetic criteria to 'A Needle in the Binding' or to *Ibn al 'Amm Online*, as there is no aesthetic pretension, even if images and emotions are generated. Form does not exercise any violence on the content here; it is reality that exercises violence and generates the form. Nevertheless, one cannot ignore that Riad al-Turk has to accept, against his will and in an exercise of ethical and political responsibility, seeing himself trapped in a game of representations.

Riad al-Turk represents the resistance of the Syrian people against the dictatorship of the al-Assads. He did not desire to represent the resistance, but simply practised resistance; he decided to fight against the regime and this had very grave consequences for his life and that of his family. His experience was transformed into a symbol, his imprisonment and torture into a powerful signifier. Yet such a signifier, which designates Riad al-Turk as representative of the resistance against the dictatorship of Hafez al-Assad, does not bestow upon him representation in the struggle against the dictatorship of Bashar. Riad al-Turk is fully conscious of this; he resists representation, preferring to remain in the second row, avoiding becoming a political representative because, as he says, the revolution is a revolution of the people.

However, Riad al-Turk has paid a very heavy price for being identified by the dictatorships of the al-Assads as representative of the political resistance against their regime. The price of representation is torture, prison, physical and psychological suffering, but also the negation of a private life, the absence of persons dear to him, the impossibility of emotions and desires. In *Ibn al 'Amm Online* (2012), al-Atassi asks him insistently about his daughter, about his family: Does he not feel any responsibility for having abandoned them? Should he not have ceased his political struggle to be with them? Riad al-Turk is moved, yet he refrains from answering the question. He ends up becoming irritated. The viewer does not understand the impertinence of some of the very direct questions posed by the director. One cannot understand them if the author did not represent himself in the apparatus of communication, if he did not introduce his body and his affects into the apparatus. This is because Mohamed al-Atassi is the son of Nureddin al-Atassi, like al-Turk from the city of Homs, a member of the Ba'ath party who was elected president of Syria in 1966. He was deposed in 1970 as a result of the military coup perpetrated by Hafez al-Assad, then general and minister of defence in the government, was arrested and sent to the military prison in Damascus, where he remained for twenty-two years. After being freed for health reasons, he travelled to Paris to receive medical treatment and died there in December 1992, only a few weeks after reuniting with his family.

Mohamed al-Atassi does not reveal his identity, because, even more radically than al-Turk, he does not pretend to raise himself to the position of a representative of Syrian resistance. Being the son of Nureddin does not bestow on him representation nor representativity. The victims, whether direct or indirect, do not receive the right of representation with their pain. For this reason, al-Atassi insists on being a journalist and not talking about his father, even if affective memory determines the realization of the film.

Mohamed al-Atassi's resisting an identity that does not belong to him, but affirming an identity in which he recognizes himself (in which being a journalist of Syrian descent in Beirut forms a part), is also the honest renunciation of a representation that does not belong to him. This does not represent an obstacle for him, as a citizen and as a journalist concerned with the situation of his country of origin, to contribute qualified – not representative – analysis and opinions.

Identity can become a condemnation when it is the result of a representation that is not desired or a representation imposed on one. A religious or political leader has to accept the construction of their identity as the result of the representation they exercise; they are not permitted to claim an alternative identity, because if they did they would be committing a fraudulent representation. In contrast, a person without representative responsibility should not see the construction of their identity conditioned by the function of their affiliation, their social function or the contingent circumstances that affect the territory or country they inhabit. Nevertheless, for power it is much easier to impede the free definition of identities and project on people the same principles of identitary responsibility that supposedly fall on the leaders. The lesser number of identity differences and nuances, the simpler it can be to govern. This mechanism of forced identification functions in any sphere of power, whether religious, military, political, cultural, micropolitical or familial.

Rabih Mroué recently addressed the problem of identity in *Grandfather, Father and Son*, an installation produced specifically for his solo show at the CA2M in Mósteles (Madrid). Fiction and reality once more intersected in a mosaic of texts, manuscript and printed documents, photographs and books. This information arrived accompanied by emotion, history competed with mathematics and imagination playfully crossed the field of illness, destruction or death to spin out the synthetic writing of three lives, that is, of three 'biographies', graphic symbols (drawings and writings) on life. In its realization the hand can let itself be guided by the drawing, not to create distance from life, but precisely to free the life in the drawing. This freedom prevents the transformation of biography into *Biokhraphia* (2002), as Lina Majdalanie explained in a previous work.

Identity cannot be constructed freely, because each individual lives in a 'library' holding the biographies of those who preceded them and those with whom one lives with in a home, a territory, in a localized or dislocated community. Very few persons have the possibility of moving from one 'library' to another. In Rabih's library 'the son' and 'the wife' attempted to: 'They flew to Cyprus to wed, as a political statement. No one seemed to notice this statement, however' (Mroué 2013: 185). The 'libraries' alter the perception of reality, in particular when that reality is the result of actions that contradict what is established in the 'books' and are carried out by particular individuals, whether they are artists or not, with a reduced capacity of speaking.

Accustomed to the stage, Rabih Mroué responded to the invitation to create an exhibition by 'exhibiting' himself. But on the walls of the museum, he went a step further: Invoking the ghosts of his relatives and the ghost of himself in a previous time, Rabih outlined the silhouette of a young communist by tradition who wrote a fictional short story that anticipated a bomb falling on the family house. He thus constructed an apparatus of memory that contained an apparatus of anticipation (the short story) and allowed the movement of ghosts – including himself – among the texts, images, objects and bodies of the visitors. In this manner the room in the museum was converted into a theatre, where the characters were people entangled in a web of affects around the young author ('the son') and the current-day actor (Rabih), against the background of a war and a labour of symbolic production. Here the actors were absences, like those imagined by Bioy Casares in his story about Morel's island. A maximum of exhibition requires, to judge by Rabih Mroué's option, an apparatus of absences. In fact, the work that concluded the exhibition's route through the museum, *The Mediterranean Sea* (2011), was a work on disappearance: that of a corpse floating in the water beside a red book, and that of the hooded cellist, two silhouettes underneath which the author, concealing his identity, once more exhibited himself.

The questioning of identity is inseparable from the issue of representation in Rabih Mroué's production. The investigation into the identity of the sharpshooters in *The Pixelated Revolution* arose from the surprise at the desire for representation, which drove the victims to continue recording the sequence with their mobile phones until the very last moment – in some cases of their own death. Since representations hide what they supposedly identify, since bodies become invisible or disappear behind the images or stories and eyes are deceived by the effect of the 'libraries' that mediate between them and reality, the representation that emerges from a commitment to reality is forced to question its own means: the archive or the library, the theatre or the museum, the fabrication of the image or the immediacy of the body.

The *Inhabitants of Images* (2010) began with an anecdote: A policeman stopped Rabih in a security zone and doubted his identity. Rabih's identity is in part his condition of being an actor, thus of being anyone. But Rabih's identity is also that of someone who, being an expert in fabrications, possesses a special ability for spotting fabrication. The *Inhabitants of Images* analyses two series of found photographs. The first one he saw on the street, when he was stopped by the police. The image repeated in numerous posters put up on the walls depicted the encounter – historically impossible – of Gamal Abdel Nasser and Rafik Hariri. Rabih knows very well that this is a propaganda poster distributed by the Independent Nasserite Movement, which emerged from the al-Mourabitoun group at the beginning of the Lebanese civil war.

But he prefers to deduce, after long argumentation, that the handshake must have taken place when both leaders were dead: The pan-Arabic Egyptian leader died in 1970 after his army was defeated by the Israelis and his Lebanese supporter in the pan-Arabic ideal was assassinated by the Syrians in 2005.

The second series of photographs is a series of posters that appeared on the streets of Beirut depicting the Hezbollah martyrs. A detailed analysis of the images and a deconstruction of their fabrication led Rabih to the conclusion that all of the martyrs shared the same body, on which a different face had been grafted to coincide with the name. Seen from a moving vehicle, the posters composed a film in which the specificity of each frame disappeared, making visible a single body and a succession of illuminated faces, which in their repetition produced a white hole, identified with God.

The contempt for the body, the mortal component of the human being, the part that can be sacrificed in the name of religion or of political reason, allows identity to be situated exclusively in the face, and particularly in the eyes, those organs that open the path of transcendence. Yet an identity deprived of a body is a fraudulent identity, it is instead the reflection of an 'idea', that is, the reflection of divinity. In fact, the homage to the martyrs is a fake homage to the individuals, as what is created is a negation of their bodies and the exaltation of the only body that is accepted, the collective body. That body is the body of an abstract subject, the party Hezbollah, and the individual identities are mere tools in a struggle where bodies are expendable and solely serve as a representation.

One then understands that 'the actor', like 'the son', prefers not to contribute to representation in the mode of presence, instead choosing absence or disappearance. Disappearance is a life strategy of one who resists the negation of the body, concealed behind a face, reduced to an image identified with a number. The body then invents an apparatus with which to evade the apparatus of the annulment of power, an apparatus in which an individual body, which affirms its presence through absence, plays with the ghosts of those whom power attempted to silence, to trap in mere static representation.

18

Memory and care

During preparations for a film project titled *Phantoms of Nabua* (2009), Apichatpong Weerasethakul visited a temple, close to his parents' home in Kohn Kaen, where a monk told him the following story:

> Ghosts will appear under certain conditions, when it is not quite dark and not quite light (at the break of dawn and twilight). At first the dead don't realize that they are dead. When they pinch themselves, it still hurts. They think they still have their own bodies. But it's just an illusion; all in the mind. They walk around talking normally to people but no one takes any notice, no one can see or hear them.
>
> Weerasethakul 2013: 192

That same monk gave him a book titled *A Man Who Can Recall His Past Lives*, which recounts the memories of a certain Boonmee, who remembers his past as a hunter of elephants, as a buffalo, a cow and as a wandering ghost. Reincarnations and ghosts will inhabit the fiction film resulting from this trip, centring on the last days of Boonmee, turned into a contemporary person as well as an 'uncle', since during his trip Apichatpong was able to interview an elderly man who claimed to be the son of Boonmee, but from what he said appeared to be a nephew instead.

In a surprising sequence, before which the viewer hesitates between being carried away by laughter or by awe, Boonmee is quietly eating dinner with his sister-in-law Jen and her nephew Tong on the porch of the principal house on his farm, with the jungle in the background, when the image of the ghost of Huay, his former wife, softly appears. She retains the same appearance as when she died twenty years ago. After overcoming their initial surprise (stronger in Tong, who had never known Huay), those three persons who decades ago shared intimacy fall into a trivial conversation. Jen asks Huay if she has received the gifts that she sent via the temple (thus subtly questioning the monks' honesty), asks if she is well, if she eats well. The same question a mother would pose to her daughter, with the paradox that in reality Jen is the younger sister, while now she looks like she could be Hauy's mother. When Boonmee asks 'how are things in heaven?', Huay responds that 'heaven is overrated, there is nothing there, we ghosts like to be near living beings.' Indeed, ghosts only exist among living beings, their memory is our memory, their pain is ours, and, consequently, when we do justice to those who suffered we are in fact healing ourselves.

The film begins with a disquieting scene: A water buffalo tethered to a tree is able to escape and crosses a field until it finds refuge among the trees. What is disquieting is the independence with which the animal seems to behave, as though it had a human will. The man who sets out to find it is not very different from the animal; he does not behave like an owner, but more like a carer. In this manner Apichatpong very subtly introduces the theme of reincarnation. Although the scene could have a much less profound interpretation: 'You know, if you grow up in or near the jungle as I did, the distance city people feel between human beings and the animal world is hardly there. You begin to understand the meaning of the different sounds the birds and beasts make hunting, mating, escaping, warning, and so on' (Weerasethakul 2013: 164). This scene at sunset, although it announces many other night scenes, ends with the appearance of an ape with red eyes.

The action suddenly cuts to the interior of a vehicle driving along a road, recording the trip in a documentary style similar to that employed in *Dokfa nai meuman* (Mysterious Object at Noon, 2000) or *Sud sanaeha* (Blissfully Yours, 2002). Jen travels from Bangkok to Nabua to visit her brother-in-law Boonmee, who is confronting the last days of an incurable illness. The first part of the film takes place in the beekeeping farm to which he has dedicated all his efforts, in which he lives alone after the disappearance of his son and the later death of his wife. His sole affective relationship is with a Laotian immigrant, Jay, who helps him every day to go through the process of dialysis.

The dialysis sequence is a long static shot, recalling the scenes of hospitals in his previous films. The camera's distance could allude to the child's gaze in the memory of the director, the son of rural doctors, a gaze that observes illness and death as something very distant, as something in the adult's world. Yet it is also a respectful gaze, similar to Pedro Costa's in Vanda's room, in turn inherited from Yasujiro Ozu's gaze in its observation of domestic interiors. The same care is given to how Jay connects the catheter, manipulates the bags, applies the surgical tape. In their modest artificiality the medical instruments vividly contrast with the surroundings, the wooden house in the middle of the jungle, the small and half-naked body of the patient. The medical instruments fracture the image of a possible paradise, with the same abruptness as the neon lights or the air conditioning do. They announce that beyond the apparently idyllic vision of the jungle and the beekeeping farm lies the immorality of men (including monks), the pressure of a productivist economy, the projection of a political model that generates social injustice and exclusion, as well as the not very edifying memory of a life and a time.

Shortly after the appearance of Huay, while around the table the diners smile, reminisce and talk with a certain melancholy, the ape with the red eyes enters – the one seen at the end of the prologue. It slowly climbs the stairs until it reaches the porch. Boonmee and Jen quickly recognize him: it is Boonsong, the son who disappeared years ago into the jungle. The scene is somewhat comic, but the naturalness with which the characters act invites one to accept the transformation as something plausible. The flashback accompanying Boonsong's story differs from the style of a conventional ghost film, a genre that Thai cinema has specialized in, and evolves instead as a meta-film exercise in which the shots of the photographer from *Blow Up* are quoted. Here Boonsong does not discover a crime, however, but the mysterious beings he will eventually turn into. 'There are many beings out there: spirits and hungry animals.'

Boonsong refers to a magic world. But he also is referring to a silenced memory. His escape into the jungle could be a fictional metamorphosis of the escape that many youths saw themselves forced to make in the 1970s, when the army established a base in Nabua. The army employed psychological and physical torture to extract information. Many peasants were accused of collaboration with the communists, were kidnapped, tortured, murdered and made to disappear. It was the intensity of this memory and not the beauty of the landscape that motivated the decision to film in that location. The challenge lies in transforming the sounds of the jungle and the latency of the ghosts into images accessible to the camera and to the gaze. Once their presence has been recognized, daylight cannot hide them anymore.

An appealing everyday quality permeates the scene of the visit to the farm, where we see the tamarinds attacked by worms, the honey and even the small construction that Boonmee has erected to receive his dialysis in the middle of the jungle. Yet precisely in that moment of maximum relaxation other ghosts appear, ghosts who do not need the half-light. These are flesh and bones ghosts. They can be called ghosts because they are invisible, just the opposite of the supernatural apparitions of the dead who make themselves visible. They are ghosts from the past, real ones: the communists that Boonmee killed on orders of the government. And the ghosts from the present, the illegal immigrants, those who lack rights and with whom Boonmee maintains a strange relationship of politeness and domination. He tries to learn French to approach them, but the words that come out of his mouth are not those of a companion, but of a boss: 'vous' 'allez' 'travailler' 'maintenant'. Here the viewer is confronted with an ethical dilemma: should we accept that we find this elderly man likeable, who in his youth killed communists under orders and who is incapable of recognizing his equality with the workers because of the aristocratic nationalism in which he was brought up? Do the historical circumstances excuse him? Is the illness his punishment? Or does he too deserve the condemnation of humans?

Jen is much more adamant with the immigrants from Laos, warning her brother-in-law on various occasions of the danger in trusting them and keeping them on the farm. With his treatment of the Laotians, however, the kind Boonmee seems to want to make up for the crimes he committed against the peasants, crimes he cannot erase. The ghosts of the past and the ghosts of the present are much more disquieting than the phantasmagorical apparitions of the beings from another world. Those ghosts, the ghosts from memory and the social ghosts, are the ones that actually torment Boonmee and the ones that Jen fears. She cannot accept that her brother-in-law puts himself in the hands of an immigrant. In fact, Jay is the only human being to take care of Boonmee in his final days and the only one who reacts in a more natural way to the appearance of Huay and Boonsong. Perhaps his condition of being a social ghost makes him more sensitive to the ghosts from another world. When he leaves, Huay takes his place in giving the patient the care he needs. Yet this substitution is one that can only announce death.

The concrete room, lit only by neon tubes that attract the flies, installed by Boonmee in the basement of his home and where he has placed the family altar, constitutes the counterpoint to the ecosystem where the ghosts, the beings from nature and the legendary fantasies (the princess and her talking catfish) live. It also heralds the final scenes of the funeral.

The division into two parts is a formal decision taken by Apichatpong (shared with other contemporary Asian directors such as Hou Hsiao-hsien or Hong Sang-soo) that was drastically realised in *Sud Pralad* (Tropical Malady, 2004) or *Sang Sattawat* (Syndromes and a Century, 2006). In both cases the aim was to contrast the urban context with the rural context, but also to represent parallel lives, possible lives or remembered lives, as well as to invite the viewer to construct the continuity of those lives. In *Uncle Boonmee,* the relaxation and melancholia that accompanies the final days of the protagonist is substituted by the tension of Jen's economic worries and the descent into an everyday life without ghosts. The emptiness of the everyday expands time, the characters fall into a waiting that is apparently indifferent, recalling the cinema of Andy Warhol. In the final scene, television replaces meditation and its talking heads rob those who watch it of their own body and with it the possibility of memory.

It is the respect for bodies that enables the coincidence of representation and care. For when we love bodies we do not reduce them to models, but sense them as multiple and different, without a hierarchy of species, genders and forms making a few bodies into representatives of others, without denying any body the right to representation. This includes animals, but also the dead.

Since bodies are only bodies when they are alive, life becomes the supreme value, demanding from other bodies a relationship of care, which does not require representation, but which does not prohibit it and even occasionally needs it, since vision reaches further than emotions. Representation, in effect, can demand the attention of the body and arouse affects where distance would hinder them, providing that such a strategy does not supplant action with a gaze, does not turn into intellectual fraud or pitying consolation.

In Apichatpong's work the function of imagination and fiction in the rendering of memory becomes evident once more. In his first film, *Mysterious Object at Noon*, imagination (improvised story) and representation (dramatization) alternated as two dimensions of the same work of fiction, inevitably contaminated by the desires and memories of the participants in the process. Representation in this case does not destroy nor fix imagination, instead one could say it strengthens and expands it. The film, shot in collaboration with peasants from various villages in Thailand, could have been extended as much as the country. Only budget limitations imposed an interruption, which in no case is a finalization.

The opening up of representation occurs in other films by means of division, repetition and duplication with variations. *Syndromes and a Century* is presented in two parts that are clearly differentiated: The first is localized in a rural hospital and its surroundings, in a region with lush vegetation and generously lit by the sun. The second takes place in an urban hospital, in a technological ambience, occasionally oppressive and depending on artificial lighting, which reaches an extreme in the scenes in the basement. The two parts correspond to the separate memories of Apichatpong's mother and father, whose reminiscences coexist in the film with fantasies, projections by the director and historical echoes.

In his fictional work, Apichatpong preserves the nature of memory permanently threatened by remembering. He thus reveals himself to be an indirect disciple of Warburg and Benjamin, who warned of the devasting effects for memory of definitive representations of the past. For this reason, Apichatpong avoids the direct representation of remembrances; they appear instead fragmented, reduced to echoes or symptoms. Personal echoes, such as the recurrent image of the doctor's office of the mother or the father's mistake, when during a job interview he deciphered 'DDT' as 'Destroy Dirty Things'. Echoes too of collective experience and of the consequences of events inscribed by political, military and economic history on people's experience.

Historical echoes resound in *Mysterious Object at Noon* in the form of archival images, fake documentaries or radio broadcasts. They bring back the suffering of Chinese immigrants in Thailand, the traces of the Japanese occupation, the military regime coincident with pro-United States propaganda, the eruption of the 'second Indochina war', the repression of students and peasants. At one point in the film, time goes back to 1945 by means of a radio that announces: 'Let us demonstrate the strength of Thailand: we the people that live together in peace, no matter where we come from, united in one country and one people.' The song, of ambiguous ideology, paradoxically inaugurated a new era of xenophobia, intolerance and violence, marked by the new wars ('cold' ones for Westerners) that devastated Cambodia, Laos and Vietnam, and inevitably affected Thais for decades. Yet the echoes of the past are not represented, they simply resonate in the ordinary life of the men and women who participate and who perform in the film, who do ordinary things such as going to the doctor, hairdresser, or restaurant, 'those simple things that people in Siam do'.

The traces of war seep into *Syndromes and a Century* through the scenes in the basement. The physicians talk and drink around a work table as though they were in a comfortable common room in the hospital, not affected by the protheses surrounding them nor by the workers fixing pipes nearby. The patients inhabit the basement as though it were their home, playing in the corridor and living with the orthopaedists who construct their legs or arms to measure. The situation is of an astonishing ordinariness, in which there is no place for the grotesque or sinister. It is life itself, life with the burdens that each one has to bear: Doctor Nohng's sister suffers from alpha thalassemia, the young Off was poisoned by carbon monoxide. But nothing is said of the reasons for doctor Nant's fondness for whisky nor of the circumstances in which the rest of the patients lost their amputated limbs.

Like Boonmee, each one assumes their karma. The symptoms of his body are also the symptoms of history, a past of violence and injustice that traversed him, without him being completely aware of it, but the responsibility for which he cannot evade. It is not a question of equating disease with war, nor an accident with torture. The pain experienced by the individual, however, can be the same. This pain enables the imagining of the pain of others, leads to the recognition of the evil perpetrated or to the care of those who can be saved, consoled or contented.

The relationship of care is rendered in a sympathetic relation between bodies. The body of the other is treated with full awareness of the pain and pleasure that contact can generate. The body is not sacralised; rather, it is naturalized. By naturalizing it, the body becomes a whole, in which skin and flesh are as essential for the life of that body as talking and imagination. Language differentiates the body of the human being from that of the animal, but not enough to detach it from nature. Fantasy and matter coincide in bodies, in bodies that do not negate representation, but who do refuse to let the image supersede touch.

Care needs time and needs listening. The female doctors in Apichatpong's films are endowed with a great capacity for listening. They listen to the complaints and fantasies of their patients with the same curiosity that they listen to the reporting of the symptoms that will serve to make a diagnosis and propose a treatment. The doctors' listening is shifted to Apichatpong's camera, who maintains the shot as long as the relations between the characters require, beyond any narrative necessities and irrespective of any rhythmic considerations.

Caring for the survivors is a way of honouring the memory of the dead, in the same way that caring for the living is way of compensating for the past or present suffering of the victims. The caring for the bodies is seen in the action of the physicians, but also in the organization of pleasurable moments related with food, rest or sex. Caring for the body also becomes visible in the functioning of the imagination, which produces fictions, or even fantasies, that allow entertainment, encounters, subjective activation or cooperation.

De Sousa Santos proposes making the revaluation of care into one of the core ideas of transformation necessary for the decolonization of knowledge and of human relationships. In his double postulation of a 'sociology of absences' and a 'sociology of emergence', the 'mechanics of progress' is replaced by an 'axiology of care' (Sousa Santos 2010: 26). The axiology of care is coherent with a new idea of humanism that not only dispenses with the perverse colonial synecdoche by which the white European (and Christian) male names (and represents) all human beings, but also with a conception of human rights based exclusively on European cultural tradition. Nevertheless, it would betray this work of decolonization if we conceive of care as a prolongation of the 'charity' practised unidirectionally by the heirs of the colonizers on the heirs of the colonized, or as a substitute for the political action necessary for guaranteeing that the relations of care are alternative and changeable, not univocal and permanent.

19

Memory and violence

Do those guilty of crimes against humanity deserve care? At what level of responsibility is the limit of exculpation situated? What advanced age or what degree of illness must be reached before we accept the commuting of a sentence or release from prison for humanitarian reasons? Does reconciliation justify the forgiveness and good treatment of criminals? Is the soldier more guilty than the guerrilla fighter, the paramilitary commander than the revolutionary leader? Is the politician less guilty than the general?

The young Boonmee obeyed his superiors' orders and without thinking killed those labelled 'communists', probably including some of his neighbours. The elderly Boonmee does not demonstrate any explicit regret, but – in contrast to the majority of war criminals – recognizes in his own body the evil he has caused. Boonmee is a representative of the banality of evil at a small scale, who only seems redeemed by the loss of his son and his naturalist's passion for the beekeeping farm. The elderly Boonmee spends his last days attended by an illegal immigrant, a young man from Laos who, had he been born thirty years earlier, could have been a target to be liquidated. Boonmee dies surrounded by his loved ones, inside a magic cave, in a premediated return to nature. His victims were not as lucky.

Boonmee, however, is a fictional character. He probably did not kill many 'communists'. Had he done so, he would have had similar scars to those shown by the actors in a documentary film made by Joshua Oppenheimer, Cristine Cynn and 'Anonymous' in nearby Indonesia. The 'communists' there did not come from abroad, they were in fact one of the political forces with the greatest support and power in the 1960s. In 1965 the PKI was blamed for the organization of a coup d'état against president Sukarno, which served as the pretext for a real military coup that finished off the fragile democracy of previous years and installed a dictatorial regime of terror led by General Suharto. During the first years of his reign thousands of 'communists' (whether they belonged or not to the party) were tortured and assassinated without any judicial guarantees whatsoever. The dirty work was carried out by death squads composed of young men, including adolescents, who thirty years later were invited by Oppenheimer to participate in the film.

The Act of Killing (2012) seems like a grotesque inversion of the cinema of relation practised by Costa, Alonso or Apichatpong, or of the theatres of the real that lend voice to the victims. The voice here is of the executioners. Not only are they offered the possibility of telling their version of the events, of reconstructing their procedures of detention, torture and murder in detail, but they are also conceded the privilege of realizing their creative dreams. In contrast to films such as *S-21, la machine de mort Khmère rouge* (S-21, The Khmer Rouge Killing Machine, 2003) by Rithy Pahn, where the testimony of the jailors is mediated by the victims' gaze, in *The Act of Killing* the criminals represent themselves as heroes and continue to represent the victims as enemies. Anwar Congo, proud of his past as a so-called 'free man' (i.e., gangster), assumes the role of director, while Herman Koto performs inside the film-within-the-film as a star inclined to transvestism.

Oppenheimer explained that his first intention was to shoot a documentary film on the survivors, but he was perplexed that in Indonesia the slaughter of more than a million people has never led to criminal proceedings nor to a process of reconciliation; the massacre has remained unpunished and the criminals continue to swagger and occupy positions of power. This could be considered a 'local monstrosity', were not the crimes committed during the Cold War, when Suharto's government was one more piece in the fight against international communism and when numerous European firms benefitted from the forced labour of political prisoners. The self-representation of the Indonesian criminals was not very different, observed Oppenheimer, from that of US-American soldiers who had committed 'excesses' during the occupation of Iraq: both were trained to kill enemies. How could they do this without regarding those enemies as not equal?

Two reasons justify the representation of the executioners in *The Act of Killing*. The first is the desire to understand reality from the conception of the world and the life of a group of persons who in principle are completely alien to the values of the filmmakers. The second is the refusal to accept any limits – including ethical limits – to the realization of an artistic work. One could add an explicative hypothesis to these two justifications: the fascination of evil, the irresistible attraction that emanates from the authors of brutal crimes and the desire to see, or to imagine, what we believe is unbearable.

In order to understand, Oppenheimer and Cynn put themselves on the killers' side and accompanied them in their everyday life. With all their 'peculiarities', these 'free men' are also human; living with them can lead to empathy. This is a risk that the filmmakers assume and, moreover, transfer to the viewers. How far should comprehension for the criminals go? To the point of ignoring individual responsibility and discharging it on a collective subject, or justifying it by a historical context? Anwar is a seductive and intelligent man; he knows that he has been given the opportunity to direct, but that to speak on an equal basis with Oppenheimer he has to also share the latter's objectives. Perhaps for this reason he agrees to take on the role of the victim. This is a key scene in the film: Anwar is subjected to torture and ends up vomiting. He then wonders if his victims felt like he did. Oppenheimer answers that they did not, that they felt worse, because they were real victims and were aware that they were going to die. 'But I was able to feel it, Joshua,' responds Anwar, 'I really was able to feel it.' Emotion, however, does not imply remorse. The risk here is that sympathy for 'one who feels' leads to suspending the demand for complex understanding, that this understanding is replaced by empathy and we end up annulling ethical and historical judgement.

Roger Shattuck analyses this tricky limit in his commentary on Albert Camus' *The Stranger* (1942), surprised by the fact that the character of a murderer could provoke sympathy in the reader, to the point that it would be relatively easy to put oneself in the place of the young Meursault in his loneliness in a hypocritical society. Camus himself later summed up his novel with the following comment: 'In our society any man who doesn't cry at his mother's burial runs the risk of being condemned to death' (Shattuck 1996: 148). This suggests that the reader's sympathy is induced by the treatment that the author gives his character, presenting him as a 'poor naked man in love with a sun that leaves no shadow', driven by a profound 'passion for the absolute and for the truth' (ibid.). In defence of Camus, we should not forget that his character is fictional, although it is true that the victim, an Algerian Arab, remains outside the representation that the novelist deliberately constructs. 'Camus' narrative has the power of magic incantation in modern dress. It makes one forget that Meursault never thinks of or refers to the human being he has killed' (ibid.: 147). The risk that the novel poses in ethical terms is that identification with the character, the exercise of immersion in his personality, determinants and context, leads to 'understanding' his criminal acts. This 'understanding' is empathetic and partial, since it implies 'looking' at reality from the experience of an individual, disregarding the experience of the victim and the moral consequences of such an understanding. Because it disregards them, understanding can easily be identified with forgiveness. How can you condemn someone that you understand?

Oppenheimer consequently avoids falling into the trap set by Anwar and denies that Anwar's feeling can be the same as the feeling of those he tortured. Oppenheimer does indeed know the victims, he has lived with them and has empathized with them. But the fact is that – limiting ourselves exclusively to the film – the victims are not summoned, nor are they represented. They are signified – grotesquely – in the representations that the executioners perform of their acts of torture, as though they were objects, since the filmic inquiry focuses solely on the subjects of these acts. The perpetrators have been transformed into material for an analysis in which Oppenheimer yields co-authorship to Anwar.

The second justification is based on the ethical neutrality of art: The artist's task is to understand, not to judge. In order to 'understand', in the way that Oppenheimer intends, he has to temporarily suspend judgement. This is achieved by creating an autonomous zone of play and visibility, that is, a zone of experience in which an art work is produced (or received). For this ethical neutrality to be tolerable, two conditions are imposed: first, the effective temporality of this autonomous zone of experience or – in other words – the fictional character of what is represented; second, the insignificance of such an experience or representation in the sphere of reality, where judgements necessarily have to be exercised. Camus' confusion in regards to his murderer and his indifference to the victim, many years after the novel's publication, leads one to think that the temporality of the suspension of judgement cannot be determined drastically. On the other hand, the fact that everything shown in *The Act of Killing* is a recreation or a fantasy of the tormentors should not make us forget that the recreations are of events that actually occurred and were never judged, while the fantasies are those of confessed murderers who have never been prosecuted. Even so, Oppenheimer, as an artist, can claim his right to go to the limit. After all, he is the one who takes the risk, he is the one who suffers exposure to the 'free men', who assumes the possibility of empathizing with those who, from a distance, would be deemed 'monsters'. The problem arises, however, when Anwar is transformed into an equal.

Oppenheimer seems constrained by a postcolonial caution. Aware of the debate sparked decades before by *Moi un noir* (I, a Negro, 1958) by Jean Rouch, he tries to respect the decisions of his actors-collaborators, with the difference that these are murderers. Jean Rouch did actually live for some months in Abdijan with the young Nigerian immigrants that feature in his film. Apparently, his camera was very respectful during the recording of their everyday life, their stories and the staging of their fantasies. Rouch, however, was censured for the way in which he intervened in the final editing of the film, in particular and harshly by one of the actors, Oumarou Ganda, who ten years later himself filmed *Cabascabo* as a response to what he regarded as the manipulation and appropriation of his voice by Rouch (Haffner 1996: 97–8).

Fleeing colonial arrogance, Oppenheimer assumes the risk of falling into a postcolonial complicity with his actor-murderer, whom he does not deny his possible condition of artist. Since the film is conceived as a work of art, Oppenheimer can argue that within it ethical judgement has to be suspended. Nevertheless, is Anwar's film a work of art in the same manner that

Oppenheimer and Cynn's film can be? The fascination with evil and postcolonial caution lead the director to treat Anwar as an artist.

Rithy Panh, who greatly respects Oppenheimer's work, was adamant about this question: he would never have left the camera in the killers' hands. In *S-21* the criminals act and speak, but they are actors before a camera subjectively operated by the director. The 'banality of evil' emerges in front of that camera. In *The Act of Killing* the criminals appear as authors and this allows them to overcome the 'banality', not to reveal themselves as monsters, but ostensibly to transform themselves into artists. Beyond the peril and dubiousness of this method, what is not permissible in any case is considering their production as artistic nor analysing it under aesthetic criteria. The fact that the film has had such an extensive second life in discussions, debates and critical commentaries does not correspond in this case to its impact as a work of art, but precisely to its incompleteness as regards ethical discourse. Since the work is not autonomous, Oppenheimer has felt obliged to complete it in the context of its reception. Only by means of this subsequent afterlife has the effective temporality of the suspension of ethical judgement been guaranteed. The artistic quality of *The Act of Killing*, in any case, resides in the gesture of the directors, in their decision to plunge into the abyss of the inferno of a reality that no one wants to see, but that thousands of people experience every day, and in their invention of a method to depict that experience. It is this gesture of the directors, and by no means the symbolic constructions of the executioners, where one can situate what is artistic in the work.

One could argue that what is least relevant about this film is an opinion about whether or not it is a work of art. Yet it is precisely in this judgement that the film's ethical condition is also determined, with the risk that, with the judgement, the postcolonial conflict once again emerges.

20

Memory and humour

From the point of view of Oppenheimer, the persistence of the narrative of crime in a society like Indonesia's eliminates the possibility of an ethics of care, making the adoption of the perspective of the perpetrator necessary. A society in which those guilty of crimes against humanity enjoy privileges (economic and of social visibility) denied the victims or survivors does not have a moral debt, but a political one. For this reason, the filmmaker feels freed from any ethical precaution. Why should art compensate with *care* what can only be solved politically? Would it not have been politically questionable to represent the survivors performing an abstraction of the dominant position of their tormentors? Oppenheimer's approach in Indonesia would have been difficult to accept in Cambodia, South Africa, Argentina or Chile, where societies have confronted – at least symbolically – the *truth* of what occurred under recent regimes (despite this not implying in many cases the complete restitution of justice or dignity to the victims nor the end of privileges for the criminals). In contrast, this is conceivable in Spain, where the transition to democracy at the end of the 1970s and beginning of the 1980s was achieved at the cost of silencing the repression carried out by the Franco regime and maintaining the privileges of the oligarchies (including those of the ecclesiastical hierarchy).

For many years, the Spanish *transición* (transition) to democracy was presented as a model process: the agreement between political parties, including the Socialist and Communist ones – who had spent many years underground – and the new UCD (Union of Democratic Centre) and Alianza Popular (Popular Alliance), which incorporated active members of the previous regime, enabled a peaceful change, allowing important social and economic advances, as well as full international acceptance. Nevertheless, the 'model' nature of the *transición* has been intensely questioned internally as well as externally. While for years these critical voices were ignored, in recent decades the resistance against the effective implementation of the law of 'Historical Memory', the obstructing of judicial proceedings against crimes committed by the dictatorship and the political convulsions aggravated by the economic crisis have compelled a revision with greater public response. The 'silence' that political parties and civil agents agreed on was justified by the risk of political regression, which in fact became apparent in the attempt to stage a coup d'état in 1981, and remained latent during the early years of democracy in broad sectors of the administration and dominant oligarchy. Democrats accepted 'silence' and 'amnesia' to assure the success of the *transición*. Yet the passage of time revealed that this 'silence' and 'amnesia' would grow into very heavy burdens. The 'amnesia' was, moreover, concretized in the Law of Amnesty (Law 46/1977), which not only exonerated those who had been politically persecuted by the dictatorship, but also those members of the state apparatus who had committed crimes against humanity – in contravention of international law.

The Report of the Special Rapporteur Pablo de Greiff (2014) exposed the contradiction between the existence of a solidly consolidated institutional democracy and the resistance to investigating the crimes of the Franco regime and compensating the victims. The report's chief criticisms refer to the difficulties in establishing the facts, due to an absence of systematic investigation of the executions and disappearances of the victims, as well as of the trafficking of stolen children. One of the most flagrant cases concerns the investigation and exhumation of mass graves, a task privatized by the State and delegated to associations, despite the magnitude of the numbers, as it is estimated that more than 45,000 people are buried without identification in over 2000 graves distributed everywhere in the territory. In contrast with these thousands of anonymous burials, the Valle de los Caídos (Valley of the Fallen), erected with the forced labour of political prisoners, where approximately 34,000 people are estimated to be interred, continues to be a symbol of the Franco regime, the mausoleum of the dictator as well as of the founder of the Falangist party, a site of fascist pilgrimage run by a religious order and a tourist destination included along the monumental route in the outskirts of Madrid.

Resistance against the truth and its judicial and political implications was upheld for decades by a historical discourse, broadly disseminated in schools and the media, according to which the Civil War and the subsequent repression were the result of a conflict between two sides, thus minimizing the responsibility of the military rebels who overthrew a legitimate and democratic government. This historical reading justified the silence and the amnesia with the refusal to 'reopen wounds'; the preservation of the oligarchy's privileges thus rested on the silence of the victims and the repression of memory. This was abetted by the absence of a purging of institutions, in particular of the military and the justice system. While the armed forces renovated themselves by opening up to the exterior, the judicial system preserved intact structures inherited from the dictatorship, exacerbating the effects of the Law of Amnesty, which up to now has obstructed any investigation into the direct or political responsibilities for crimes against humanity – crimes that do not prescribe and cannot be protected by any national law.

The filmmaker Basilio Martín Patino anticipated the denunciation of the 'silence' and 'amnesia' on which the supposedly exemplary Spanish *transición* was constructed. He shot *Queridísimos verdugos* (Dearest Executioners, 1973) during the last stages of the regime, a documentary film featuring three of the last 'administrators of justice' still active in Spain. It could not be premiered until 1977, once the process of transition had been launched after the dictator's demise.

The three executioners present themselves as humble workers, carrying out their tasks in order to survive, always at the disposal of the justice system when the authorities need them. Antonio is the friendliest and the one with whom the viewer can most easily sympathize. Vicente is more introspective, but likewise sincere. Bernardo affects the role of a gentleman, ardently reciting poems and strolling through his neighbourhood in Granada as though the life and death of his neighbours depended on him. The three relate their experiences before the camera frankly, comment on their cases, show off the technical mastery of their profession and give their opinion on the defendants, without questioning the judicial decisions. In one sequence they briefly recreate the protocol of execution: the garrotte operates by strangulation, in the same way that wires were later employed by the 'free men' in Indonesia. Yet its rudimentary mechanics conserves the memory of the Empire, the Inquisition and humanist modernism, by reason of which Ferdinand VII transformed it into the exclusive instrument of execution in Spain. Like Anwar and his friends, Antonio and his colleagues speak freely, since they are part of the system and limit themselves to carrying out the law; they have nothing to fear and to be ashamed of. Martín Patino spurs them on, with bottles of wine and generous meals, which they consume in traditional taverns and humble outdoor restaurants, typical of the poor and bleak Spain they physically and mentally inhabit. A narrow perspective could lead one to pity them for their fate, as one might feel sorry for the protagonist of Luis García Berlanga's *El verdugo* (The Executioner, 1963), a hangman who ends up accepting his task without being very aware of the circumstances that led him to it. Martín Patino provides enough information at the beginning of the film, however, to keep the viewer aware that these poor men could have chosen other options. Antonio López Sierra enlisted as a volunteer in the army fighting against the government of the Republic, fought subsequently with the División Azul (Blue Division), the troops that – despite Spain's neutrality – fought in the Second World War with the Nazis. Vicente López Copete belonged to the fascist Falange party, joined the Spanish Foreign

Legion in Morocco, took part in the repression of the 'revolution of 1934' in Oviedo, and later engaged in smuggling. Bernardo Sánchez Bascuñana was a member of the Guardia Civil, of the purest lineage of the many Granadians immortalized by García Lorca in his poems, whom he – a fascist to the bone – would not have hesitated in the least to kill, like anyone who 'sins or dares to disagree'. No one forced them to take the decisions they took; what is more, their illiterateness does not excuse them from the ideological current they joined. Martin Patino animates the exhibitionism of these executioners who speak so loquaciously, while his sarcastic gaze tears into the most sinister one of them: the patriarch from Granada, who does not hesitate to recite before the camera in the purest fascist style nor to dance with Roma women in a cave in Sacromonte, he a dark stain in the sordid tavern of colonized vitality. However, in contrast to Oppenheimer, he does not lend his camera to the realization of their fantasies, nor concede the slightest discursive value to their arguments or artistic value to their caprices or – in the case of Bernardo – to his poetic inclinations. The songs, dances and settings that accompany their testimony introduce an ironic counterpoint, occasionally relativizing the brutality that is narrated and depicted, but at no point concealing it and much less aestheticizing it. The director achieves an aesthetic of the grotesque by means of the *mise en scène*, the framing, and above all by the montage of sound and image. In addition, the grotesque here – in the best tradition of the *esperpento* (a Spanish literary tradition using the grotesque for social criticism) – contributes to the ironic and veiled denunciation, yet never to the aggrandizement of the protagonists.

During the shooting of the film the Franco regime maintained the instruments of repression and ideological control intact. The denunciation is thus levelled against this regime by challenging its administration of justice. The executioners themselves sporadically express their compassion for some of the condemned persons. More explicit are the testimonies of the lawyers and physicians. Even though no one questions the sentences and all of them – without exception – carry out the duties assigned them within the protocol of execution, it becomes apparent that the garrotte is not as 'dignified' nor as 'humane' as Ferdinand VII imagined it to be; justice, moreover, continues to fall implacably on the weakest in the system. Not one of the documented cases affects a person of means; the majority of those sentenced to death were poor, illiterate and sometimes even disabled. The case of Ramón Oliva Márquez, 'Monchito', vividly recalls that of Jorge del Carmen Valenzuela Torres, the main character of *El chacal de Nahueltoro* (The Jackal of Nahueltoro, 1969) by Miguel Littin. For Jorge and his family, the 'death penalty' is nothing more than the consequence of a 'life penalty': poverty and ignorance have sentenced them before the court did. The fate of these men and women who bore the 'life penalty' makes apparent that the destiny of the executioners was not predetermined. If poverty does not serve as an excuse for commuting a death penalty, then it cannot be cited, not as extenuating, but for justifying, a decision freely taken. How to explain to the young Roma from Almendralejo that there are deaths punished with execution and others rewarded with thousand-peseta bills?

Together with the poor, however, other people were condemned as well: some historical, such as Michele Angiolillo, the anarchist who assassinated Cánovas del Castillo and was executed with great theatrical and media display. Others, more recently, such as Francisco Granados and Joaquín Delgado Martínez, members of the Federación Ibérica de Juventudes Libertarias (The Iberian Federation of Free Youth), sentenced without any evidence for a bomb attack on the DGS (Directorate General of Security) and executed on 18 August 1963. The affable Antonio López Sierra, that amusing and friendly man who assumes the role of entertainer for the group of executioners, was responsible for putting Salvador Puig Antich to death on 2 March 1974. Puig was an antifascist militant and member of the anarchist Movimiento Ibérico de Liberación (Iberian Movement of Liberation) falsely accused of a policeman's death: his execution was one of the last State crimes carried out by the Franco regime. The image of his face alone suffices for all of the film to turn into a biting attack on the regime.

The four former ministers of the Franco government who signed the order of execution against Salvador Puig Antich did not have to face any criminal proceedings after the proclamation of the Spanish Constitution in 1978. Neither did the hundreds of senior officials and civil servants belonging to the police, the Guardia Civil or the army who were responsible for crimes violating fundamental human rights. They were protected – paradoxically – by the Law of Amnesty of 1977, originally introduced to exonerate antifascist militants who had fought against the Franco regime during the dictatorship from any criminal and legal responsibility. The superiors in the chain of command ordering those miserable executioners portrayed by Martín Patino preserved their professional, social and economic status after the political transition, some of them adopting poses as swaggering as those of the leaders of the Indonesian Pancasila. Successive petitions and recommendations for the repeal of the Law of Amnesty have been ignored, while attempts to begin criminal procedures, initiated by judge Baltasar Garzón in Spain and subsequently by judge María de Servini in Argentina, have run into the immunity guaranteed by a system whose elites have hardly changed.

Humour was the means used by Martín Patino during the last stages of Francoism to express the pain of a people oppressed by poverty, religious fanaticism and fascist ideology. Direct denunciation was not possible at that time, although Martín Patino did not limit himself to allegory, as so often in that epoch, and went very far in his documentary approach. Laughter is one of the strategies of resistance of the oppressed. It serves to physically fight against the depression of punishment. It serves socially to forge community. And symbolically it serves to relativize the dogma on which all authoritarianism rests.

The Spanish *transición* not only assured the impunity of fascist criminals and the perpetuation of the privileges of the great economic clans, it moreover had a numbing effect on cultural production in Spain. The idea that everything that could be done in terms of a democratic normalization had already been accomplished became installed like a new dogma, materialized in the new Constitution of 1978. The myth functioned, to the point that very few dared to question the 'model' character of the process of transition. Just as occurs today in Indonesia, the victims that tried to claim their rights were regarded as pariahs and wet blankets. Thirty years had to pass before 'historical memory' once again appeared on the political agenda. The awakening occurred in March 2004, sparked by Al-Qaeda's attack on four regional trains near the Atocha station in Madrid. Martín Patino was the only artist who dared to confront the immense shock produced by the assault. The political manipulation of the attack at a national scale exposed the modern liberals as the heirs of the old fascists. The pain of the workers revived the memory of the attack on the capital by the rebel nationalist army. This was how Martín Patino understood it in his work *Homenaje a Madrid* (Homage to Madrid, 2004), a multi-channel installation in which images of the terrorist attack alternated with those of the bombings during the last moments of resistance of the people of Madrid against the rebel army. The Roma from Almendralejo would likewise have had difficulty in understanding the difference between one violence and another, especially because many insisted on attributing the crimes to ETA. The *transición* had not accomplished everything it could have in recuperating democracy.

His last film, *Libre te quiero* (I Want You Free, 2012), testified to this recuperation in a more festive vein. It documents the occupation of the Puerta del Sol square in Madrid on 15 May 2012, which has given birth to numerous proposals for the realization of a second transition to real democracy.

21

Histories and memories

Historical memory arises from the collocation of two apparently incompatible terms. Memory is the past that is present in our doing, thus extending into the future. Memory generates a dense present, one rich in nuances. Memory is that sediment of experience where suffering and pleasure are deposited, where they fuse together and react, stimulating new realities. History, in contrast, is what makes us conscious of the past, warns us and unconsciously conditions our acts. History prepares us for criticism, for organizing life together and for projecting the future. We can, of course, conceive of the negative version of both terms, imagining memory as that which crushes us, which materially binds us to the behaviour of the past, and history as that which imposes itself on us as the narrative of the past, condemning us to a future we have not chosen.

Historical memory results from the resistance to a history that dispenses with a part of itself, that disembodies itself, but it is also the result of a dissatisfaction with a subjective and silent memory that does not achieve representation and is therefore politically innocuous. Memory and history feed back into each other: memory supplies history with testimony; history recuperates the lapses of memory; history edits and interrupts the stream of memory; memory resists the falsification of history.

History (in its scientific mode) and memory (personal or collective) can work together in recuperating the past, but they can also conflict with each other. There is a memory of power, complicit with official historical narratives, employed by nation-states in the nineteenth and twentieth centuries to construct their identities. And there is a countermemory, which peoples and groups excluded from those narratives or from the official sites of memory turn to. The further that official history and memory lie from individual and group history and memories, the more likely that traumatic symptoms will emerge.

All history has its fictional component, accepted as an inevitable price of the process of transmission. When fiction is presented as fiction and does not decisively affect ordinary memories and histories, it is a symptom that the relationship between past and present is fruitful and productive. However, when these inevitable fictions begin to supplant ordinary memories and histories and to exert a claim to truth or universality, they create a weight that progressively crushes the shared game and the projection of new social visions. This fictionalized history claiming truth was what sparked Nietzsche's reaction against history in his 'Second Untimely Meditation'.

History becomes dangerous when it determines life. Memory becomes dangerous when it withdraws from it. History has to be useful for life through criticism, but criticism cannot determine life. Memory has to be useful for life through the renewal of life, but without the experience of the past devouring that of the present. History and memory only make sense when they are useful for living together.

Can history continue to be differentiated from memory? Traditionally, history was distinguished from memory because the former was written down in the form of a hegemonic narrative and the latter was oral and corporeal, circulating in a multitude of songs, popular stories, rituals, customs and visual representations. Memory constructed identity out of bodies and therefore from a local territory; history constructed identity from words and thus from a territory that was not necessarily geographically limited. Both indices of distinction have disappeared in recent decades. In the first place, memory has been externalized by physical or virtual prosthetics, which also introduce the risk of amnesia. In the second place, memory has been de-localized, since the mobility of people and information detaches memory from place and leads to something as apparently contradictory as a global memory.

Pascal Gielen cites the results of a survey taken among a sample of people in Flanders on which type of historical event occurring in their lifetimes they remembered. Those who had been born before the Second World War primarily remembered historical events that had taken place in Belgium, while those born after the war mainly recalled those from the rest of the world (Gielen 2009: 61). We could imagine that the dissociation between individual memory and historical memory relates to that poverty of experience that Benjamin discussed in the 1930s and which Agamben recently insisted on in *Infanzia e storia* (Agamben 1978: 6). According to Benjamin, the poverty of experience is tied to the disappearance of oral culture in favour of solitary writing, of archives. But also to the destruction caused by the World War. This did not contribute to an enriching of experience, but rather to its impoverishment. Modernity for Benjamin was the age of a new barbarism, a flight forward where the necessity of the new had shattered experience.

One could say that many contemporary artists have followed the path of the novelist discussed by Benjamin, the individual in solitude, and when they want to recuperate experience they see themselves obliged to travel. 'When someone goes on a trip, he has something to tell about,' says a German proverb, 'and people imagine the storyteller as someone who has come from afar.' But, adds Benjamin, 'they enjoy no less listening to the man who has stayed at home, making an honest living, and who knows the local tales and traditions' (Benjamin 1936: 84).

Occasionally artists go out in search of the memory of others in an exercise of ethical responsibility, to make pain and injustice visible, but also in a certain manner to look for borrowed experiences. In exchange for the memory that others lend them to realize their film, book or performance, they offer the elaboration of a symbolic apparatus or even of a fiction, which they give back in return. Groupov travelled from Brussels to Ruanda to realize a lengthy investigation and make amends for the guilt of Western media in the genocide portrayed in *Rwanda 94* (1999). Joshua Oppenheimer similarly went to Indonesia to document the lives of the survivors of the Indonesian genocide and ended up shooting, in collaboration with Cristine Cynn and 'Anonymous', *The Act of Killing*. Other voyages are regional, such as that made by Ong Keng Sen from Singapore to Phnom Penh to stage the testimony of Em Theay (the last surviving repository of court dances, herself persecuted by the Khmer Rouge) in *The Continuum. Beyond the Killing Fields* (2002). Others are local, like that embarked on by Yuyachkani from Lima to Ayacucho to accompany the memories of the victims in the audiences during the sessions of the Commission on Truth and Reconciliation in 2002. This text is itself an aggregate of histories and memories, borrowed for the realization of an exercise of accompanying and of intellectual reflection. This does not lend an inferior ethical or artistic value to the works cited above, in comparison with those realized based on personal memories (such as Apichatpong or Panh) or by artists who do not need to travel (like Martín Patino).

Artistic nomadism has invaded the field of memory. In itself, there is nothing bad in an artist putting their enunciative capacity at the service of memories silenced by impotence or shame. Yet the result of the sum of personal stories and borrowed histories is an interchange of memories at a global scale, as stimulating as it is dangerous. There is no global memory because there is no global body and no global territory. What exists is an accumulation of histories, a multiplication of trajectories. As Pascal Gielen suggests, there is no shared historical memory any more, not even an official memory confronted against a countermemory, but instead the field of histories has been opened to competition (Gielen 2009: 64). In this new context, memory is neither previous nor parallel to history; memory is born intertwined with histories, the histories themselves shaping memory. This is a memory that no longer serves to construct indenty, but has other causes:

justice, ethical investigation, defence of human rights, affirmation of the individual. Today, those who work with memory in the artistic field proceed not so much from a local or national perspective, not even from a community perspective, but from an individual subjectivity that contributes its history to a network of construction of meaning in which criticism and action are possible.

Nevertheless, in the game of histories in competition those who have something to say about their own past have to be aware that their memory will enter the memory market. As a site of exchange the market can be positive, as a site of speculation it can be perverse. In the field of competing histories as described by Gielen, the capacity that individuals and groups have for making their histories heard is generally more limited than the ability of big communications media to sell theirs.

Working with memory becomes necessary when minority individuals or groups are attacked in the face of the indifference or impotence of the majority. Film, theatre, literature and the visual arts have served as a space of enunciation for individuals or groups to claim symbolic compensation at least. The initiative can be the result of a personal necessity, a shock, an emotional mobilization, an assumed responsibility or be the consequence of organized militancy. Needs, wants and desires can be instrumentalized for the benefit of illegitimate representations or simply decay into an institutionalized routine that produces closed representations, transforming memory into a monument. This risk threatens memory as much as countermemories. Artistic projects necessary at a certain moment lose their efficacy as manifestos of resistance against official history, turning into new ways of monumentalizing the past. The monumentalization of the past can serve in some cases to disguise the present-day violence of new powers. Oppenheimer's cruelty can be regarded as a resistance to a monumentalization of the past that does not take into account the persistence of the structures of behaviour and power that today constitute the true danger. Yet other modes of resistance exist, similarly based on humour and on the game of representation, which can also be deployed by artists, without having to give the camera to the executioners in exchange for their memory.

The transition from need and agitation to artistic proposals based on fiction and anger is clearly demonstrated in the recent history of Argentine cinema. The most widely distributed films in the 1980s that dealt with the dictatorship's repression were made by directors with no direct relation to the actual events on which these films were based: *La historia oficial* (The Official History, 1985) by Luis Puenzo and *La noche de los lápices* (Night of the Pencils, 1986) by Héctor Olivera. They represented, fictionally, what Argentinian society had refused to accept during the previous decade. Yet the necessity of these representations was soon adulterated by sensationalism on the one hand and a sedating closure on the other: the terrible events depicted in the films belonged to the past and the representations served to do symbolic justice. This justice, however, contrasted with the impunity granted by the laws of 'Punto final' (End Point) and 'Obediencia Debida' (Law of Due Obedience), as well as with the open wounds in the families of the disappeared and of stolen children.

Several years passed before in 1999 Marco Bechis, survivor of a detention camp, filmed *Garage Olimpo* (Olympic Garage), based on direct testimony by people who, like him, had suffered isolation and torture. In contrast to previous fictions, this one did not demonstrate the same indulgence for the viewers, that is, with those who at that time had not wanted to see and who were uncomfortable seeing again (Noriega 2009: 87). Argentina was living under the false miracle of the Menem era, who amnestied the few officers that had been sentenced in 2002. The voices of those who dug into the past were annoying, as irritating as the 'the crazy women' of the Plaza de Mayo square when they challenged the military regime. Perhaps for this reason, the film enjoyed much less distribution than the previous ones. The same fate befell the first films made by children of the disappeared: *(H) Historias cotidianas* (Everyday Stories, 2001) by Andrés Habegger, son of Norberto Habegger, a Montonero militant disappeared in Brazil in 1978, and *Papá Iván* (Father Ivan, 2004) by María Inés Roque, daughter of Juan Julio Roque, founder of FAR (Fuerzas Armadas Revolucionarias [Armed Revolutionary Forces]) and a Montonero leader assassinated in 1977. These films are contemporaneous with the activism launched in 1995 by the association HIJOS (Hijos por la Identidad y la Justicia contra el Olvido y el Silencio [Children for Identity and Justice against Forgetting and Silence]) and coincide in their refusal to forget. One of the tools of public action employed by HIJOS was the *escrache*, a protest targeting a person at their home or workplace, in order to draw attention to unpunished criminals and to denounce the legacy of Argentina's dictatorship at the end of the twentieth century. Activism in favour of memory joined the activism against the neoliberal policies of Menem's government, policies that led to economic collapse during de la Rua's tenure and the freezing of bank deposits, known as the *corralito* decree, which reflected the democratic bankruptcy.

The representation of pain joined with that of anger in two films that broke the canons regarding the documenting of memory: *Los rubios* (The Blondes, 2003) by Albertina Carri and *M* (2007) by Nicolás Prividera. Both are children of victims of the military dictatorship, but their inquiry does not concentrate on the recreation of the past and the demand for reparations, but in finding an answer to personal perplexity. Both are conscious that their stories 'compete' on the global 'market' of memory. They are just as aware that the identitary solution proposed by previous directors – and still upheld by the activism of HIJOS – does not resolve their questions. In his film, Prividera resorts to a performative mode, presenting himself as the protagonist of an irritated and irritating inquiry. In her film, Carri questions representation itself, using theatricality and mediation as procedures of distancing, reflection and irony. Both directors rebel against the burden of memory, against the condemnation that society imposes on them as children of the disappeared. In Prividera's case, his rebellion is transformed into a denunciation of a society predisposed to accept, in Carri's case, into a staging of the false normality that hegemonic representations favour.

Albertina Carri hardly knew her parents. She was three years old when Roberto Carri and Ana María Caruso were 'disappeared' by agents of the dictatorship in March 1977. As a filmmaker who is a child of disappeared victims, she is supposed to have a moral duty to make a film about her parents. This dominant morality is accompanied by certain political and aesthetic rules, which translate into the manner of representing the disappeared and their social circle, whose memory is to be vindicated. Carri accepted her responsibility, but strove to free herself of the moral imperative and, consequently, questioned representation as a way of subverting the rules. Why should someone who never really got to know her parents be able to take on the representation with greater understanding than anyone else? Carri thus decided to avoid the representation demanded of her; what the film depicts, as Gustavo Noriega observes, is a 'void', 'the impossibility of film to reconstruct what is irreparable' (Noriega 2009: 19).

The multiplication of mediations, the humour, the meta-filmic means, the self-representation, all have a single goal: that of staging a process of empowerment by an artist who will not accept the role of a victim nor the denial of her singularity, in favour of a past to whose repetition she seems doubly condemned (by the disappearances themselves and by the moral obligation of representing them). As the aim is to depict a process of empowerment, the protagonist of the film is the filmmaker herself. Yet since this is not a personal initiative of her own, but a response to a moral obligation, Carri opts for representing herself, duplicating herself in front of the camera with the collaboration of the actress Analía Couceyro. 'My name is Analía Couceyro, I am an actress and in this film I play Albertina Carri,' states the actress in a close-up at the beginning of the film. The idea is to create distancing, to encourage the viewer's critical reception. Carri is not supplanted by Couceyro, since she is seen in numerous occasions together with the actress during the filming process, which is likewise documented in the film. The hyper-representation clearly situates the axis of inquiry, but at the same time it reduces attention on the protagonist and directs it to the actual object of inquiry: the viewer no longer pays attention to the woman (daughter/filmmaker), but to what the two Albertinas look at and listen to. The alienation, moreover, evades the risk of sentimentalism; thanks to this alienation Carri is able to include a highly emotional sequence: a childhood recollection of a three-year-old girl whose only repeated desire is the return of her father and mother. The filmmaker knows that this return is impossible, just as any attempt to reconcile the past is, since the past will continue to be what it was and no representation can change it. Far from accepting her condition of victim, Carri employs pain in her artistic work; humour contributes to constructing an activating fiction.

The concealing hyper-representation of the daughter is coherent with the refusal to represent her parents. In fact, they are not depicted as adults, that is, as parents, in the entire film; only a few photographs show them as children. 'I did not want the viewer to leave the film believing they were taking away an image of Roberto and Ana María. That would have been more reassuring' (60). For a person is not understood by their photograph, as the filmmaker knows very well; she probably tried, unsuccessfully, to extract something from the mute photographs. Similarly, her parents' companions are not directly depicted: they always appear on a screen, which serves the fictional Albertina to advance in her investigation. It is through the glance, the voice and hand of the actress how the film offers the testimonies: reproducing videos of the interviews, reading letters and documents or drawing the detention centre as described by someone who did not want to be recorded on camera. It is precisely during one of those moments, as Couceyro is analyzing an interview with a person close to the parents, that she observes: 'Depicting memory in its own mechanism. By omitting, it remembers.'

This treatment of memory was questioned by the INCAA committee responsible for allocating funds to the production. Carri decided to include a sequence in her film that recreated receiving a fax justifying the refusal of funding. Couceyro reads the document, which calls for 'greater documentary rigour', at the same time emphasizing the necessity of doing justice to the figure of the assassinated militants. The INCAA asked for a documentary depiction of the events. Yet Carri was not prepared to satisfy their demands: 'That is the film that their generation needed. I understand that, but that is a film that they have to make, not me. They need that film and I understand that they need it. But it is not my task to make it' (26).

The only true representations as such almost constitute a provocation of the dominating morality. '*Los rubios* is a film that attacks the rules of Good Remembering, against the official mnemonics that dominates the intents of interrogating the experience of the 1970s in Argentina' (81). In the first place, the arrest is reconstructed in an animated sequence with Playmobil figures, the same ones that are used to reconstruct other moments in the life of the three girls in the country home where they were taken by relatives after the disappearance of the parents. This is not a realist reconstruction, but one of a child's imagination, in which the Playmobil couple are kidnapped by a UFO. In the second place, identity is produced artificially, by means of blonde wigs worn by the entire film crew. The first representation was criticized for reducing a political occurrence to an infantile fantasy. Yet this infantile fantasy was a way of representing the actual memory of a little girl, now a filmmaker, who is asked to carry out a work of restitution. The purported depoliticization is actually refuted by the second sequence of the wigs, which could be regarded as more frivolous. Carri's family was known in their neighbourhood as 'the blondes', despite not being blonde. It was a way of naming their strangeness: they did not belong to that place, on account of their social condition and political ideas. By designating them as 'blonde', the neighbours anticipated the actual denunciation. For this reason, Carri is unsparing with the neighbours, whom she exposes directly to the camera, whose voices she records live with the best equipment possible. For they, though innocent, were implicit collaborators – just like the silent society denounced by Bechis in his aerial shots of Buenos Aires – in the crimes of the dictatorship. Being 'blonde' is not part of a biological, cultural or genetic identity. 'The blondes' were the strangers, those who could be dispensed with, because of their behaviour and ideas. By putting on the blonde wig, Carri changes her genetic identity – the one that obliges her to be a victim, the daughter of disappeared parents – for a political identity, shared with many others, whether or not they are children of the disappeared, whether or not they are victims.

In this manner Carri rebels against being classified as a 'victim', since being a 'victim' – as Badiou elaborates – entails the risk of being regarded as less than human. The victim is excluded from society; as a suffering body, deprived of subjectivity, it occupies a territory shared with the tormentor, different from the rest of human beings (Badiou 1993: 10–11). In order to remain human ('immortal' in Badiou's terms), Carri does not accept this categorizing. Only by preserving her freedom of being a non-classified human can she also maintain her capacity of artistic and discursive enunciation.

The final costuming is not a gesture of forgetting, but of memory. This is a memory that includes forgetting. Herein resides the politics of memory, which results from a decision to avoid the closure of representation. In a previous sequence, Analía Couceyro – in the role of Albertina Carri – undergoes a blood test at the Forensic Institute. Obviously, Carri herself has to subsequently take the same test, since blood in itself cannot be represented.

Yet the genetic heritage does not politically determine, nor offer, ethical guarantees. The wig does.

The blonde wig is the conclusion of the process of empowerment. It has nothing to do with the wigs worn by Koto in Oppenheimer and Cynn's fiction. In that case, the wig was a symptom of a trauma. In this one, the wig is the acceptance of the void and the overcoming of any type of melancholic paralysis in contemplating such a trauma. In *The Act of Killing* Oppenheimer offered the camera to Anwar. Carri keeps the camera and asks Couceyro to momentarily represent her identity. The results are very different, but in both cases the tranquillizing closure, the perpetually looming risk of monumentalization, is avoided.

22

End of the party

Utilizing fiction, irony, humour and masking are risky decisions when artists work in human contexts affected by ongoing violence or its consequences. Roberto Bolaño and Angélica Liddell justified these means in an exercise of dedication and in cruelty to themselves. Walid Raad, Rabih Mroué and Albertina Carri considered them necessary for creating distance, thus maintaining their critical and artistic capacity in the face of a reality – imposed on them – of an identity they could not choose. Apichatpong put the lives of the survivors before the representation of the victims, inviting viewers to participate in the labour of memory, conceived primarily as a game. Oppenheimer and Patino gave voice to the executioners, echoing their humour and fantasies, so that its grotesque visualization would physically incite repulsion, without underestimating the power that permitted their arrogance.

The strategies of representation are diverse, but common to all of them is theatricality, mediation and in some cases – literally – masking. For various reasons the authors consider the mere presentation of information and testimonies as insufficient. Since they go beyond presentation a fiction emerges that can be constituted as an artistic discourse. This is what contributes a truth that otherwise would escape the contemplation of bare faces and unedited testimonies.

Rolf and Heidi Abderhalden similarly employed masks and the deployment of scenographic means to confront the history of violence in Colombia in their theatre triptych *Los santos inocentes* (The Holy Innocents, 2010), *Discurso de un hombre decente* (Discourse of a Decent Man, 2011) and *Los incontados* (The Unaccounted, 2014). The latter draws on material from the previous two to map out an itinerary that penetrates successive layers, leading from a bourgeoise 'normality' to a tropical *fiesta*. The ravages of corruption, guerrilla warfare, paramilitary forces and drug trafficking echo among the dance rhythms, ostentatious costumes and colourful music. The association between *fiesta* and violence is disconcerting, as bizarre as the *ranchera* songs of Angélica Liddell, the appearances of ghosts in Apichatpong or the wigs of Albertina Carri.

The setting for *Los santos inocentes* (2010) consists of a multitude of masks, costumes and coloured balloons, stuffed into a small space furnished with chairs and tables that recalls a humble traditional restaurant. This cramped space is unthinkable for celebrating a large party, were it not for the danger lurking in the street. In this closed space, contrary to the space of carnival, a party has taken place, or rather, a party has been interrupted that could be restarted at any moment. In fact, actors portraying dancing figures hide between the objects, waiting for the moment when the music will return. The vibrant colour and the promise of dancing are in keeping with the brand image of the new Colombia, which is leaving behind violence and opening up once more to national and international tourism with its beaches, music, carnivals and exuberant vegetation. Nevertheless, there is something perplexing in this reproduction of the brand aesthetic, a sinister inversion that announces what will shortly occur.

The core of the piece consists of the documentation and recreation of the festivity of the Holy Innocents in Guapi. In this small village on the Colombian Pacific coast the day designated by the Christian calendar as 'Holy Innocents' Day' is celebrated by an extraordinary festival celebration. Men cross-dressed as women, disguised with grotesque masks and armed with whips roam the streets and thrash their neighbours. Other men offer themselves as victims so that the festivity can take place, with some whipping and others being whipped, the latter attempting to jump to avoid their legs being hit, the former pursuing the victims. The whippers threaten and are proud to play the role they have taken on that day, one that privileges them from early on in the morning until the onset of night. The origins of the ritual can be traced back to the eighteenth century, when the ancestors of these young men inverted the established order for a day; instead of letting themselves be thrashed by their overseers, they seized the whips to beat their equals. Later on, a syncretic process shifted the festivity to the Day of the Holy Innocents, when Christians commemorate the massacre of the children decreed by Herod to prevent the coming of the Messiah. With this double genealogy forgotten, the festivity is explained nowadays as an attempt to relive the pain suffered by their ancestors, a voluntary practice of not-forgetting, through which the inhabitants of Guapi strive to physically remember the experience of slavery, humiliation, uprootedness and punishment. Its grotesque character is heightened by alcohol, which makes the tormentors lose control and hinders the victims from avoiding the whip; the collective drunkenness ends up transforming the festivity into a kind of nightmarish trance.

Heidi and Rolf Abderhalden understood that this festivity, instead of celebrating liberation, expressed the symptoms of a trauma in its repetition, each year recalling the memory of suffering and injustice. They saw that it could have a broader reading within the context of a country that had embarked on a process of overcoming decades of violence. The work is developed as a theatrical action integrating music, visual and documentary video. Two marimbas, played by Genaro Torres and Dioselino Rodríguez, flank the narrow central performance space, above which a projection screen is suspended.

The action commences with the story of an actual journey: that of Heidi Abderhalden, who shares with the audience her decision to celebrate her birthday, on 28 December, in Guapi. During the performance Heidi, as an alien witness, relates her impressions and participation in the ritual, while Genaro and Dioselino, as local witnesses, perform a variety of songs and works for marimba. It is Genaro Torres who observes, while lamenting the recent violence, that it is nothing but the latest episode in 'two hundred years under the yoke of marginalization, racial discrimination and neglect'. For this reason, he explains, he came up with the idea of suggesting to a poet he has befriended that Guapi, Timbiqui and Lopez be declared 'independent states of the Republic of Colombia'. Genaro does not like this festivity that celebrates violence, does not like the disorder provoked by the alcohol, the races and the whippings. He prefers to take refuge in his home, far from the village, to which he travels in a small boat.

The documentary images of the village in the moments before the day of the celebration and those shot in the streets populated by the *matachines* [the costumed tormentors] alternate with the representation of the festivity on stage by figures who are masked, dance wildly, wreak havoc and whip. They include Julián Díaz, the 'famous actor' invited by Mapa Teatro to walk around Guapi and subsequently relive on stage the memory of that action, himself transformed into a *matachin*. The presence of a well-known television actor impacts the diverse accumulation of the performance, reinforcing the confusion of a reality in which *telenovelas* (soap operas) and festivity are interwoven with the news of crimes of all types, within the setting of a society in which brutal cultural and economic inequalities persist.

The recordings and the stage recreation of the festivity are juxtaposed with documents projected on the screen, supplying information on Ever Veloza García, alias HH, drug trafficker and former paramilitary leader, member of the ultra-right-wing Autodefensas Unidas de Colombia (AUC, United Self-Defence Forces of Colombia), extradited to the US in March 2009. HH was responsible for massacres and perpetrated thousands of killings; he is in effect the Herod of the region, a slaughterer of innocents. But his decision, like that of the biblical ruler, was not merely the outcome of mental imbalance, perverse superstition or individual evil. It was a consequence and part of a network of power, which delegates to unscrupulous people tasks of control and pacification that it later – hypocritically – finds shocking. HH went too far, thought the officers who protected, tolerated and probably encouraged him, yet HH would not have existed without them and without the ideological orientation encouraged by the government. They preferred to extradite him to the US, to be tried there for drug trafficking and not for the thousands of murders committed in Colombia, which cannot be attributed to any one man. A projection of the facts extracted from the horrifying confession of the committed crimes, with the names and dates of his victims, ends the performance.

Yet this conclusion is a false end, because the violence in the area did not cease with the extradition of HH, nor will it finish with the demobilization of the guerrillas. The 'armed truces' do not mean the true cessation of actions by any of the involved groups, whether by the army, police, ex-guerrillas or former paramilitary members. The trauma of the bodies, moreover, will take much longer to cure, and this trauma is manifested in repetition.

In fact, the festivity in Guapi in 2009 was almost cancelled due to the threat of guerrilla action. One of the documentary videos shown during the performance depicts images of a march through the streets of the village against the violence. The marches continue to be held, years later, because the deaths have not ceased since then.

Mapa Teatro avoids mimetic representation and practises a type of *mise en scène* that is more of an 'indisposition'. In the ritual recorded on video, the 'Holy Innocents' are not shown, but rather indicated by the bodies of those who receive the whippings of the tormentors. Neither are they shown on stage; the responsibility is left to the audience of establishing the continuity between the children massacred in the Christian commemoration, the freemen whipped as slaves in the ritual of inversion and the present-day innocents: the peasants, the indigenous people and the victims of the dirty war, of paramilitary violence and drug trafficking. Some of the names appear on HH's list. Not all of them, because the list continues to grow.

In the face of this, what can the witnesses do? Genaro and Dioselino, outside the inner space, prefer to cross the river, distance themselves from the festivity and play the marimba, competing with difficulty against the roar of the *fiesta*, whips, screams and shots. Heidi, situated in an intermediate theatrical space, seems moved by what surrounds her and opts for inebriation. It is the inebriation brought about not only by the alcohol of the festivity, but also by an excessive combination of vitality and death, of exuberance and the grotesque. The complicity becomes obvious between her figure, as a witness who reflects, and that of the musician don Genaro, the marimba master, as a witness who does not reflect, or reflects by fleeing into his music – or rather who, via his music, opens up a space of reflection or purification.

The witness is not free of punishment. At the end of the ritual, Heidi recognizes that 'the camera was not a good mask'. She adds: 'When I asked a well-known *matachín* why he had whipped me so much and so hard, me, who had come to celebrate my birthday party, he answered, "for being innocent. For being innocent". Innocence, like silence, is guilty. The representation does not close. Responsibility falls on the spectator.

What is most surprising about the ritual in Guapi is that the inhabitants voluntarily offer themselves to be whipped by the fake tormentors. Four hundred years ago, the Spanish monarchy authorized the trade in African slaves to the American colonies. This trade made unscrupulous slavers rich; thanks to the loss of freedom, forced labour and the death of thousands of persons denied their dignity, privileged Spaniards and other Europeans enjoyed a high standard of life and amassed riches. Today the scars of the whip once more bleed on the bodies of the descendants of those women and men subject to violence and inhumanity. Why do the great-great-grandchildren of those who were once freed continue to inflict on themselves a punishment that no one above them has decreed? Why add pain to poverty? Why must the dispossessed also be humiliated?

One could interpret that they unconsciously do this to avoid greater evils. This is the logic of the ritual sacrifice: the pain accepted during the ceremony serves to create a bountiful future and drive away evil. This principle was incorporated into Christianity, becoming the ideological core of asceticism as much as of the contemporary 'tragic sense of life'. But it also served to Christianize festive rituals of pain. What is unique about the Guapi ritual is that, in contrast to Christian or Muslim believers, the whipped persons are not penitents who inflict injury on themselves, but 'innocent' bodies who accept the pain inflicted by representatives of evil, without any guilt nor expecting any specific recompense. Do they believe that the performance will keep away the real presence of evil figures, who are no longer slaving colonists, but the guerrillas, the paramilitary and the assassins for powerful men, who far away from Guapi observe the world from so high above that they do not recognize other bodies different from theirs? Are the whippings meant to replace bullets, the wounds mutilation, the pain death? Or is the performance instead a symptom of dependence on the tormentors and of the fascination triggered by evil in the 'innocents'? An inhabitant tries to offer an ingenuous, but at the same time terrible, explanation: 'This is a tradition whose roots are lost in time. You have to be from here to understand it. You have to be from here to feel a certain pleasure in the pain.'

These words conclude the last piece of the triptych. *Los incontados* is at the same time a synthesis of the two previous pieces and an attempt on the part of Heidi and Rolf Abderhalden to offer a poetic response to the history of a country marked by violence. The roots of the evil can be traced back to Spanish colonization, but the recent origins have to be situated in the 1950s. The artists invite the audience to go back to an imaginary context that could be a childhood memory. The stage is even more cramped than in *Los santos inocentes*, but it seems the party has not yet begun: behind the glass that separates the audience from the stage house (a true box), a group of children await the beginning, equipped with musical instruments and a few coloured balloons. The scene reproduces a photograph by Jeff Wall titled *A Ventriloquist at a Birthday Party in October 1947* (1990), in which Mapa Teatro found the three components that triggered their work: the children's party, the middle-class living room and the ventriloquist.

Heidi Abderhalden, like a ghostly witness, walks around the reconstructed living room and activates the mechanism of memory: voices from the past sound from the radio, speaking of the different meaning that words have for the oligarchy and for the lower classes: 'violence', 'pressure groups', 'revolution', 'structural change', 'agrarian reform', 'political parties', 'social sensibility', 'the press'. The children do not understand the meaning of these words and remain mute; they likewise do not understand the story of the little bear recruited against its will. They simply await the signal to play their music as a 'marching band' and afterwards exit the stage. The children of the past, those whose memory Heidi mediates, must also not have understood those words. But the truth is that those years marked the beginning of contemporary violence in Colombia (Adelman 2002).

The stage is like a magic box, full of springs and surprises. When the girl opens the radio's lid voices sound from it, which cease when the lid is closed. A ventriloquist's dummy appears ready to speak. Yet what happens is that a curtain of smoke descends from the spotlight in the ceiling, from which a magician emerges. The magician-ventriloquist evokes the figure of 'Alejandro', a friend of the Abderhalden family, whom they knew as a 'family father' with an ordinary life, but behind which was concealed Hernando Pizarro Leongómez, leader of the ELN (Ejército de Liberación Nacional, [National Liberation Army], an insurgent organization with Marxist ideology and a pro-Cuban stance). He was responsible for a massacre committed in 1995, when he fell into a trap set by the Colombian intelligence service that made him suspect more than 160 comrades of betrayal. The disguising of the violent Hernando behind the peaceful figure of 'Alejandro' was one more of the multiple camouflages, concealments and ruses used during the years of violence by guerrillas, the military and the paramilitary. Ventriloquism was also one of them, a technique taught to young guerrillas to outwit possible spies from the enemy side.

The guerrilla fighter, disguised as a magician, performs his tricks before the children, who are oblivious to the double identity of who entertains them (and with whom they live together). He does not pull out a colourful handkerchief from his hat, however, but a red one with the hammer and sickle. A little while later a red record, protected by a cover with the face of Che, is turned into a blue record. By then the voice from the past has returned, mixed with noises and bursts of other broadcasts lost in time. Is it the dummy who is speaking? The ventriloquist? Ventriloquism is also a term used to question political leaders whose speeches repeat the dictates imposed by superior economic authorities or external powers. In this case, the addressee of the voice that emerges from the radio could be the girl who is still listening, or the other girl, now an adult, who returns as a ghost: 'Tell her not to make any noise. And to be disciplined. Tell her that if she is loyal, you will take her for a walk. To be firm before the enemy and not to move. Tell her that if she does not move they will leave as if by magic. And to be happy. Because the revolution is a *fiesta* . . . '.

The words retrieved from the smoke were spoken by Camilo Torres Restrepo (1929–66), a priest who was a pioneer of liberation theology and participated in the foundation of the Frente Unido del Pueblo (United Front of the People). This movement was a clear response to the abduction of democracy by the Frente Nacional (National Front), demanding solutions for the poverty and injustice in the countryside as well as in the cities. It joined the ELN founded shortly beforehand. Torres died in his first military action against the army in 1966. That same year the FARC (Fuerzas Armadas Revolucionarias de Colombia [Revolutionary Armed Forces of Colombia]) was founded, a movement with Marxist ideology and inspired by Che Guevara, led for years by Pedro Antonio Marín, *Tirofijo* (Sureshot). The *fiesta* had begun.

Camilo had promised the girl that if she did not move, the 'bad guys' would disappear as if by magic. The girl watches the magician's tricks attentively. Yet what is true is that Camilo died before the *fiesta* was over. During it many innocent people were gravely injured or lost their lives. This girl is fortunate: Julián Díaz, the 'famous actor', will take her away from the stage before the *fiesta* turns into a nightmare. Danilo Jiménez, in contrast, was not so lucky: he needed sixteen years to recover from an attack that ultimately took the life of his wife and that of some of his fellow members of the Marco Fidel Suárez band.

He was a victim of a new war, which exploded in the early 1970s when drug traffickers joined the games of power and money and the old oligarchs faced the competition of the narco-capitalists. Cocaine became a business alternative to an economy based on clan oligopolies dedicated to the production of coffee, chocolate, tobacco, beer and textiles (Hylton 2003).

The layers of memory continue to be peeled away. The curtains open and close, until a second stage space is revealed. In front of the microphone Heidi recuperates the memory of her trip to Guapi and fragments of the first piece are depicted on stage, but also on an ancient television monitor. The party of 2009 could also be the one from 1979, or that of 1989. The violence has changed names, but not in intensity. The bodies of the innocents have suffered the whippings with the same resignation or the same impotence.

Together with Heidi, the rapper Jeihhco, his torso naked, is ready to sing an apparently infinite list. While *Los santos inocentes* closed with a list of victims, this layer of *Los incontados* opens with a list of killers, named by their surnames, first names or nicknames. Among them, Carlos Castaño Gil, alias 'El Fantasma' (the Ghost) or 'El Pelado' (the Hairy One), a leader of the Autodefensas Unidas de Colombia, formed at the beginning of the 1980s to illegally fight against the guerrillas and who – like them – financed themselves through drug trafficking. Also named is his comrade 'HH', 'Hernán Hernández' or 'El mono Veloza' (the Monkey Veloza), the Herod of the Innocents in the Guapi festivity. A brother of 'El Fantasma' served as the liaison between 'El Fantasma' and the narco who shortly afterwards would become his enemy, Pablo Escobar, the 'boss of evil'.

23

The fascination of evil

Infamous criminals fascinate us. Some can even seduce us. It was the fascination of evil that impelled Hannah Arendt to travel to Tel Aviv and cover the trial of Eichmann. That Arendt discovered the 'banality' in her report does not imply that the evil carried out by human beings is banal nor that all criminals are as apparently contemptible as the elderly Nazi war criminal. Oppenheimer was in fact seduced by Anwar and his fantasies, which, although tasteless and even despicable, cannot be qualified as banal, since they manifest the trauma of the murderer.

Back in 1993, during the difficult years of violence in Colombia, Mapa Teatro first approached evil when it staged Heiner Müller's *The Horatian* with a group of prisoners from La Picota, one of Colombia's maximum security prisons. *The Horatian* raises a problem very similar to the one discussed above in relation to the ethics of the executioner: why is the executioner a murderer who is paid and the socially disadvantaged criminal a murderer who is condemned? In *The Horatian* the dilemma is even greater: between the heroism for those who kill for society's benefit and the death sentence as well as dishonour for those who kill for personal reasons. What ethics situates the act of killing on the side of good or on the side of evil? In 1993 Rolf and Heidi Abderhalden managed to have a group of 'evil men' leave the prison and pose this moral conflict before an audience in a Bogotá theatre, surrounded by police armed to the teeth.

The same year that Mapa Teatro took a group of dangerous criminals from prison for a few hours, Pablo Escobar was riddled by bullets while attempting to flee from his last hiding place in Medellín. Escobar was without a doubt a seductive criminal. He continues to be so after his death, to the extent that a television series on his life logged one of the highest audience ratings on Colombian television in recent years. The series' success, moreover, confirmed the popularity that the murderer still enjoys in broad sectors of the population in Antioquía. This is undoubtedly related to his expansive personality, but also to his humble origins, beneficent gestures, sporadic fights against the oligarchy and his status as a rebel able to stand up to the police, the army and the DEA (Drug Enforcement Administration). Escobar was one of the monsters spawned by the illegal trade in marijuana and cocaine between Colombia and the United States. He became one of the richest men in the world and was responsible for hundreds of attacks, kidnappings and murders. He flirted with political leftists, was a member of parliament and even imagined himself as the president of the republic. Out of spite he ordered the assassination of the presidential candidate running for Nuevo Liberalismo, Luis Carlos Galán, one of the most decisive of the many crimes he ordered against politicians, judges, prosecutors, members of the military and of the police. His war against the state, however, concealed a sordid collaboration with the powers that be, with those who could reap benefits from the death of a candidate who strove for the moral renovation of the institutions. The 'patrón del mal' (boss of evil) would not have existed without that power, whom he served as its armed wing and at the same time financed. The caricaturist Carlos María Gallego summed this up succinctly: 'How corrupt was the Colombian political class that it even corrupted Pablo Escobar?' (Salazar 2001: 210).

Discurso de un hombre decente is based on a possible text written by Pablo Escobar to be given on the occasion of his inauguration as president. It is not absurd to imagine that in a context of violence and corruption, when the distinctions between 'good' and 'bad' persons, business people and *mafiosi*, revolutionaries and drug traffickers were blurry, that Escobar dreamed of ascending to the presidency of the republic. The 'speech', written without the necessity of ceding the typewriter to the murderer, was 'recomposed' by Camilo Uribe, who in the programme appears as the 'logographer', purportedly drawing on fragments from several documents written by the drug baron.

The priorities of his governmental programme were derived from what constituted reality for him: armed forces, prisons, kidnappings, tools of repression. His measures, which included the integration of his henchmen in law enforcement agencies and the installation of electric chairs with integrated incinerators in all prisons, proposed the design of a blatantly authoritarian State focused on security. The most polemical point, nevertheless, was his promise to legalize the drug trade. Escobar's perspective – in Uribe's version – is that of a businessman transformed into a politician: legalization would eliminate benefits for the mafias, increase product quality, for which a 'certificate of origin' could be claimed, while the earnings generated by the sector would increase income – via taxes – for the State.

The idea is not without merit and numerous experts have promoted it. In fact, *Discurso de un hombre decente* begins with an interview with an expert on the advantages and risks of legalization. Agnes Brekke, in the role of the objectified female TV host (based on Pablo Escobar's lover, Virginia Vallejo), poses the questions in a type of preamble to the work. The scene simultaneously denounces the superficiality with which the media treat policies regarding the consumption and trade of narcotics, as well as confirming that the experts generally agree on the advantages of their legalization and regulation.

The possible speech serves to launch a poetic reflection on a sullied paradise, defiled first by the oligarchies, later by drug traffickers, paramilitary forces and corrupt politicians. The balloons and masks of *Los santos inocentes* give way to tropical vegetation, brilliant colours and games of projected transparent images. The scenographic exuberance could allude to the parties that Escobar organized in his Hacienda Nápoles, his 3000-hectare luxury retreat in Puerto Triunfo, a town in Antioquía province near Medellín. The imagining of Escobar, however, has been undertaken to eliminate the vulgarity: the work is not a homage to him, but to what he (as the tool of a more complex evil) destroyed.

The *fiesta* that envelopes the speech is a bitter one, stained by the thousands of lives cut short and by the rivers full of blood that nearly drowned the exuberance of a beautiful tropical city in the Colombian highlands. Life is not yet entirely life in Medellín. For this reason Mapa hides its actors behinds veils, covered in plants, immersed in the music straining to break through. Real life has to be protected and life is the life shared by humans, animals and plants, including the cocaine plant, that friendly and terrible hybrid played by Heidi, who renounces the word to be one with the *mata* (bush) (*la mata que mata* [the bush that kills]).

Mapa utilized Pablo Escobar to raise a debate on one of the nuclei of violence in Colombia as well as in other Latin American countries. Yet it avoids ceding the limelight to the criminal. Some photographs of him are shown, as well as a few fragments of film. His speech is presented via the projection of a microfilm that supposedly reproduces the notes found in the pocket of the shirt he wore the day he was gunned down by the police, with many words and phrases censured by the CIA before its hypothetical declassification. But no one represents Escobar in the work, he is denied the right of representation. One sees an animated body whose figure does not correspond with the very popular one of the narco. One hears, moreover, the voice of Jeihhco Caminante, who recites the text in a tone more apocalyptic than seductive. Jeihhco is the stage name of Jeison Castaño, a rapper who founded the hip-hop collective La Élite in 2002 'as a call for peace and non-violence' (La Élite 2011). Jeihhco's reading of Escobar's speech took place while his organization, made up of eighty-five artists and cultural managers and twenty-five DJ, rap, graffiti, Bboy and Bgirl groups, represented one of the most serious resistances to the legacy of violence left behind by Escobar, his associates and his armed enemies in the hills flanking the river Aburrá. Which does not mean that in the *barrios* of Medellín the rappers, mimes and artists, like many other young people, continue to die.

If Jeihhco represents a youth that does not let itself be fascinated by evil, Danilo Jiménez represents the survivors of the *fiesta*. He first appears alone, singing a cappella, and later with his entire band on a raised platform, surrounded by vegetation, which recalls the stages of the parties at the haciendas surrounded by tropical vegetation. Danilo and his band used to play for the drug barons and visited the Hacienda Nápoles several times. While Danilo sings, a LED board provides anecdotes from these parties, as well as reporting on the car bomb attack that he and his companions suffered near the La Macarena bullring. Shrapnel lodged in his skull obliged him to relearn how to read and write. Only ten years later was he able to sing again.

Danilo is one of the 'innocents' affected by the violence. An 'innocent' collaborator, because he did not turn down the drug barons' money. In contrast to young Jeihhco, old Danilo has one foot on each side of the invisible line that demarcates moral responsibility. Invisible lines similarly separate the territories controlled by each one of the gangs in the neighbourhoods. Crossing them is risky. As much as remaining neutral is.

The invisible lines that score the hills of Medellín are delineated by violent people. Who draws the invisible lines of morality? Danilo was an innocent collaborator. One could say the same of all those who worked for Escobar without wielding arms. Or of those who did business thanks to the violence. Who profited directly? Who made this possible? How could Escobar have imagined himself president without the thousands of millions he earned from selling cocaine in the United States and Europe? What would have happened to Escobar without the celebrity cocaine addicts, without the publicity of cocaine as something fun, something trendy, almost necessary for being where you have to be in the world of business, art, sports, culture? Even innocent Charlie Chaplin, as a projection reminds us almost at the end of the work, enjoyed the effects of the white gold from South America.

Escobar's death did not end drug trafficking, but it initiated a period when politicians tried to distance and differentiate themselves from drug traffickers. President Samper (1994–98), who had been accused of receiving support from the Cali cartel for his campaign, put himself at the service of the United States government and ordered the arrest of the drug traffickers who had contributed to the downfall of Escobar. Álvaro Uribe's ties with drug traffickers and paramilitary groups had been much stronger during his tenure as governor of Antioquia (1995–97). He was in charge of executing the Plan Colombia, which foresaw the extreme militarization of the conflict and brought tremendous benefits for the United States as well as for those who had opposed the peace process with the guerrillas: banana multinationals, oil companies, agro-industrialist business people, drug traffickers and paramilitary groups. The Plan Colombia proposed the fumigation of cocaine plantations with highly toxic products and the military harassment not only of the FARC and the drug traffickers, but also of peasants, many of them indigenous. The indiscriminate fumigation was denounced by the peasants of Guapi as one of the principal threats affecting them, as terrible as the armed violence. Once again the policies that favour governments and multinationals condemn the most vulnerable to exclusion.

What fault does the *mata* (bush) have? The bush is the role played by Heidi Abderhalden in *Discurso* and in the second part of *Los incontados*. This is a playful and dancing bush, half bird and half monkey. The growers brought it from Bolivia and Peru, where it had originally been cultivated. With the passing of years it became another inhabitant of Colombia. The bush is, without any doubt, the most innocent of all of the roles in this story. It does not at all resemble the malaria mosquito (presented in a documentary video during *Discurso*), which is more similar to the drug traffickers. The bush jumps back and forth, it puts itself at the service of the peasants, so that they can do whatever they want with it. A fumigator constantly pursues it, but the bush manages to escape and reproduce itself again and again.

The dependence of thousands of peasants in Bolivia, Peru and Colombia on growing coca leaves is not an indicator of their complicity with evil, nor of their desire to obtain great benefits, but of neoliberal policies, which applied to agriculture privilege the activities of large companies specialized in monocultures. The expansion of the cultivation of coca leaves was a strategy of survival for many peasants and displaced workers. The harassment of the peasants provoked in Bolivia the response of the coca farmers, who together with Aymara groups, miners and students organized themselves in a movement that took Evo Morales to the presidency in 2005. He was the first indigenous president of Bolivia. This meant the end not only of neoliberal policies, but also of a republican tradition according to which an inherent inequality existed between indigenous people and mestizos, with indigenous people believed to be incapable of governing the country (García Linera 2006: 79). Morales transformed the coca leaf into a symbol of his government and into an instrument of foreign policy. His was a postcolonial attempt to re-signify what during the 1990s had become, together with weapons of mass destruction and Islamic fundamentalism, one of the indicators of the new axis of evil, replacing communism. 'Drugs are the great enemy of humankind', repeated Reagan and Bush, echoed by Latin American leaders in whose territories the raw material was cultivated. The war on drugs launched in the countries that are their consumers not only rests on a tremendous hypocrisy, but is also obviously inefficient and counterproductive. Milton Friedman himself, the ideologist of neoliberalism, warned president George W. Bush at the end of the 1980s: 'You are not mistaken in the end you seek to achieve.

Your mistake is failing to recognize that the very measures you favour are a major source of the evils you deplore.' (Friedmann 1989).

In a country with development rates statistically superior to those of Bolivia, but run by a political and economic class loyal to the neoliberal dogma, Heidi Abderhalden's action invited a symbolic rebellion. Tropical and festive theatricality saw all of its postcolonial and critical potential summed up in the jumping of a bush with sunglasses.

24

The ethics of the witness

Mapa Teatro's artistic approach emerges from the necessity of understanding the violence pervading the politics as well as everyday life of Colombia. Their work examines the past, but also questions the current situation in its political and social complexity. In the same way that filmmakers employ theatricality in search of a truth that raw images cannot offer, Mapa Teatro uses the document, but with the certainty that documents by themselves are insufficient and that representation is necessary for achieving understanding. Although Mapa forsake dramatic theatre, and thus the notion of representation associated with it, the works that make up the triptych cannot be described as a new version of documentary theatre, since their efficacy as tools of truth resides to a large extent in the poetic impact they contain and wield. It is poetry that fulfils the function of vexing the audience, more than the documents about the violence, the direct political speeches or the presence of guests alien to the world of art or theatre. This is a poetry that works against the grain: against the reigning morality regarding the stories of memory, against what is socially agreed regarding drug consumption or against political correctness regarding the peace process. The poetic action is carried out from the position of the witness, the position that Heidi Abderhalden assumes in *Los santos inocentes* and retains in the following works, including when she changes into a dancing cocaine bush.

The ethics of the witness implies a certain distance in respect to sensitive material or real testimony, which refer to other lives and to a pain that cannot be shared. It is the same distance that Albertina Carri assumed in relation to her parents, since in spite of being very close to them she hardly knew them personally and did not share their struggle. The ethics of the witness implies respect for experiences and emotions that do not belong to those who observe or relate them, but it also implies the empathy necessary for feeling the suffering of the other. Acknowledgement of the difference of bodies is consistent with equality of rights, yet a recognition of alterity cannot serve as an excuse for watching from the sidelines. In Artaud's terms, these witness are 'interested' witnesses, they do not let themselves be deceived by the sirens of objectivity, they are not afraid to empathize, to take to the streets at the risk of being beaten nor to be accused of being biased. They are 'affected' witnesses, in a double sense, since the suffering that others underwent or undergo affects them as much as the energy of those who work for a change, affected too because the political and social reality they observe is their own reality, a reality that has conditioned their lives and their artistic careers.

Witnesses represent no one but themselves. They do not, however, avoid the responsibility of representation. Their ethical stance is similar to that of Carri, Mroué or Apichatpong: speaking about a near reality requires an effort to understand it, but does not confer the privilege of a dramatic nor an enunciative representation of the Other. In this artistic effort to comprehend, theatrical (or visual) representation is constructed with a maximum degree of artistic and ethical commitment. In such a representation, however, there is no space for representatives. Heidi does not represent anyone else than herself in her role as witness of the Guapi celebration, as a cocaine bush during the reconstruction of the speech or in the combination of both at the end of the *fiesta* in *Los incontados*. In fact, Heidi did actually travel to Guapi on the day of her birthday, and she depicts what she saw – though re-elaborated in a mode of poetic representation, in which impressions and emotions coexist with historical constructions and unexpected interferences. As a cocaine bush, she assumes the neutral function of the bush, in itself innocent as regards the process it is subject to, the violence it generates and the profit obtained from it by the drug traffickers, as well as the consequences that its derivatives can have in the bodies of unknown human beings. The neutrality of the bush does not imply the indifference of the witness, but it is the spectator who has to take sides, as the artists have done in selecting materials and deciding on the *mise en scène* that has produced the theatrical representation.

The ethics of the witness is realized in a constant making of decisions about the benefits of inaction and the necessity of intervention. Inaction here in fact means active listening, that is, the focusing of attention. Intervention does not intend to produce changes or manipulations, but rather to restore the complexity of experience in the sphere of representation, via the introduction of sensitive or documentary elements, even if these are not directly or literally related with what actually occurred. The labour of the witness requires self-restraint. Mroué resolved this by constructing himself as fiction, Carri by doubling herself with the aid of an actress, Apichatpong with the collaboration of anonymous narrators, non-professional actors or ghosts. Rolf and Heidi Abderhalden likewise employed fiction to superimpose the recent history of Colombia on their own biographical experience. In order for the superposition to be ethically tolerable, however, they had to give a voice to guests.

The guests are not 'the others', they do not take the stage as victims (although some of them might have that condition in other contexts) nor are they on stage as representatives of the perpetrators, since the actions of these persist in the traumatic memory produced by their acts and they themselves should not be represented, other than to reiterate or to confirm their condemnation. The guests comprise a complex 'us', a difficult 'us', an 'us' that strives to constitute itself as subject without naively ignoring alterity, but without letting itself be dissuaded by the caution arising from the acknowledgement of the heterogeneity of bodies and with it the impossibility of their aesthetic or dramatic representation.

Don Genaro, one of the marimba players in *Los santos inocentes*, does not represent the musicians, he is a musician; he does not represent the victims, he is an indirect victim of marginalization and violence; he does not represent the audience, he is a spectator himself, even if he watches the *fiesta* from the stage. Musician and spectator at the same time, simultaneously acting as himself and as a musician, he is at the same time an actor in the performance and a spectator of it. Don Genaro is active and passive, like Heidi, the witness-creator, like Rolf, the invisible creator-witness. Don Genaro does not represent, but he is also not a representative. Each individual has a story to tell. Each place has its own stories. For Don Genaro, telling a part of his story on the stage designed by Mapa Teatro brings him personal satisfaction, for no one listened to him when he tried to tell it in the village.

Similarly, Don Danilo, the singer in *Discurso*, does not represent any group; although one of the direct victims of the conflict, this condition does not transform him into their representative. On the other hand, he does represent a role: that of a musician in a band entertaining at public festivities or private parties. The fact that he can once again represent the role that he fulfilled before the attack is undoubtedly a personal achievement for him, one whose potency is transmitted to the audience when it reads – while simultaneously listening to his songs – the information regarding his story.

Don Genaro and don Danilo occupy their own space of performing within the interior of the theatrical apparatus: although it might coincide in time, their action never intermixes with that of the other actors. This is obvious in *Los santos inocentes*, where after the first scene the spaces of performance are clearly differentiated, for the musicians the peripheral space of the stage and for the actors the internal one of the festive box. But this also occurs in the following two works: though don Danilo might wander the same internal space in these works, one could say that his body occupies another dimension of representation, a dimension similar to that of the girl who remains on stage for many minutes, sitting on a chair, a witness to the *fiesta* in *Los incontados*.

The separation of the musicians and the girl are a sign of the care with which Mapa treats its guests: Heidi and the rest of the actors make sure that for them each performance constitutes a gain and not a sacrifice. The suffering has to remain on the other side, on that of everyday reality, or reserved, on the side of the representation, for those who voluntarily lend themselves to it out of ethical or artistic necessity.

The presence on stage of Don Genaro and Don Danilo had a precedent in the presence of other guests in previous works by Mapa Teatro, in particular the collaboration of Juana María Ramírez in *Testigo de las ruinas* (Witness to the Ruins, 2005). Like the musicians, Juana was asked only to be present to do what she knew best and had done for years in her home in Cartucho: prepare *arepas* [cornmeal rolls] and chocolate. When Mapa Teatro decided to create a stage work with the memory of the long process of the demolition of Cartucho, they asked her to put her body together with the projections in which her former neighbours were depicted virtually, as well as with the bodies of Rolf and Heidi, transformed into ghost witnesses. Their presence on stage expressed the artists' recognition of the unbreakable vitality of the neighbours who had worked with Mapa and had made possible an artistic project that accompanied the destruction of their homes. 'This woman's vitality, her final burst of laughter in the middle of the empty and lonely park, serve as brutal testimony to the survival force in human beings before the disaster produced by the paradoxes and arbitrariness of power' (Mapa Teatro 2005). Juana, Genaro and Danilo appear on stage not as witnesses, but as bodies whose very life offers testimony. This life requires care and it is care that dominates their relationship with the other actors who protect them.

Other guests do not need the same treatment, since they act more as collaborators than as bodies bearing witness. This is the case of the rapper Jeihhco or the 'famous actor' Julián Díaz.

Jeihhco recites the words supposedly written by Pablo Escobar, but he does not represent the drug baron dramatically; Jeihhco continues to be himself. In contrast to the musicians, however, he does represent a group, a function he took on when he founded La Élite. This is not something that arises from his participation in Mapa's work, as his representativity predates the theatrical representation. Symbolically and emotionally, the representation derives benefits from his representativity. Jeihhco has gone through a process of empowerment in a social milieu absolutely hostile for an enterprising young man. He has been able to occupy his place and, together with others, contribute with his music and art to the transformation of morality and of models of self-realization.

Julián Díaz, accustomed to dramatic representation in his habitual work as a television actor, abandons this mode to represent himself as a 'famous actor', but also as a 'successful Afro-Colombian'. His presence in *Los santos inocentes* serves to counter any temptation to see the celebration as an example of extreme alterity. In contrast to the witness-bearing bodies, Julián is a denouncing body, taking upon himself the cruelty of the representation: he accepts the white suit, the mask and the *matachín's* whip in order to satisfy the gaze seeking the tranquillity of the cliché, the cliché that pleasure in pain is something innate to blacks, to the grandchildren of slaves who bear their trauma. Against this cliché, Mapa reserves the final monologue of *Los incontados* for this masked *matachín*: Vladimir Mayakovsky's dream, as narrated by Antonio Tabucchi. In this dream, which in the Italian writer's imagination the Russian poet had every night during the last year of his life, Mayakovsky 'awakes' from the revolution with the obsession of washing his hands with a bar of soap, which reappears as a symptom in various moments of the story (Tabucchi 1999: 67).

Yet witnesses cannot be neutral. And poets cannot renounce creating verses. What witnesses and poets cannot be forgiven is that they continue washing their hands.

25

The apparatus of memory

Anatomía de la violencia en Colombia (Anatomy of Violence in Colombia) reveals itself as an apparatus of memory. Each one of the works makes up in itself an apparatus that functions by means of the aggregation of objects (whether physical or not), actors (whether professional or not) and information extracted from public archives. This becomes evident in the last of the works, *Los incontados*, where the space constructed by Mapa determines the composition of the work. This is a physical and aural space, in which the entrances and exits of the sound correspond to the opening and closing of the successive curtains, which in turn reveal diverse layers of reality and meaning. The outcome of this display, increasingly rapid, is a noisy polyphony of voices, gestures and images, which chaotically intersect in the interior of the machine: a personal celebration, a ritual celebration, the announcement of a revolution, the beginning of a party, the end of a party, the consequences of armed struggle, a possible speech, various real speeches, a questioning of drug consumption, a debate on drug traffic, the sound of the bands, that of the whips, of the bombs, of the bodies that have lost control of themselves. The great noise lies very close to the great silence. Just like the shedding of blood lies very close to soap.

Los incontados presents an apparatus of memory that returns a poetic and humorous reflection of Colombian society, transmitting to those outside the gaze of several witnesses affected by what they have experienced, what they have seen and what remains to be done. It is also an apparatus of internal memory, a memory of poetic construction itself. In the triptych, *Los incontados* fulfils a function similar to that of *Testigo de las ruinas* in regards to *Proyecto Prometeo*, but in this case not as an introspective epilogue, but as a comprehensive third part.

In effect, *Testigo de las ruinas* (Witness to the Ruins) was the final manifestation of a long process that had begun in 2001, when Mapa Teatro was commissioned to symbolically preserve the memory of the Santa Inés (El Cartucho) neighbourhood, then in the process of demolition. The commission came from the recently elected mayor of Bogotá, the charismatic Antanas Mokus, who could no longer prevent the disappearance of the neighbourhood and the construction of what would become the uninspired Parque del Milenio.

His desire was that at least some trace would be conserved of what life had been like in that neighbourhood for decades. The outcome was *Proyecto Prometeo* (Prometheus Project), which consisted of a labour of relation with the neighbourhood's residents, leading to numerous actions and audio-visual documents, as well as two public actions: *Prometeo* (Prometheus, 2002), a guided tour along Avenida Jiménez, and *Prometeo, segundo acto* (Prometheus, Second Act, 2003), an installation on the immense site of the neighbourhood, with the participation of some of the displaced residents.

Yet the process did not conclude with the presentation of the theatre spectacle, which Mapa called an 'install-action'. The materials were reused in successive works by the group: *Re-corridos* (Re-tours, 2003), an interactive installation in a house very similar to those torn down in the Santa Inés neighbourhood; *La limpieza de los establos de Augias* (Cleaning the Augean Stables, 2004), a video installation that contrasted the images of the past with those of the process of construction of the park occurring at that moment; and *Testigo de las ruinas* (2005), a theatrical video installation, in which the memory of the neighbourhood and of its destruction was presented as an act of resistance.

This series of works is a clear indication of Mapa's desire not to conclude a process whose nucleus is memory. It would be incoherent and ethically problematic to conceive a work on memory that ended in a theatre performance, in an installation or in a book. The very nature of the presentations indicated this direction: the presence of the neighbourhood's residents, not as actors, but as living memory; the use of sound as a medium for transmitting the past and the physical implication of the new witnesses that visited the installation (2003); the broadcasting in real time of the construction of the park (2004), a sign of the irreversibility of time, but also of the instability of recollection, of the impossibility of fixing the traces – and, consequently, the commitment to their permanent reactivation; the recognition that the memory of the process belongs not solely to those who lived in the neighbourhood and were displaced, but also to those who accompanied them as witnesses and remained physically marked by the experience of a shared time.

In a new version of this last work, Rolf and Heidi Abderhalden invited Antanas to participate in *Testigo de las ruinas: un archivo vivo* (Witness to the Ruins, A Living Archive, 2012). The politician, by this time retired, appears on stage seated on a sofa behind a translucent screen on which are projected the images shot in El Cartucho and the recordings of the artistic works produced by Mapa in the last ten years. He attentively listens to Rolf, at the front of the stage, who informs the audience of the circumstances and the process in an unclassifiable manner, something between a lecture, a recitation and a testimony. At one point in the work, Juana María Ramírez appears on stage and, before she begins to make *arepas*, sits down for a moment together with Antanas. Surprisingly, he invites her to dance. The shared bolero between the former mayor and one of the last inhabitants of El Cartucho rises to become a poignant moment within the framework of the work. As Carolina Ponce de León observes, the dance does not close the wounds, in the same way that the presentation of *Prometo, segundo acto* did not heal them. For this reason, the presentation is not a show, nor the deployment of an archive, but the event of a living archive, in which the artists (Rolf and Heidi Abderhalden), as much as the guests (Juana María Ramírez and Antanas Mokus), act as 'agents'. 'Each one of them represents a path of access; their memories and experiences – tangible as well as intangible – are an integral part of the archive' (Ponce de León 2018: 354).

The living archive challenges the closure of representation without negating theatrical representation as a means. The living refers to the performing of the 'actors' on stage, but also to the persistence of memory in the images, gestures, memories and ideas that currently condition their lives. As the Brazilian philosopher and curator Suely Rolnik notes, this is 'living memory' (Rolnik 2006).

Rolnik developed the concept of the 'living archive' while approaching the musealization of Lygia Clark's oeuvre. This artist had abandoned sculpture for non-objectual art in her decision – shared with many other artists of her generation – to resist the representation and objectification that made art profitable for the capitalist market. Nevertheless, she had become aware of the risks that artists faced when they opted for the 'living'. Clark completely abandoned artistic practice, believing there was no way of avoiding the capitalization or bureaucratization inherent to the art institution. Was the reactivation of her practice in a museum space thirty years later not a betrayal of a decision taken very consciously to evade 'the perverse effects of cultural capitalism'? Rolnik decided to assume this risk, implicitly sharing Susan Sontag's analysis, who in *The Aesthetics of Silence* affirmed that the abandonment of creative practice by writers and artists such as Rimbaud, Wittgenstein or Duchamp did not negate their previous work. 'On the contrary, it imparts retroactively … a certificate of unchallengeable seriousness', that of not considering art (or philosophy) 'as something whose seriousness last forever, an "end", a permanent vehicle for spiritual ambition' (Sontag 1969: 6).

The strategy chosen by Rolnik to reactivate Clark's practice, without objectifying or representing it, was orality.

> The idea was to produce a living record of the effects of the body constituted by Lygia in her exile from art, as they appeared in her cultural

and political environment both in Brazil and in France. The goal was to revive the memory of the potentials of these proposals, via an immersion in the sensations they brought forth in lived experience.

Rolnik 2006: 7

Rolnik was concerned, too, with producing the memory of the context marked by the dictatorship and by strategies of resistance at times mutually opposed, such as the guerrilla and counterculture movements, without reducing practice to a consequence, an illustration or an anecdote. For this it was necessary to carry out a labour of relation, to unblock the sensitive and intimate memory of the collaborators (witnesses-participants); this labour of relation was in itself an homage to Clark's own practice and a recognition of her legacy: 'it was a matter of producing a memory of the bodies that the experience of Lygia Clark's proposals had affected and where it was inscribed, to give it a chance of pulsating in the present' (Rolnik 2006: 7). The living archive was realized as a series of sixty-six filmed interviews, subsequently screened in diverse museums. Rolnik assumed the inherent contradictions of the project and justified in her text the return to the museum of an artist who had exiled herself from it. Her principal argument was based on the attempt to overcome the preservation of the 'actions' in the form of a 'dead archive', in order to restore the condition of 'living memories' to them and thus reinvigorate their effectiveness.

The use of orality as a strategy of restitution to circumvent representation has been employed in other artistic mediums and to many diverse ends. Claude Lanzmann avoided images and dramatic re-enactments in his monumental film *Shoah* (1985), dedicated to the memory of the Nazi Holocaust. In the field of theatre, Olga de Soto likewise resorted to orality to reconstruct the work *Le jeune homme et la mort*, a ballet by Jean Cocteau choreographed by Roland Petit, with Jean Babilée and Claire Sombert, and premiered at the Théâtre des Champs-Élysées in 1946, a few months after the end of the Second World War.

In the verbalized recollection the body is not supplanted, it is not represented, its singularity is not questioned nor subject to closed structuring principles. The voice of someone recounting, remembering and reconstructing is maintained in a singularity that, nevertheless, is not betrayed by its transition to an apparatus of restitution or memory. In their stories the artists are equally respected in their singularity, even if inside they function as characters.

Yet the voice and the story are not the only procedures for manifesting 'living memories'. Images too can resist representation and offer themselves as an exercise of corporeal memory. Even writing, or a certain type of writing.

And why not the body, in its gesture, its presence, its movement? It is not so much a question of substituting one medium for another, but rather of highlighting certain characteristics proper to orality: physical correspondence, the situation of listening, non-linearity, the openness to the reply and conversation etc.

Sontag noted long ago that many of the characteristics valued by McLuhan in orality were present in important writers of the twentieth century: 'Joyce, Stein, Gadda, Laura Riding, Beckett, and Burroughs' – to which could be added Cortázar, Perec, Bolaño or Goytisolo – 'employ a language whose norms and energies come from oral speech, with its circular repetitive movements and essentially first person voice' (Sontag 1969: 28). Michel de Certeau described the apparatus of writing as powerful tools of power, segregation and colonization; nevertheless, he distinguished the writing produced by society as 'text' from that of other forms of writing that are nothing more than the necessary mediations of the 'unproductive' voice (De Certeau 1980: 196). In his criticism of logocentrism Jacques Derrida contrasted the book as 'totality of the signifier' with writing as 'destructive irruption'.

The living archives of Mapa Teatro are inscribed in this anti-representational logic. They are theatrical representations that challenge any attempt towards the closure that can result in a mimetic, dramatic or political representation. The presence of the guests fulfils the function of avoiding the objectification of their testimony in a closed representation. Living bodies can always continue to resist – and to surprise. The presence of the witnesses-affected localizes the authorship physically, a shared but not irresponsible authorship, exposing the vulnerable nature of creation and memory. Living memory always depends on the memory of bodies. The enemies of memory are the same ones who attacked and continue to attack bodies.

The history of this book

The prehistory of this book stretches back to the spring of 2011. I was finishing up the last months of a visiting professorship at the University of Roehampton in London, when Yuyachkani invited me to participate in a conference on 'Memories and Representations', to be held in Lima in July to celebrate the fortieth anniversary of the founding of the theatre group. The question of 'representation' was not a part of my reflections at that time. In fact, I had dedicated my sabbatical year to a series of philosophical and literary readings, guided by the idea of 'in-transcendence' (see Chapter 27), to experiences related to research and creation, as well as to a series of miscellaneous studies and reflections that led me to launch a blog: *Parataxis 2.0*. Its title was drawn from another project I was immersed in at that time, the curating, together with Lara Khaldi, of the fifth edition of the Jerusalem Show, 'On/Off Language'.

In London I followed the news from Spain closely and enthusiastically. The mobilization of the citizenry initiated on 15 May in Madrid triggered a process of political transformation in which we are still immersed. It rekindled hope for those who had seen themselves stripped of rights and of a future by an economic crisis that 'no one saw coming', abandoned by representatives who lacked any type of response. At that time, the true dimensions of the corruption that the business and political oligarchy had set up for itself in Spain were not known. But enough was evident for productive political fictions to emerge such as 'we are the 99%', which were joined by other mobilizing slogans like 'NO, NO, NO, THEY DON'T REPRESENT US', 'THEY CALL IT DEMOCRACY, BUT IT ISN'T', 'REAL DEMOCRACY NOW', 'STOP EVICTIONS', 'TAKE OVER THE STREET'. Young people, and in general the populace of southern Europe, were experiencing first-hand what the people of Latin America had lived through in the previous decades, as a consequence of the corruption of their politicians and the application of the IMF's neoliberal recipes.

I travelled to Lima with a couple of texts, one in which I reflected in a somewhat confused manner on these questions and another one in which I presented some proposals on the relationship between representation and memory. They were very conditioned by a recent visit to Palestine and by some of the projects exhibited at the Jerusalem Show. At Yuyachkani's 'house' I met many of the artists who have stimulated the reflections contained in this book (Miguel Rubio and Teresa Ralli, Rolf Abderhalden, Héctor Bourges), as well as with some thinkers with whom I have shared interests and experiences, among them Ileana Diéguez and Silvana García.

While in Lima, I received another invitation, this time from the University of Antioquía (Colombia). The organizers of the II International Congress on Theatrical Studies, 'Indisposing the Stage', invited me to give another lecture. This was an opportunity to develop what until then had only remained roughly sketched out. The title proposed for this talk was 'The Ethics of Representation'.

When I returned to Madrid, what I found was not the occupation of the Puerta del Sol square, but the visit of Pope Ratzinger and an unbreathable atmosphere of jubilant cant. Fortunately, I was just passing through Madrid, only staying long enough to take a plane to Palestine. Those were intense months of learning and working, together with Lara, Jack Persekian, Jumana Emil Aboud, Isa Frej and many other professionals in the fields of culture, art and politics. With their practice and their thinking they resist, day after day, the genocidal occupation by the State of Israel.

Israeli colonialism seems from another epoch, but it is precisely for this reason that it exposes the inhumanity implicit in all colonialism. 'Inhuman' means regarding other human beings as inferior in rights; in Palestine this is embodied in the brutal reality of the wall. Its disproportion, in regards to the bodies of the men, women and children that it constrains, every day and effectively, is also a metaphor for the impotence of the individual who resists becoming less than human.

It was difficult to return to academic activity in Spain. The university was in the same depressed state as the rest of the country. The shock provoked by the debt crisis had awoken the middle classes and intellectuals from any kind of perverse neo-colonial dream. It pitted them against the crude reality of a new world order, governed by financial markets, big corporations and a select group of political representatives, organized in alliances hardly conceivable until then. The voracity of the market unleashed new types of internal colonialism, which in a kind of historical vengeance brought up to date the barbarism let loose by European colonialism 500 years before. It was replicated in Palestine, was rendered and is once again rendered into the negation of dignity, the trade in bodies and the appropriation by a few of rights theoretically assigned to all.

The crisis of representation and the growth of inequality, no longer regarded as defects of the system but as its agenda, demanded a political reaction. The crisis of humanism and the deterioration of human rights, transformed into a 'religion' that no one respects, demanded an ethical reaction. How were artistic practices that have traditionally worked with representation providing a response to these two imperatives?

'Ethics of Representation' was presented in lecture format at the University of Antioquia on 16 March 2021. There I met Ileana Diéguez again, as well as Emilio García Wehbi, Enrique Vargas and the professors of the Faculty of Arts Luzdary Alzate, Anamaría Tamayo Duque, Natalia Restrepo, Lina Villegas and Eduardo Sánchez, among others. The lecture offered a precise sketch of the discursive structure of the book, referring to the work of artists whose practice has been fundamental for its composition: Angélica Liddell, Rabih Mroué and Mapa Teatro. I had attended the presentation of *La casa de la fuerza* by Angélica Liddell at Matadero (Madrid) on 5 November 2009, and again at the Centro Párraga (Murcia) on the 29 of the same month in a chamber presentation during the International Seminar on New Dramaturgies. I was able to see Rabih Mroué's work *The Inhabitants of Images* on 9 October 2010 at Toynbee Studios (London), within the context of the project Performance Matters, coordinated by Adrian Heathfield and Lois Keidan, and again on 12 April 2013 at the Museo Reina Sofía in Madrid, during the seminar *No hay más poesía que la acción* (There is No More Poetry Than Action) organized by Artea. I travelled to Munich to see *Los santos inocentes*, on 29 November 2011 at the Carl Orff Saal / Gasteig, and subsequently to Berlin, to witness the performance of *Discurso de un hombre decente*, on 26 May 2012.

One of these trips produced a brief text, partially integrated into this book: 'Three Memories and an Anticipation'. The issue of representation in the sense of speaking for another is central to it. Together with the work of Mapa Teatro, in this text I recounted my visit to an exhibition of Doris Salcedo at the White Cube Gallery in London. A few months previously I had also been able to see the show *Miraculous Beginnings* (2010) by Walid Raad, several of whose performance lectures I had previously attended: 'The Loudest Muttering Is Over: Documents from The Atlas Group Archive', at MNCARS, Madrid (18 February 2009) and 'My Neck is Thinner Than a Hair: a History of the Car Bomb' at the Idans festival in Istanbul (22 May 2009). At that same festival I saw 'The Continuum: Beyond the Killing Fields' by Ong Keng Sen, a 'docu-performance' on which I wrote in the first version of 'Ethics of Representation' and more extensively in the second edition of *Prácticas de lo real* (Practising the Real).

The idea of making a second edition of *Prácticas de lo real* came from Rodolfo Obregón; it was realized thanks to the efforts of Jaime Chabaud and his publishing company Paso de Gato in Mexico. It was presented in Mexico in October 2012, at the same time as the massacre of Tlatelolco was being commemorated. Edwin Culp invited me to give a lecture on the same topic at the Universidad Iberoamericana, where a few months before a conflict broke out with the governor and future president Peña Nieto, which sparked the rise of the *YoSoy132* movement.

From Mexico I travelled to Porto Alegre, as Marta Isaacson had invited me to give a lecture at the VII Congress of ABRACE (Brazilian Association of Research and Post-Graduate Studies in Theatre Studies). In addition to meeting up with Brazilian colleagues working on similar issues, I met Tania Farias and some of the members of the group 'Ói nóis aquí traveiz', whose work I had seen many years ago. Some of the materials resulting from this encounter have been important for the elaboration of the final part of this book, although they had previously been incorporated into the third edition of *Prácticas de lo real,* published in English as *Practising the Real*, which I worked on during 2013 and which included a translation of 'Ethics of Representation' as an appendix.

During the last few years the issue of the real has intersected with a new questioning of 'theatricality'. *Teatralidades disidentes* (Dissident Theatricalities) is the title of a research project directed by a team composed of Victoria Pérez Royo, Fernando Quesada, Isis Saz, Esther Belvis, Idoia Zabaleta, Isabel de Naverán, Ana Harcha, María José Cifuentes and Ixiar Rozas. Other artists and thinkers, such as Jaime Vallaure and Rafael Lamata, Héctor Bourges, Tomás Aragay, Amalia Fernández, Santiago Alba Rico, Rolf Abderhalden, Anna Vujanović, Adrian Heathfield, Simon Bayly, Leire Vergara, Jordi Claramonte and Suely Rolnik have also collaborated in it. This book owes much to the work sessions that took place in that context and to the texts written for the publication *No hay más poesía que la acción* (There is No Poetry but Action), among them a text by Óscar Cornago on the *Desplazamiento del Palacio de la Moneda* (Moving of the Palacio de la Moneda), in which he introduces the category of the 'dispositif' or apparatus. I proposed a first engagement with 'the art of the dispositifs' in a lecture given at the Centro Dramático Nacional, on the invitation of José Luis Raymond, titled 'The Eloquent Image'.

The final writing of this book likewise owes much to the lectures and seminars I have imparted in recent years on 'the real' and on 'dissident theatricalities': in Bilbao (19 December 2012), Salamanca (14 May 2013), Santiago de Chile (7 July 2013), Buenos Aires (11 July 2013), Bogotá (20 August 2013), Madrid (17 May 2014) and Sao Paulo (1 September 2014). I would like to highlight the doctoral seminar I gave at the University of Chile, invited by Mauricio Barría, titled 'The Irruption of the Real', and express my gratitude to the instructors and students who participated in it and contributed ideas and references very productive for the ongoing research. Just as decisive was the conference in Bogotá, during the Master's Programme in Theatre and Live Arts, directed by Víctor Viviescas and Alejandro Jaramillo, and the seminar they organized, titled 'The Obscene / The Stage: What You See What You Do Not See'. In the course of this seminar I was able to have informal conversations with Rolf and Heidi Abderhalden, Alejandro Valencia, Bruno Tackels, Antonio Araújo, José Alejandro Restrepo, Adriana Urrea, Yoshiko Chuma and Héctor Bourges.

This book is traversed by a painful separation and a terrible absence. The emotional suffering was transformed into a physical one; for days I endured pains that only invasive chemical treatments could mitigate. Yet individual suffering is sterile if it is not activated as communication, if the mere event does not turn into an inscribed experience. That petty incident, being individual and forced, opened up a path of empathy and the possibility of approaching the pain that others had undergone as the result of active struggles for equality and justice, or of artistic decisions supporting those struggles.

Among the many activities that I could not realize in that time, I was sorry not to be able to attend – although I tried – the opening of Rabih Mroué's exhibition at the Centro de Arte 2 de Mayo (Madrid). I saw it weeks later and the impression it made on me was decisive for the new focus of this book. Then is when I wrote a brief note titled 'The Formal Gesture'. Another project in the same museum occupied me during the following weeks: the drafting of a text for the catalogue of the exhibition *Per/form. How to Do Things with[out] Words*, commissioned by Chantal Pontbriand (2014). In the contribution, 'Act, Realize, Manifest', I dealt with the problem of 'performativity' in a neoliberal society, offering several observations – partially integrated into this book – on the relationship between 'representation' and 'manifestation' and on laughter as a means of resistance.

Two other texts published in this last year contain references and critical proposals included here. The first is a contribution solicited by Teresa Calonje (2014) for her book *Collecting Live Art*, 'The Cabinet of Events', in which I advanced some ideas on the function of orality in relation to memory. The second is a very brief vision of the recent history of Latin America, which serves as an introduction to a book on the work of Rodrigo García edited by the Malta festival in Poznań (Poland). Some passages from 'Ameryka Lacinska: Historia Nieobiektywna' (originally published in Polish) have been reused here to contextualize the approaches by some of the Latin American artists dealt with in this book.

Rodrigo García, who was the invited curator at the Malta festival, saw how his own work *Gólgota Picnic* was censured due to the threats of an ultra-Catholic group. In Lima three years before, Yuyachkani's action at the Plaza de Armas square had met with the response of hundreds of candles, lit by Catholic believers after leaving a mass held by the bishop. There they had prayed for the health of the dictator Alberto Fujimori, responsible – with others – for crimes whose memory was commemorated by the groups called together by Yuyachkani. During the last few years, the Catholic church has regained power and influence in Spain, thanks to a government that includes leading members of the Opus Dei, sympathizers of the Legionnaires of Christ and leaders for whom the alliance with the Catholic hierarchy brings great moral and economic benefits. The old morality once more imposes itself on democracy, making ethical reflection unnecessary.

The resurgence of Catholic power and of conservative morality occurs parallel to the rise of radical Islam in the Arab world, but also in the marginal neighbourhoods of major European cities. The spectre of Islamism is used by European politicians (like those depicted by Santiago Sierra and Jorge Galindo as 'in charge') to revive a war of religions and with it a new fanaticism, falsely democratic and falsely Western. At the cost of renouncing the secular tradition of European Enlightenment, it is employed to justify a brutal cutback in liberties and rights, in the field of morality as much as in economics and political debate.

In Spain, cuts in social spending (in public health, pensions, aid to those dependent on state support) have been accompanied by cuts in civil and labour rights (increasing the precarity of the job market by promoting temporary and partial contracts, restrictions on the rights of demonstrations, rollback of the justice system with the introduction of new taxes, etc.). The education and cultural fields have also seen themselves dramatically affected these last years. The strongest attacks have been on public education: first on its primary and secondary levels, and subsequently on the university level. With the excuse of guaranteeing freedom, increased government funding has been designated to private schools that receive state aid – the majority belonging to religious organizations – to the detriment of state schools. In addition, the ethics and values course 'Education for Citizenship' has been eliminated, while religion classes have been incorporated into the official syllabus, with the alternative offering – what irony – of a course called 'Ethics'. Vocational training has been promoted, with the excuse of correcting the excess of overqualified labour, while the public university system is legally and economically demolished; at the same time – paradoxically – the business of private universities expands, many of them owed by denominational groups.

The cultural sector has also suffered the blows of austerity policies, in some cases literally harassed for political reasons, in others simply abandoned by decisions on priorities that rarely benefit cultural projects. Like in all fields, the weakest – in this case, artists – are the most affected. Nevertheless, initiatives are multiplying, some centres of artistic creation continue to modestly support production and research, while independent initiatives and groups preserve spaces for exhibition and debate open. Inscribed in such networks are the master's programme in Theatrical Practice and Visual Culture and the above-mentioned Dissident Theatricalities, both contexts that have offered me the possibility of sharing some of the ideas that have ultimately made their way into this book.

The writing of this text began in June 2014. My first intention was to compose a book out of the two lectures mentioned above. I imagine that rereading *Los detectives salvajes* (The Savage Detectives) and, above all, reading *2666* by Roberto Bolaño, foiled these plans. I finished reading it in Hamburg, without the faintest idea that the park where I strolled in those days was the same one in which the elder Archimboldi spoke with Alexander Fürst von Pückler while they enjoyed an ice cream, where Bolaño abandoned his character before Archimboldi took a flight to Mexico. It was undoubtedly one of the most intensive reading experiences of the last few years – so intense that a few times I almost missed the performances scheduled during the International Summer Festival at Kampnagel.

* * *

The first edition of this book was published in Mexico under the title of *Ética y representación* (Ethics and Representation) by Toma, Ediciones y Producciones Escénicas y Cinematográficas AC, through the publisher Paso de Gato, with the editorial coordination, proofreading and care of Leticia García Urriza under the direction of Jaime Chabaud. That edition consisted of forty-three chapters. A tragic coincidence, not sought out, with the number of students from the Escuela Normal de Ayotzinapa, disappeared in Iguala during the night of 26/27 September 2014. Two years later, as I write these pages, on 2 November 2016, the facts are still unclear. The Attorney General's Office tried to falsely close the investigation by placing responsibility for the death and the incineration of the bodies on the Guerreros Unidos group, restricting the political responsibility for the case to the local sphere and exempting the various police and army forces. The report by the Attorney General was invalidated by other reports, among them by the Interdisciplinary Group of Independent Experts, whose members included Alejandro Valencia, with whom I met on various occasions in Mexico and Bogotá.

The systemic corruption in the State of Mexico, the inefficiency, the indifference in the face of the lie and the cynicism of political representatives can explain why an essay on 'ethics and representation' was so well received there. It is true that this text did not specifically address those very serious problems, but it does speak to the unease, pain and anger of those affected by these problems and who fight to denounce them and propose solutions.

On 31 July 2015 the anthropologist, activist and advocate of human rights Nadia Vera was murdered in an apartment in Colonia Narvarte, Mexico City, very close to the place where I write these words. Similarly tortured and killed were the photojournalist Rubén Espinosa, a young factory worker, Yesenia Quiroz Alfaro, a Colombian model, Mile Virginia Martín, and the domestic worker Olivia Alejandra Negrete Avilés. Nadia Vera was twenty years younger than me. The sister of the choreographer Shantí Vera, she had collaborated in the production of an international festival of dance, 'Cuatro por Cuatro'; she was an affable person, loved by many of my friends in Mexico, Ecuador, Chile and Colombia. Nadia had made the governor of Veracruz, Javier Duarte, publicly responsible for what could happen to her, as a consequence of her actions denouncing the violence treacherously employed by the State against critical journalists. Once again the Attorney General falsely closed the case and cleared the PRI politician of any responsibility. Fifteen months later, the crime remains unsolved, although two weeks ago Duarte fled Mexico, with the complicity of his party and several powerful people.

The situation in Mexico, the destitution of Dilma Rousseff in Brazil, the social decomposition in Venezuela, the defeat of Bernie Sanders by Hillary Clinton, the failure of the referendum for the peace agreements in Bogotá and the inauguration of Mariano Rajoy in Spain (president of a party formally accused of illegal financing and whose ranks include dozens of corrupt politicians) have led me to question the focus of this book. Should one instead take a step back and propose the question in terms of public morality? Is it not urgent to put firm limits to the neoliberal depravation of political representatives, civil servants, corrupt business people, as well as of those who support them with their votes, their economic and media power?

Since I finished the book a year and a half ago I have given numerous seminars and lectures on the theme: between 24 and 30 April 2015 at the Universidad Iberoamericana in Mexico, invited by Professor Edwin Culp; afterwards, at the Centro de las Artes de San Luis Potosí and in the Casa de Cultura de Tlalpan (May 2015), at the Museu de Arte in Rio de Janeiro (August 2015), at Experimenta Sur (September 2015), at the University of Paris-Sorbonne (October 2015), at the MPECV in Madrid (November 2015), at the MITAV in Barranquilla (August 2016) and at ITESO in Guadalajara, by invitation of ENIAV (October 2016). I am grateful to all of the participants in those seminars for their contributions.

Being able to attend the performance of *Los incontados*, at Mapa Teatro's centre in Bogotá on 15, 17 and 19 March 2016, in the company of Suely

Rolnik, was decisive for me. There I also gave a lecture on 'Poetic Dispositifs'. The outcome of that experience was the text 'After *Los incontados*', with which I attempted to respond to the challenge levelled by Mapa Teatro at the end of their work, when the stage lights go down, the proscenium glass goes dark and responsibility is placed on the spectators. Those days in Bogotá provided me with access to some of the keys to this work, which I have integrated in this edition.

The topic of the 'dispositifs' was developed in successive lectures in Brussels, Los Angeles, Madrid and Puebla, although I have decided to not include those materials in this book, since they have generated or will generate independent texts. Parallel to this, on the invitation of Ruth Estévez, curator of Redcat (an artistic centre linked with CalArts, Los Angeles), I began research into the work *Palabras ajenas* (The Words of Others, 1967) by the Argentine artist León Ferrari. This work consists of a collage of texts of very diverse origin, with which Ferrari positioned himself against imperialist United States barbarism and against Christian religion, the latter serving as the moral and ideological foundation of 'Western civilization'. The work's monumentality is comparable with that of *2666* or *La casa de la fuerza*, responding to the same ethical demand: that of putting oneself on the side of those who suffer, of approaching the pain of others by means of immense efforts in the realization of the artistic task.

A few years after the publication of *Palabras ajenas,* imperialist barbarism attacked Argentina, with the help in this case of the Military Junta. As in so many other countries in Latin America, local military officers took charge of the dirty work, which US-Americans did not want to do any more after Vietnam. León Ferrari went into exile in Brazil, but his son Abel refused to leave Buenos Aires. He was 'disappeared' a few days after the coup. The bodies of others were no longer those of others. The words of others savagely hurt our bodies.

Following the suggestion of the editor of 'La uña rota', Carlos Rodríguez, the book's title was changed for its Spanish edition (Segovia, 2017). The idea arose during a meeting in Segovia on 12 October 2016. Both of us had forgotten that it was a holiday: Hispanic Day, the national day of Spain, a festival that unjustly celebrates the beginning of the colonization of the Americas. Was it because both of us refused to celebrate anything that we fixed our work meeting for that date, that instead of delighting in Castilian roasts we found refuge in the sophisticated friendliness of Syrian cuisine?

The Bodies of Others is a homage to León Ferrari and to all those who, after denouncing brutality and injustice, have suffered in their own flesh the vengeful sword that Jehovah wielded in ancient times, which was wielded by Spanish conquistadores in the name of Catholic kings and emperors, and is now wielded by the cynical and ignorant, oblivious to the life that unites us in its immanence, blinded by ambition, power, ideology, nostalgia for old transcendencies – or by the brutal project of that new transcendence called neoliberalism.

* * *

The English edition of this book closes a cycle of almost ten years. Following a suggestion from Giulia Palladini, professor at the University of Roehampton, I wrote to Joe Kelleher, director of its Department of Drama and Performance, who in 2010 accepted my application to spend a sabbatical year there.

The Preface to the English Edition here lays out some of the discursive axes that perhaps would have been more prominent if the book had been written today. The articulation of these new axes was possible thanks to numerous experiences, readings and encounters. Very significant for me was my participation as dramaturg and co-director, together with Ruth Estévez and Juan Ernesto Díaz, in the staging of León Ferrari's *Palabras ajenas,* which was presented in Los Angeles, in September 2017 and subsequently in Miami, Madrid, Bogotá and Mexico City. Working with Ferrari's text allowed me to specifically work on an ethics of distance, but it also permitted me to experience the pedagogic power of art (in the Brechtian sense of 'great pedagogy'): The power of the poetic material to politicize the very bodies of those who re-present it, something I reflected on in an article, written in collaboration with Ruth Estévez, published in the journal *Degres* (issue 177, 2019).

While working on *Palabras ajenas* the necessity arose of bringing the piece up to date, using appropriations and collages that would question our discursive and artistic urgencies. This is how the project *Torre de Babel* (Tower of Babel, Madrid 2018 and Mexico City 2019) arose, a laboratory of research and learning that concluded with the presentation of a performative choral lecture. Starting from the question, 'What are today's wars?', the participants brought together numerous new materials, current and historical, in order to reflect on the possibility of political art in the present-day context. The memory of political theatre, of documentary theatre, of the activist happening, intersected with the memory of fascism in Spain and Latin America, with news on repression, censorship, male violence, neo-slavery, child abuse and violence against migrants. One month before the presentation planned for Madrid we received the news of Marielle Franco's execution in Río de Janeiro. The next day Mame Mbaye died on a street in Madrid. These two deaths, the direct consequence of institutionalized racism and homophobia, brutally confronted us with the limits of representation. *Torre de Babel* ended with a long silence, our perplexed silence at not knowing how to respond to this brute expression of violence and evil. We decided to give voice to Marielle, reproducing her last speech at the Municipal Chamber in Río. Her re-presented body emitted an overpowering strength, a vital enthusiasm compatible with the intelligence and power necessary to face the political adversaries who interrupted and opposed her, but who were unable to repress either her words or her joy. They had to resort to bullets.

Palabras ajenas and *Torre de Babel* allowed me to rethink in practice some of the issues that in *The Bodies of Others* had been approached from observation, from accompanying or from theoretical reflection: the appropriation of others' testimonies or experiences from a place of representation, the ethics of care in contrast to the discourses of hate and the construction of an apparatus of collective enunciation.

The question of justice was necessarily present in this practical process, although it had already been formalized in a roundtable conference on 6 April 2017, in which I took part with Roger Bernat and Gabriel Yépez after the presentation of *Please Continue (Hamlet)* at the Museo del Chopo, as part of Ambulante, the festival of documentary cinema in Mexico. This same festival, which that year focused its programme on the theme of justice, screened the film *The Moscow Trials by* Milo Rau. This first talk was a subsequent expansion of a lecture titled 'They Have the Word: Notes on Theatricality and Justice', which I gave in different versions in Bogotá (2017), Madrid (2018) and Mexico (2019).

The preoccupation with the commitment of art to denouncing impunity, situating itself on the limits of autonomy, became manifest in the text 'The Limits of Fiction' (2018), which had its origin as a master class for the inauguration of the academic year at the UCLM in Cuenca (Spain) and was developed in subsequent lectures in Santiago de Chile and Cuenca (Ecuador).

Finally, working with different groups on the presentation of *Palabras ajenas* and *Torre de Babel* allowed me to elaborate with greater precision some notes on 'the power of fiction' (Mexico and Madrid 2019) and the concept of 'poetic bodies' (Lima, Istanbul and Madrid 2019). They revolved around the constitution of a collective subjectivity of enunciation and creation, in which a multiplicity of singularities worked together, based on shared emotions.

The pandemic interrupted various projects, among them the presentation of *Palabras ajenas* in its Portuguese version, at the Bienal de São Paulo, and a meeting with the artist Lukas Avendaño, whom I had invited to participate in a Congress on Arts and Diversity, to which Paul Preciado and Mujeres Creando – among many others – were also invited. I was supposed to have met with Lukas in Oaxaca in May, and he to have presented his performance in Murcia in November. In December the corpse of his brother Bruno was discovered. That meeting is still pending. And the demand for justice is still open. There are feelings that exceed what one can write in a book. My words reveal their inadequacy in the face of pain and of struggle. Yet I cannot abdicate the responsibility of writing. Not even now, in this forced solitude, confronted by the uncertainty that assaults us, moved by the indignation before so much unjustifiable evil; yet even so maintaining alive the desire for a society nourished by the potency of life and a political justice ultimately reconciled with ethics.

Madrid, 2015, 2016, 2017, 2020.

27

Without / End

These were the two words with which the 'cinemalchemist' José Val del Omar signalled the end of his films. Val de Omar, a restless inventor who during his life patented a great quantity of devices related with the recording and reproduction of images, sounds and even tactile sensations, believed that the only reason for all the 'technical efforts' should be a 'concern for man' (Val del Omar 2004: 10). A humanist ethics did indeed guide the entire technical and aesthetic adventure of the creator of *Tríptico elemental de España* (Elemental Triptych of Spain), whose ethics was an ethics of modesty. Val del Omar valued life, the time of life; if a director expects that the audience dedicates time from their lives to see a film, the director has to act responsibly and not make them waste their time. As a practice, film (like theatre) implies an experience of intersubjective enrichment. This distinguishes it from other forms of industrial cinema (or commercial theatre), in which the sole objective is economic benefits in exchange for entertainment. The industry's accounting does not apply to the films made by Val del Omar, but instead the 'mathematics of God': 'who gives the most ... has the most', one reads and hears in *Aguaespejo granadino* (Granada Water-Mirror, 1955). It is ethically unacceptable that a filmmaker conceives of their work as mere distraction, because in this case they are acting like a thief, someone who does not give, but who solely steals the time of others. In exchange for the attention, immobility and temporary silence of the audience, the director has the obligation of offering them the possibility of an intense experience. For this reason, Val del Omar, a magician of filming and a master at editing, regarded as most important in cinematographic art not the director's work, but the moment of reception. 'This cinema has to be a spectacle based on the concentration of spectators. A cinema that operates with the potency and pressure of the group. More than emotion, this cinema is commotion; today the adventurers and barkers of "haunted caves" are already disputing it' (109).

Val del Omar, in his modesty as a 'cinemalchemist', shared with Antonin Artaud the desire for a theatre that was realized as a 'kind of event' and 'that reunites us with life, instead of separating us from it' (Artaud 1973: 229). Artaud imagined a theatre of physical images, while Val del Omar dedicated a good part of his life to developing inventions that permitted the physical communication of film: diaphonic sound, tactile-vision, as well as other procedures for the physical stimulation of the spectator. Val del Omar sought commotion, Artaud hypnosis and trance.

Angélica Liddell is an heir to this position. The spectators, whom she challenges and insults as participants in a hypocritical and unjust society, paradoxically deserve a maximum of respect as human beings. For this reason, every evening she devotes herself to the realization of her works, encouraging her collaborators to practice this same devotion. Hers is a theatre of commotion and a theatre that can induce trance. In her last work, numerous sequences could be regarded as trance rituals: the long drum march, the singing of the Ukrainian trio, the flagellation of the men while they clean the floor ... In a certain manner, *You are My Destiny (Lo stupro de Lucrezia)* (The Rape of Lucrezia, 2014) is the inversion of *La casa de la fuerza* (2009). Whereas in the latter everything was pain and the necessity of care, *Lucrezia* teems with fury and celebration, vengeance and festivity. The production's dimensions permit the format to be expanded: the scenery represents the Ducal Palace of Venice, with two levels of action occupied by Liddell, dressed as a princess, three Ukrainian vocalists, ten children with capes and balloons, a woman-girl (the actress Lola Jiménez, who will eventually be Lucrezia), a splendid rapist-lover, an elderly woman in the body of a young man, a rooster and ten handsome men to be mistreated and cared for. Numerous elements refer to the previous work: the girl has been multiplied by ten, the champion 'strongman' has been replaced by ten young actors, the *mariachis* by three Ukrainian vocalists, the work of the women by that of the men, the flowers have multiplied, the car now descends from the gridiron with an enormous felt lion, replacing the little stuffed animals that covered the body of the strongman. There is continuity in the drama, in the personal drama of Angélica, but in the social drama too: the victims of Gaza and Ciudad Juárez have now been unconsciously joined by those from Syria, Ukraine and Ayotzinapa.

Lucrezia is the historical figure of a chaste and beautiful woman raped by a macho man blinded by jealousy, power and ambition. Lucrezia killed herself in front of her husband and father so that her body would remain as a permanent memory of the affront. Yet, why does a woman have to accept the destiny imposed on her by the dominant morality? Why does an offended woman have to live out her grief, instead of celebrating her freedom? Why does a violated woman have to accept death as the only option? What use is memory for a dead woman? One has to go on living. Angélica proposes appropriating the macho that raped her and transforming him into her lover, deciding to fall in love with him because he is the only man who has spoken to her of love and not of politics. Lucrezia rebels against her condition of victim, so that men cannot manipulate her for a vengeance that solely benefits them. Lucrezia rebels against those who seek to subjugate her for life with greater conviction than against he who raped her in a moment of anger. Why weep over the loss of chastity when that act of violence can be the catalyst for liberation?

Angélica Liddell abandons grieving and chooses celebration. This Lucrezia's revenge is not carried out by inflicting on the aggressor a pain proportional to that imposed on the victim, but by abandoning the logic that made the man a criminal and the woman a victim, while the rest of the actors appear as witnesses, without any ethical or political responsibility falling on them. By changing the logic, new responsibilities are revealed, but also new courses of action.

The abandonment of grieving, moreover, distances Angélica Liddell's work from the danger that Rancière warned about in 'The Ethical Turn of Aesthetics and Politics': that the aligning of art with ethical causes (in particular with issues of memory) disguised an effective abdication of political action. According to Rancière, such an abdication has been achieved following two models. The first derives from those artistic practices of the early twentieth century that aimed to take art to everyday life, thus contributing to a revolutionary society by means of a new aesthetic configuration of life (the festival model). The second model, which Rancière calls 'soft ethics', derives from the failure of these projects and their subsequent appropriation by the institutions: the goal is no longer to participate in a project of global transformation, but to contribute to improving conditions of life in local contexts (intervening, for example, in depressed social environments through architecture or art).

The ethical turn of aesthetics and politics can also be explained as the inversion of historical time as conceived by modernity. If emancipatory projects conceived of history as a lineal progression with a cut marked by the revolutionary process, the post-historical experience has situated us at a point on that same line, traversed by the cut of a revolution that could have been, but never was and remains irreversibly behind us. When this cut is no longer situated in the future, but in the past, 'the ethical option seems an option for endless mourning'.

> Breaking with today's ethical configuration, and returning the inventions of politics and art to their difference, entails rejecting the fantasy of their purity, giving back to these inventions their status as cuts that are always ambiguous, precarious, litigious. This necessarily entails divorcing them from every theology of time, from every thought of a primordial trauma or a salvation to come.
>
> Rancière 2004: 132

'Ambiguous, precarious, litigious' are three adjectives that can easily be applied to the artistic approaches of Lemebel, Mroué and Majdalanie, the Abderhaldens, Apichatpong or Carri, and very explicitly to the work of Bolaño or Liddell, in that declared tension of strength and vulnerability, lust and poetry, horror and beauty. In her last work, Angélica renounces mourning and opens up a space of freedom beyond death. What dies in *You are My Destiny* is an idea of love, burdened by Christianity and by romanticism, on which the model of 'hard ethics' rests, that of those who resist and cry, but have lost view of the horizon of transformation. Angélica is aware that the ethics of care can easily degrade into that model of the ethics of the lament.

In fact, *You are My Destiny* is performed as a prolonged lament, yet it is a lament that leads to celebration. It is not a question of recuperating the horizon, but the present, as the body of the raped Lucrezia continues to be a body ready for pleasure and for fighting. The goal is to transform pain into life, impotence into anger, failure into power. At the end, after the first applause, the actresses that were princesses, the young boy who was an elderly lady and the men who during the second part were dressed as mourners, take off their masks and join the festivity. The bodies dance, laugh, some naked, others masked, while Angélica once more offers free sex (as she related in *La casa de la fuerza*), this time symbolically in front of the audience. Sex can no longer be a motivation for being condemned to death, not even for becoming a victim for life, because romantic love has been dispensed with, a love that sustained the narrative of fidelity and private property, bestowing on men the right of exclusive enjoyment of their property acquired in accordance with the prevailing law.

The inversion of the discourse does not suspend representation; on the contrary, it exacerbates it. Occasionally one could imagine that Angélica parodies herself; the sacrificial figure that emerges in *La casa de la fuerza* is transformed into a grotesque body, irate and full of vitality. Angélica frees herself of physical suffering on stage: now it is the men who shoulder the pain. Exposed in their fragility, Angélica submits them to long sequences that take them to the limits of physical endurance. There are no tricks in these scenes, they do not pretend to suffer, they actually suffer. The tortures, however, are not endless, they are part of the game, because they are part of the performance. This is a theatre that is nourished with real emotions, with real experiences, and that is realized with real actions, but which does not forgo representation.

The last scene does not contradict the show. The liberation of the masks does not cancel representation. The final affirmation of the bodies is part of the performance. For only in representation is the actress-dramaturg able to achieve that unity of mystery and of the sacred that belongs to a maximum intensity of life. It is the distance (which Angélica here calls 'sacred') that guarantees the symbolic impact of the performance. As well as its political impact.

* * *

Perhaps this is a good spot to cease the commentary and to try to summarize what I have learned with this book. A résumé that will obviously not coincide with what each reader may make, based on the reflections or ideas these pages may have triggered, and whose complexity or intensity cannot be retrieved in a few pages.

First of all, I have confirmed a hypothesis: representation is ethically tolerable when it is conceived within a framework of an in-transcendent paradigm. In-transcendence results from comprehending transcendence as a power of expansion or duration that does not require the postulation of a metaphysical dimension, but is possible thanks to empathy, fiction, commitment, imagination or memory. It is a transcendence that strives to recuperate the experience of the mysterious and of the sacred, but that takes place in an immanent dimension: in a space that opens up between living beings without them renouncing their organic materiality. In-transcendent representations are of necessity temporal, ephemeral and always in flux. This can be said of aesthetic representation (whether mimetic or theatrical) as much as of political representation.

Theatrical representation, as a temporal apparatus of symbolic construction and as a generator of community, can continue to function as a metaphor of the transitory modes of representation operating in the fields of knowledge, aesthetics and politics. The ethics of theatrical representation is sustained on several axes of tension: repetition-singularity, reality-fiction, distance-involvement, corporality-simulation. Different artists give precedence to one or another of these axes in their work.

The in-transcendence of representation is that of the body itself. The body inhabits a specific place and lives in the present – those are its limits. For this reason, there is no place for inherited representations (those that live on after death), not even for those representations not affected by transformations of the body. There is no place either for representations of those who inhabit other places that the body itself is ignorant of. Nevertheless, the limits are permeable, since empathy, imagination and fiction – with the collaboration of telematic communication media – permit the transcendence of the body and strengthen the effective instrumentality of ghosts. In one way or another, the ethics of the body requires involvement in a place or in a time, or the construction of a delayed or shifted presence that verifies and encourages involvement.

Presence and representation are not incompatible concepts. The body that represents can be a body that is present and in presence; consequently, immediacy without representation does not guarantee involvement in a given situation. Presence and representation can be synonymous terms, as Derrida reminds us, citing Bergson. This is not a terminological nor a conceptual question, but an ethical one. The presence contained in representation is manifested in the gesture that accompanies the body (and the ghost) when it commits, risks, dedicates itself to a shared situation. Aesthetic representation can be opposed to care and action, but theatrical representation and political representation do not necessarily exclude them.

The repetition inherent in theatrical representation can be a tool to construct meaning and community. In-transcendent repetition recuperates the cyclical structures of rituals, which in turn imitate those of natural cycles, in order to generate temporary communities. These communities are in-transcendent because they are temporary, but sustain themselves in connections that cannot be explained solely by immediacy and presence. The singularity of the individual is not threatened by its integration or participation in repetition, when it is conceived by the individual – and those with whom the individual shares the situation – as a tool for communicating and for constructing community, whether aesthetic or political. The singularity of the emotion or of the discourse are likewise not degraded, as long as (and only as long as) the repetition functions as an instrument for activating that which triggers emotion or that which the discourse addresses. Repetition is the nucleus of physical and linguistic games, by means of which new aesthetic and political subjects are constructed.

The in-transcendence of representation requires sharing with those who at each moment are spectators the techniques of construction of these modes of transitory transcendence occurring in empathy, imagination or in play. To this end one resorts to irony, manifested in the modes of fiction and meta-theatricality. Meta-discursivity occurs in the modes of theatre within theatre, film within film, literature within literature, but also in the exaggeration of theatricality as histrionics, in the self-referentiality of images and audio-visual sequences or in the multiplication of narrative puns until any linearity or transparency is suspended.

The irony revealed in the in-transcendence of representation can similarly occur in the superimposition of fiction and reality. If representations are temporal or in-transcendent, the montage of fiction and reality alerts us to the pretensions of fixation or of immutable truth. This does not imply equating reality and simulacrum, but warning us of the ease with which representations of reality can be manipulated, in order to replace them with fantasies that discharge the viewer of any responsibility and make involvement impossible.

Humour is the most direct means of relativizing what is allegedly immutable. Humour relativizes the subject, relativizes the discourse, critically alerts us to dogmatic pretensions. It opens communication with others, even in those situations in which imminent violence or traumatic pain seemingly hinder any possibility of play.

The disproportion in the struggle between individuals and machines of representation leads to the construction of an apparatus or counter-apparatus. The apparatus shatters the logic of representation, not because it puts an end to representation, but because it situates the action in a moment before or after the performance. The apparatus allows bodies to participate in the repetition and in the game without abandoning their singularity, on the condition that those same bodies have – or had – the capacity of knowing how the apparatus functions or can profane them at any moment.

To play, one has to be free. Play can only occur in a situation of shared freedom. Representation cannot be contrary to freedom. And freedom makes no sense if it is not for keeping the game active. The possibility of play has to be defended politically, by means of action, since the ludic is inseparable from freedom, a precondition for the ethical relationship. Ethics is not a substitute for political action, but both are inalienable in the constitution of a game that can also stage disagreements. Play takes place in modes of conversation, in cooperation, dance, struggle, memory, performance, action. Emotion depends on the intelligence of the players. Emotion and intelligence can be synonymous in a situation of play, just as much as presence and representation. The in-transcendent game is that played by bodies that involve themselves in it. Representation is one of the possible tools of play and involvement.

References

Adelman, Jeremy (2002), 'Andrean Impasses', *The New Left Review*, 18: 41–72.
Aeschylus (1926), *The Eumenides*, trans. Herbert Weir Smyth, Cambridge (MA): Harvard University Press.
Agamben, Giorgio (1978), *Infanzia e storia*, Turin: Einaudi 2001.
Agamben, Giorgio (1990), *La comunità che viene*, Turin: Bollati Boringhieri 2001.
Alba Rico, Santiago (2007), *Capitalismo y nihilismo*, Madrid: Akal.
Alexievich, Svetlana (1997), *Voices from Chernobyl*, Normal/London: Dalkey Archive Press, 2005.
Amnistía Internacional (2003), *Muertes intolerables. 10 años de desapariciones y asesinatos de mujeres en Ciudad Juarez y Chihuahua*, Madrid: Amnesty International Publications.
Arendt, Hannah (1958), *The Human Condition*, Chicago: University of Chicago Press.
Artaud, Antonin (1973), 'Théâtre Alfred Jarry', in *Œuvres complètes*, 2: 229–30, Paris: Gallimard.
Artaud, Antonin (1976a), 'Fragments of a Diary from Hell' in *Selected Writings*, ed. and with an introduction by Susan Sontag, trans. Helen Weaver, 91–6, New York: Farrar, Straus and Giroux.
Artaud, Antonin (1976b), 'Van Gogh, the Man Suicided by Society', in *Selected Writings*, ed. and with an introduction by Susan Sontag, trans. Helen Weaver, 483–512, New York: Farrar, Straus and Giroux.
Artaud, Antonin (2004), 'Pour en finir avec les jugement de Dieu', in *Œuvres complètes*, 13: 1639–63, Paris: Gallimard.
Avendaño, Lukas (2020), 'Gratia plena': https://www.facebook.com/lukas.avendano.39/posts/10221569862027880 [27 December 2020]
Badiou, Alain (1993), *Ethics. An Essay on the Understanding of Evil*, trans. Peter Hallward, London: Verso 2001.
Bakhtin, Mikhail (1924), *Toward a Philosophy of the Act*, trans. Vadim Liapunov, ed. by Vadim Liapunov and Michael Holquist, Austin, TX: University of Texas Press 1993
Bakhtin, Mikhail (1941), *Rabelais and His World*, trans. Helene Iswolksy, Bloomington, IN: University of Indiana Press 1984.
Bazin, André (1971), *Jean Renoir. Períodos, filmes y documentos*, Barcelona: Paidós, 1999.
Belting, Hans (2001), *Antropología de la imagen*, Madrid: Katz 2007.
Benjamin, Walter (1936), 'The Storyteller. Reflections on the Works of Nikolai Leskov', reprinted in *Illuminations*, trans. Harry Zohn, 83–110, New York: Harcourt Brace Jovanovich 1968.

Bernstein, Anya (2014) 'Caution, Religion! Iconoclasm, Secularism, and Ways of Seeing in Post-Soviet Art Wars', *Public Culture*, 26 (3): 419–48.
Bolaño, Roberto (2001), *Putas asesinas*, Anagrama, Barcelona.
Bolaño, Roberto (2004a) *2666*, trans. Natasha Wimmer, London: Picador 2009.
Bolaño, Roberto (2004b), *Entre paréntesis*, Barcelona: Anagrama, 2012.
Butler, Judith (2004), *Precarious Life. The Powers of Mourning and Violence*, London/New York: Verso 2006.
Butler, Judith (2020), 'Los poderes de la memoria en las pequeñas cosas', online lecture Museo Reina Sofía, 8 October 2020: https://www.museoreinasofia.es/actividades/judith-butler [accessed: 23 July 2021].
Cavarero, Adriana (2013), *Inclinations. A Critique of Rectitude*, trans. Amanda Minervini and Adam Sitze, Stanford, CA: Stanford University Press 2016.
CIDH (Corte Interamericana de Derechos Humanos) (2009), *Caso González y otra ("Campo Algodonero") vs. México*: https://corteidh.or.cr/docs/casos/articulos/seriec_205_esp.pdf [accessed 28 August 2021].
Cixous, Hélène (1994a), *La Ville Parjure: ou Le Réveil des Erynies*, Théâtre du Soleil, Kindle edition, pos. 3321.
Cixous, Hélène (1994b), 'Le Coup', in Théâtre du Soleil, *La ville parjure ou La reveille des Erynies* (theatre programme).
Clark, Lygia (1971), 'L'homme structure vivante d'une architecture biologique et celulaire', in *Lygia Clark, da obra ao acontecimento*, São Paulo: Pinacoteca del Estado 2006.
CONADEP (1984), *Nunca más. Informe de la Comisión Nacional sobre la desaparición de Personas Físicas.* http://www.desaparecidos.org/arg/conadep/nuncamas/7.html.
Crimp, Douglas (1989), 'Duelo y militancia', in *Posiciones críticas. Ensayos sobre las políticas de arte y la identidad*, 99–113, Madrid: Akal 2005.
Crimp, Douglas (1994), 'Representaciones no moralizantes del SIDA', in *Posiciones críticas. Ensayos sobre las políticas de arte y la identidad*, 122–36, Madrid: Akal 2005.
Damasio, Antonio (1994), *El error de Descartes*, Barcelona: Crítica 2010.
De Certeau, Michel (1980), *L'invention du quotidien 1*, Paris: Gallimard.
Derrida, Jacques (1989), 'Envoi' in *Psyche. Inventions of the Other*, ed. Peggy Kamug and Elizabeth Rottenberg, 94–128, Stanford, CA: Stanford University Press 2007.
De Soto, Olga (2010), 'historia(s)', in Isabel de Naverán (ed.), *Hacer historia*, 125–34, Barcelona: Mercat de les Flors, Institut del Teatre.
Didi-Huberman, Georges (2002), *La imagen superviviente*, Madrid: Abada.
Didi-Huberman, Georges (2008), *Cuando las imágenes toman posición*, Madrid: Antonio Machado Libros / Círculo de Bellas Artes, 2013.
Echeverría, Bolívar (1998), *La modernidad del barroco*, Mexico City: Era.
Echeverría, Bolívar (2011), *Discurso crítico y modernidad*, Mexico City: Ediciones desde abajo.
Expósito, Marcelo, Jaime Vindel and Ana Vidal (2012), 'El activismo artístico', in *Perder la forma humana*, Madrid: Museo Reina Sofía.

Foucault, Michel (1975), *Surveiller et punir. Naissance de la prison*, Paris: Gallimard.
Friedman, Milton (1989), 'An Open Letter To Bill Bennett', *The Wall Street Journal*, 7 September 1989.
García Linera, Álvaro (2006), 'State Crisis and Popular Power', *New Left Review*, 37: 73–85.
Gielen, Pascal (2009), *The Murmuring of the Artistic Multitude*, Amsterdam: Antennae Valiz.
Gilligan, Carol (1982), *In a Different Voice. Psychological Theory and Women's Development*, Cambridge MA and London: Harvard University Press.
Goffman, Erving (1959), *The Presentation of Self in Everyday Life*, New York: Doubleday.
Gorini, Ulises (2006), *La rebelión de las madres*, Buenos Aires: Norma.
Haffner, Pierre (1996), 'Les Avis de cinq cineastes d'Afrique noire', *CinémAction*, 81: 89–103.
Heller, Agnes (1987), *Beyond Justice*, Oxford: Basil Blackwell.
Hylton, Forrest (2003), 'An Evil Hour. Uribe's Colombia in Historical Perspective', *New Left Review*, 23: 51–93.
La Élite, *Red de Hip Hoppers Elite* (2011): http://reddehiphopperselite.blogspot.com.es/ [accessed 31 July 2012].
Lévinas, Emmanuel (1961), *Totality and Infinity. An Essay on Exteriority*, trans. Alphonso Lingis, Pittsburgh: Duquesne University Press, 1969.
Liddell, Angélica (2008), 'El sobrino de Rameau visita las cuevas rupestres', in *Perro muerto en tintorería*, Madrid: Nórdica Libros.
Liddell, Angélica (2009a), *La casa de la fuerza*, http://archivoartea.uclm.es/obras/la-casa-de-la-fuerza/ [accessed 26 July 2012].
Liddell, Angélica (2009b), *La casa de la fuerza*, Segovia: La Uña Rota, 2011.
Liddell, Angélica (2014), 'Conferencia Wittgenstein', in *El sacrificio como acto poético*, 61–2, Madrid: Con tinta me tienes, 2014.
Maakaron, Samar (2008), 'Looking for a Missing Employee in Shizuoka, Japan & Live from Beirut', https://www.khtt.net/en/page/5985/looking-for-a-missing-employee-in-shizuoka-japan-live-from-beirut [accessed 31 July 2021].
Mapa Teatro (2005), 'Testigo de las ruinas', http://archivoartea.uclm.es/obras/testigo-de-las-ruinas/ [accessed 17 August 2021].
Mroué, Rabih (2013), *Fabrications. Image(es), mon amour*, ed. Aurora Fernández Polanco, Madrid: CA2M.
Noriega, Gustavo (2009), *Estudio crítico sobre 'Los rubios'*, Buenos Aires: Picnic.
Pavlovsky, Eduardo (2001), *La ética del cuerpo*, Buenos Aires: Atuel.
Pegna Herçog, Alex (2020), 'En nome de Deus. Primeiro ano de governo Bolsonaro é marcado por ataques à cultura', 19 January 2020, in https://diplomatique.org.br/primeiro-ano-de-governo-bolsonaro-e-marcado-por-ataques-a-cultura/ [accessed: 12 December 2020]
Phelan, Peggy (1993), *Unmarked. The Politics of Performance*, London and New York: Routledge.

Ponce de León, Carolina (2018), 'La Ceremonia Secreta', in Marta Rodríguez (ed.), *Mapa Teatro. El escenario expandido*, 343–59, Bogotá: Universidad Nacional de Colombia.
Pontbriand, Chantal (ed.) (2014), *Per/Form: How to Do Things With[Out] Words*, Madrid and Berlín: CA2M / Sternberg Press.
Rancière, Jacques (2004), *Aesthetics and Its Discontents*, trans. Steve Corcoran, Cambridge: Polity Press, 2009
Ricoeur, Paul (1983), *Time and Narrative*, vol. 1, trans. Kathleen McLaughlin and David Pellauer, Chicago / London: University of Chicago Press 1984.
Rivera Garza, Cristina (2015), *Dolerse. Textos desde un país herido*, Mexico City: Surplus; translated by Sarah Booker as *Grieving. Dispatches from a Wounded Country*, New York: The Feminist Press 2020.
Rolnik, Suely (2006), 'The Body's Contagious Memory. Lygia Clark's Return to the Museum', http:// transform.eipcp.net/transversal/0507/rolnik/en/print#_ftn5> [accessed 30 July 2021].
Rolnik, Suely (2018), 'Mapa Teatro: Creating from an Affect', in *Of Lunatics, or those Lacking Sanity*, 19–24, Madrid: MNCARS.
Rolnik, Suely (2019), *Esferas de la insurrección. Apuntes para descolonizar el inconsciente*, Buenos Aires: Tinta Limón.
Rubio Zapata, Miguel (2006), *El cuerpo ausente*, Lima: Grupo cultural Yuyachkani.
Salazar J., Alonso (2001), *La parábola de Pablo*, Bogotá: Planeta.
Sánchez, José A. (2014), *Practising the Real on the Contemporary Stage*, Bristol and Washington: Intellect.
Sánchez, José A. (2019), 'Presence and Disappearance', *Performance Research*, 24:7: 6–15.
Scott, James (1990), *Domination and the Arts of Resistance. Hidden Transcripts*, New Haven, CT / London: Yale University Press.
Sennett, Richard (1976), *The Fall of Public Man*, London: Penguin Books, 2002.
Shattuck, Roger (1996), *Forbidden Knowledge. From Prometheus To Pornography*, New York: St Martin's Press.
Sontag, Susan (1969), 'Aesthetic of silence' in *Styles of Radical Will*, New York: Farrar, Straus and Giroux.
Sontag, Susan (1993), 'El siglo XXI comienza con el sitio de Sarajevo (entrevista con Alfonso Armada)', *El País*, 25 July 1993.
Sontag, Susan (2003), *Regarding the Pain of Others*, New York: Picador.
Sousa Santos, Boaventura de (2010), *Descolonizar el saber, reinventar el poder*. Montevideo: Trilce.
Spivak, Gayatri Chakravorty (1988), 'Can the Subaltern Speak?', in *Marxism and the Interpretation of Culture*, C. Nelson and L. Grossberg (eds), 271–313. Basingstoke: Macmillan Education.
Spivak, Gayatri Chakravorty (2013), *An Aesthetic Education in the Era of Globalization*, Cambridge MA/London: Harvard University Press.
Tabucchi, Antonio (1999), *Dreams of Dreams and The Last Three Days of Fernando Pessoa*, trans. Nancy J. Peters, San Francisco: City Lights.

Todorov, Tzvetan (2009), *Vivir solos juntos*, Barcelona: Galaxia Gutenberg, 2011.
Val del Omar, José (2011), *Desbordamiento*, Granada: Centro José Guerrero.
Van Gogh, Vincent (2014), *Vincent van Gogh. The Letters,* ed. Leo Jansen, Hans Luijten and Nienke Bakker, Amsterdam & The Hague: Van Gogh Museum & Huygens ING, Letter to Theo van Gogh, 13 April 1885, http://vangoghletters.org/vg/letters/let493/letter.html [accessed 27 July 2021].
Vergès, Jacques (1968), *Estrategia judicial en los procesos políticos*, Barcelona: Anagrama 2009.
Warr, Tracy, (ed.) (2000), *The Artist's Body; survey by Amelia Jones*, London: Phaidon.
Weerasethakul, Apichatpong (2013), *The Memory of Nabua.* A Note 011 tlle [sic] Primitive Project, https://www.1fmediaproject.net/2013/03/07/apichatpong-weerasethakul-primitive-fondazione-hangarbicocca-milan/ [accessed 27 July 2021].

Index

Abderhalden, Heidi xxx, 143, 145, 158
  see also Mapa Teatro
Abderhalden, Rolf xxx, 143
  see also Mapa Teatro
absence, stage xxix, 12–13, 99–104, 105, 110–11, 119
ACT UP (AIDS Coalition To Unleash Power) xv, xvii
activism (artistic) 59–60
Aeschylus, *The Eumenides* xx–xxi
Agamben, Giorgio, *La comunità che viene* 7
AIDS activism in the 1980s xv–xvi
al-Atassi, Mohamed
  Ibn al 'Amm 105–6
  Ibn al 'Amm online 106, 108
al-Atassi, Nureddin 108
al-Turk, Riad 105, 107–8
Alba Rico, Santiago, *Capitalismo y nihilismo* 41–2, 49, 50, 51
Alexievich, Svetlana, *Voices from Chernobyl* xi
alterity, radical xxvi–xxvii
Antigone 31, 38
anyone and someone 55
apparatus 2, 42, 44, 80, 81, 100, 103, 106–8, 110, 111, 135, 163, 166–7, 172, 185, 187
Arendt, Hannah
  banality of evil 53, 151
  The Human Condition vii, xxix
Argentina
  HIJOS (Children for Identity and Justice against Forgetting and Silence) 137
  recent film history 136
  repression in 1970s 55–6
Artaud, Antonin xxvii, 12–13, 79–81, 84, 157
  'Théâtre Alfred Jarry' 181–2

  Pour en finir avec le judgement de Dieu 80
  theatre of cruelty 79
  Van Gogh le suicidé de la societé 79
Atlas Group, The, *see* Walid Raad
attacks on artists
  in Brazil x
  in Southern Cone 55
Avendaño, Bruno xix–xx, 179–80
Avendaño, Lukas xix–xx, 179–80
  Buscando a Bruno xix
  Las dos Fridas xix
Ayotzinapa, murdered students 175

Badiou, Alain, *Ethics* xxv, 6–7, 37
Bakhtin, Mikhail
  Rabelais and His World 85
  Toward a Philosophy of the Act 83
Bassi, Leo 87
Bechis, Marco, *Garage Olimpo* 137
Beckett, Samuel, *Waiting for Godot* 73
  see also Susan Sontag
Belting, Hans, *Antropología de la imagen* 12
Benjamin, Walter, 'The Storyteller' 134–5
Bergson, Henri 24
Bernat, Roger, *Please Continue (Hamlet)* xxi–xxii, 179
Bioy Casares, Adolfo, *La invención de Morel* 28, 100–1
Black Lives Matter xii, xiii
body and representation 47–52
Bodies of Others, The
  1st section, ethics and representation xxv–xxvii
  2nd section, ethics of the body xxvii

3rd section, representation and absence, disappearance, and memory xxviii–xxx
epilogue xxxi
Bolaño, Roberto 65–6, 143
  2666 xxvii, 66, 69–70, 74, 87–9, 175
  Estrella distante 65
  on Las Yeguas del Apocalipsis 62
  Los detectives salvajes 65 175
  Nocturno de Chile 65
Brecht, Bertolt 55, 85, 178
  Kriegsfibel 72
  Mann ist mann 95
Brekke, Agnes 152
  see also Mapa Teatro
Bulgakov, Mikhail 70
Butler, Judith
  'Los poderes de la memoria' xiii
  Precarious Life xiv–xvi, xxvi–xxvii

Camus, Albert, *L'étranger* 123
care and bodies 118–19
Carri, Albertina, *Los rubios* 137–41, 143
Casafranca, Augusto 38–9
  see also Yuyachkani Cultural Group
Casas, Francisco 61
  see also Las Yeguas del Apocalipsis
Castaño, Jeison, *see* Jeihhco
Catanzaro, Beatrice, *A Needle in the Binding* 106–7
Certeau, Michel de, *L'invention du quotidien 1* 167
Chekhov, Anton, *Three Sisters* 75, 77
CIDE report on femicide in Ciudad Juárez 68–9
Ciudad Juárez, *see* femicide in Ciudad Juárez
Cixous, Hélène, *La Ville Parjure* xx
Clark, Lygia 165–6
cocaine, cocaine bush 154–5
Colchado Lucio, Óscar 39
commedia dell arte 15–16, 17, 21

CONADEP (*Nunca más* report) 56
conceptual art in 1960s–70s Latin America 59
Correa, Ana 39–40
  see also Yuyachkani Cultural Group
Cortázar, Julio 66, 167
Costa, Pedro 114, 122
Couceyro, Analía 138–41
Covid-19 lockdown effects vi, 179
Crimp, Douglas, 'Duelo y militancia' xv–xvi
Cynn, Cristine, *see* Oppenheimer, Joshua, Cristine Cynn and 'Anonymous'

Damasio, Antonio, *El error de Descartes* 12
Deleuze, Gilles, *Spinoza. Philosophie Pratique* viii
Deneuve, Catherine 94
Derrida, Jacques 32, 167, 186
  'Envoi' xxvi, 23, 24
Dewey, John 60
Díaz, Julián 145, 160–1
Didi-Huberman, Georges, *La imagen superviviente* 97
Dispositif, *see* apparatus
Duras, Marguerite, *see* Resnais, Alain

Echeverría, Bolívar
  Discurso crítico y modernidad xxxi
  La modernidad del barroco xxxi
  theorization of Baroque modernity xxxi
Em Theay, *see* Keng Sen, Ong
Escobar, Pablo 151–3
ethical neutrality of art 124
ethics
  and artists 11
  of care 82–3
  and judicial decisions xx
  in micropolitics and macropolitics ix
  and morality xxv, 5–8

and representation xxiv–xxv
  of the witness xxx, 157–61
evil xxxi–xxxii

fabrication and history 96
fabrication and representation 41–6
fascism 60–1
fascism in 1960s–70s Latin America
  61
Favio, Leonardo, *Gatica, el mono* 18
femicide in Ciudad Juárez 66–9
Ferrari, León 177
  Palabras ajenas 177–8
fiction and representation xxviii,
  186
fool 85–6
Foucault, Michel *Surveiller et punir.
  Naissance de la prison*, vii
Foucault, Michel and Gilles
  Deleuze, 'Les intellectuels
  et le pouvoir' 32
Franco, Marielle xviii, 178–9
Fujimori, Alberto 38, 174

Galeano, Eduardo xx
Ganda, Oumarou, *Cabascabo*
  124
García, Rodrigo 173
García Berlanga, Luis, *El verdugo*
  (1963) 129
García Linera, Álvaro, 'State Crisis
  and popular power' 155
Genet, Jean 51
Getino, Octavio 43
Gielen, Pascal, *The Murmuring of the
  Artistic Multitude* 134
Gilligan, Carol, *In a Different Voice*
  xvii, 82–3
Goffman, Erving, *The Presentation of
  Self* 22
Grotowsky, Jerzy 54, 55
Grupov, *Rwanda 94* 135
Guattari, Felix
  La révolution moléculaire vii
  micropolitics vi

Habegger, Andrés, *(H) Historias
  cotidianas* 137
Hadjithomas Joana, *see* Joreige, Khalil
  and Joana Hadjithomas
Heller, Ágnes, *Beyond Justice* xxi
HIJOS (Children for Identity and
  Justice against Forgetting and
  Silence), *see* Argentina
history and memory, *see* memory and
  history
Hong Sang-soo 116
Hou Hsiao Hsien 116
humour 187

identity and representation
  108–9
in-transcendence and representation
  185–6
in-transcendence and transcendence
  169, 185

Jeihhco (Jeison Castaño) 150, 153,
  160
  see also Mapa Teatro
Jerusalem Show 106–7, 169–70
Jiménez, Danilo 154, 159
  see also Mapa Teatro
Jones, Amelia 101
Joreige, Khalil and Joana
  Hadjithomas, *Je veux voir* 94
justice
  ethico-political vs. socio-political
  xxi
  and fiction xxiii
  and representation xxi, xxiv

Khoury, Elias, *see* Mroué,
  Rabih, *Three posters*
  (2000)
Keng Sen, Ong 171
  The Continuum 135
Kogut, Sandra, *Adieu Monde* 45

Lacan, Jacques 6
Lanzmann, Claude, *Shoah* 166

Las Tesis feminist collective, *Un violador en tu camino* xiii–xiv, xviii
Las Yeguas del Apocalipsis xix, xxvii, 61–3
  Homenaje a Sebastián Acevedo 64
  La conquista de América 63
  Refundación de la Universidad de Chile 62
  Tu dolor dice: Minado 64
Lebanon, civil wars 93–4
Lemebel, Pedro 61–2
  see also Las Yeguas del Apocalipsis
Lévinas, Emmanuel, *Totality and Infinity* xvi
Liddell, Angélica xxvii, 47, 143
  Actos de desobediencia 76
  Anfaegtelse 76
  La casa de la fuerza xxvii, 76–9, 81–4, 171
  Lecciones incompatibles con la vida 82
  Perro muerto en tintorería 47–52, 86
  Te haré invencible con mi derrota, Jackie 76
  Y cómo no se pudrió Blancanieves 47
  Y los peces salieron a combatir contra los hombres 47
  You are my destiny 182–3, 184–5
Littin, Miguel, *El chacal de Nahueltoro* 130
living archive 165–7
Llosa, Claudia
  Madeinusa 34–6
  La teta asustada 34, 36
Londoño, Luis Alfonso 44
  see also Mayolo, Carlos and Luis Ospina
López Petit, Santiago 80, 81
ludic, *see* play

Madres de la Plaza de Mayo 55–7
Magnani, Anna 16, 21, 28

Majdalanie, Lina 93
  Biokhraphia 109
  see also Mroué, Rabih
Mapa Teatro 157
  Discurso de un hombre decente 143, 152–4, 171
  La limpieza de los establos de Augias 164
  Los incontados 143, 147–50, 163, 176–7
  Los santos inocentes 143–5, 150, 171
  Proyecto Prometeo 163–4
  Re-corridos 164
  Testigo de las ruinas 160, 163
  The Horatian 151
  Tríptico de la violencia xxx–xxxi
Marker, Chris 91
Martín Patino, Basilio
  Homenaje a Madrid 132
  Libre te quiero 132
  Queridísimos verdugos 129–32
Marx, Karl, *Der achtzehnte Brumaire* 32
Mayakovsky, Vladimir 161
Mayolo, Carlos and Luis Ospina, *Agarrando pueblo* xxvii, 43–4
Mbaye, Mame xix, 178
memory and history 133–6
meta-theatricality 47, 186
Mexico, systematic corruption and repression 176
migrants 60
mimesis and fiction 90
Mockus, Antanas 163–5
moral codes 9–10
Morales, Evo 155
morality and gender xvii
Mroué, Rabih 93, 143, 173
  Grandfather, Father and Son 109
  Looking for a missing employee 102–4
  The Inhabitants of Images 110–11, 171
  The Pixelated Revolution 110
  Three posters 94–6

Mroué, Rabih and Lina Majdalanie
  33 rounds et quelques seconds 102–3
  Who is afraid of representation 101–2
Müller, Heiner
  Die Hamletmaschine 51
  The Horatian 151
Murúa, Lautaro, *La Raulito* 43

neoliberalism x, 170, 174, 176
neorealism in Latin America film 43
Nut, Pau de 75, 76, 78, 159

Olivera, Héctor, *La noche de los lápices* 136
Oppenheimer, Joshua, Cristine Cynn and 'Anonymous', *The Act of Killing* 121–6, 127, 135
orality 166–7
Ortega, Julio
  Adiós Ayacucho 39–40
  see also Yuyachkani Cultural Group
Ospina, Luis, see Mayolo, Carlos and Luis Ospina

Pahn, Rithy, *S-21, la machine de mort Khmère rouge* 122, 125
pain and representation 70, 71–3
Palestine, Israeli colonialism in 170
Pane, Gina, *Action Escalade non-anesthésiée* 63–4
Pasolini, Pier Paolo 74
Pavlovsky, Eduardo xxvii, 53
  El señor Galíndez 53–4
  El señor Laforgue 53
  La ética del cuerpo 54, 54
  Paso de dos 53
  Rojos globos rojos 53, 54
  Telarañas 53
Pegna Herçog, Alex, 'En nome de Deus' x
phantasm and ghost 99

Pinochet, Augusto 61
Pizarro Leongómez, Hernando 148
play (ludic) xxxi, 4, 187
poner el cuerpo, see putting the body on the line
popularism, authoritarian xi
porno-misery film 43
presence and disappearance xxix
presence and representation 105, 186
Prividera, Nicolás, *M* 137–8
public sphere vi–viii, xxii–xxiii, xxix, 10
public realm and theatricality 20–1
Puche, Sindo 47
Puenzo, Luis, *La historia oficial* 136
Puig Antich, Salvador 131
putting the body on the line 59

Raad, Walid 93, 97, 143, 171
Ralli, Teresa 38
  see also Yuyachkani Cultural Group
Ramírez, Juana María 160, 165
  see also Mapa Teatro
Rancière, Jacques, *Aesthetics and Its Discontents* 183
Rau, Milo
  The Congo Tribunal xxii
  The Moscow Trials xxii–xxiii, 179
Renoir, Jean
  French Cancan 17–18
  La carrose d'or xxvi, 15–22, 27–9, 33
  La régle de jeu 18
representation
  core concept of 1–4
  definitions of 23–7
  delegated 26, 29, 31–1, 32
  mental 24
  in micropolitics and micropolitics ix
  mimetic 23–4, 28
  theatrical 25
Resnais, Alain, *Hiroshima, mon amour* 91

Ricoeur, Paul, *Time and Narrative I* 90
Rivera Garza, Cristina, *Dolerse* xxvii–xxviii
Rodríguez, Dioselino 145, 146
  see also Mapa Teatro
Rodríguez, Jesusa 87
Rohmer, Erich 15, 16
Rolnik, Suely
  'The Body's Contagious Memory' 165–6
  Esferas de la insurrección vii
  macropolitical and micropolitical insurrections vi–ix, xxvi
Roque, María Inés, *Papá Iván* 137
Rouch, Jean
  Moi un noir 124
  Petit à petit 45
Rousseau, Jean Jacques 6
Rubio Zapata, Miguel 37, 39
  see also Yuyachkani Cultural Group

Sábato, Ernesto 56
  see also CONADEP (*Nunca más* report)
Sánchez Martínez, José Antonio
  essay for *Per/form* 173
  Ética y representación 175
  History of this Book xxv
  Practising the Real 171–2
  Teatralidades disidentes 172
  Torre de Babel 178–9
Sarajevo, siege of 1992–6 72–3
Scott, James, *Domination and the Arts of Resistance* 86
Sennett, Richard, *The Fall of Public Man* 20–1
Shattuck, Roger, *Forbidden Knowledge* 123
shock doctrine 61
Sissako, Adberrahmane, *Bamako* xxii
Solanas, Fernando 43
Sontag, Susan
  'Aesthetics of silence' 167
  'El siglo XXI comienza con el sitio de Sarajevo' 73
  Regarding the pain of the others 71–2, 73
  staging of *Waiting for Godot* 73
Soto, Olga de, *Le jeune homme* 166
Sousa Santos, Boaventura de, *Descolonizar el saber* xxv, xxx, 119
Spain
  effects of neoliberal austerity policies 170, 174–5
  May 15 political movement 169
  political resurgence of Catholic church 174
  repression under Franco 130–1
  transition to democracy 127–9, 132
Spinoza, Baruch, *Ethics* viii
Spivak, Gayatri Chakravorty
  An Aesthetic Education xxvi
  'Can the Subaltern Speak?' 32–3
Syria, civil war 106

Tabucchi, Antonio, *Dreams of Dreams* 161
Third Film in Latin America 43
Todorov, Tzvetan, *Vivir solos juntos* 6
Torres, Genaro 145, 146, 159
  see also Mapa Teatro
Torres Restrepo, Camilo 149
transcendence, *see* in-transcendence and transcendence

Val del Omar, José 181–2
  Aguaespejo granadino 181
  Tríptico elemental de España 181
Van Gogh, Vincent 79–80
Veloza García, Ever (alias HH) 145–6, 150
Vera, Nadia 176
Vergès, Jacques, *Estrategia judicial* xxiii

Villaflor, Azucena xix, 56
  see also Madres de la Plaza de Mayo
virtuosity 29, 50, 55, 74, 75

war on drugs (USA), 155–6
war photography 71–2, 73
Warburg, Aby 117
  Der Bilderatlas Mnemosyne 97
Warhol, Andy 116
Warr, Tracey 101
Watanabe, José 38
Weerasethakul, Apichatpong
  Mysterious Object at Noon 117–18
  Phantoms of Nabua 113
  Sang Sattawat 116

Sud Pralad 116
Sud Sanaeha 116
Syndromes and a Century 117–18
Uncle Boonmee Who Can Recall His Past Lives 113–16, 121
Welles, Orson, *F. for Fake* 44
witnesses and representation 146

Yasujiro Ozu 114
Yuyachkani Cultural Group xxvi, 37–8, 135, 169, 174
  Adiós Ayacucho 39
  Antígona 38, 39
  Rosa Cuchillo 39–40

www.ingramcontent.com/pod-product-compliance
Lightning Source LLC
Chambersburg PA
CBHW062217300426
44115CB00012BA/2107